DAVID LYNCH
IN THEORY

edited by
FRANÇOIS-XAVIER GLEYZON

Prague 2010

Litteraria Pragensia Books
www.litterariapragensia.com

 Published 2010 by Univerzita Karlova v Praze
Filozofická Fakulta

Litteraria Pragensia Books
Centre for Critical & Cultural Theory, DALC
Náměstí Jana Palacha 2
116 38 Praha 1, Czech Republic

The publication of this book has been partly funded by research grant MSM0021620824 "Foundations of the Modern World as Reflected in Literature and Philosophy" awarded to the Faculty of Philosophy, Charles University, Prague, by the Czech Ministry of Education.

Cataloguing in Publication Data

David Lynch in Theory, edited by François-Xavier Gleyzon. – 1st ed.
          p. cm.
     ISBN 978-80-7308-317-5
     1. Film Studies. 2. Critical Theory. 3. David Lynch.
     I. Gleyzon, François-Xavier. II. Title

Printed in the Czech Republic by PB Tisk
Cover, typeset & design © lazarus
Cover image by Andrzej Dragan

CONTENTS

FRANCOIS-XAVIER GLEYZON
INTRODUCTION: DAVID LYNCH'S SEISMOGRAPH

Los Angeles, January-February 2010

In David Lynch's workshop, pell-mell, are to be found a variety of implements: hammers, paintbrushes, brushes, cameras, old radios, frames, canvases, photographic film, a soldering iron, drills, etc. In this workshop or laboratory, a veritable cabinet of curiosities built in reinforced concrete, the thin rectangular windows are placed high up and, by a certain trick of perspective, the balmy, orange-colored light of Los Angeles comes into it at a slant and pours out copiously onto the artist's work-table. In order to seize these light-filled moments – *these Californian epiphanies* – David Lynch gets up early. Then he contemplates his work-table. Away from the attentions of the curious, the artist works in the midst of all his implements, his tools – he *experiments*. Among the latter a certain category of implement seems to take pride of place, a place apart, a place of choice. Measuring apparatus with needles enabling us to record tensions and vibrations occupy priority space in David Lynch's workshop. Wearing a blue heavy-duty apron showing part of a white short-necked shirt carefully buttoned to the top, Lynch places his implements, captors, receivers and other measuring apparatus next to one another. After having made short work of cleaning his work-top, he then grabs hold of the first measuring instrument to his right. This is the most interesting of them. It is also the most imposing. The apparatus recovered in an old decommissioned factory in Minnesota consists of three dials. The first is circular with a long needle affixed directly to a paper on which patterns may be traced. The two other dials indicate very clearly with an A and a V that we are looking at an ammeter and a voltmeter. Lynch plugs the apparatus into the mains. He seizes the female electric lead to bring it into contact with the male terminal of the apparatus. A noise both muffled and metallic makes itself heard several times over. David Lynch stops and attentively observes the needles becoming agitated, wriggling under the impulses of the electric shock – frenetic, even hysterical, deviations of the needle then convert this agitation, this energy into movement. A few seconds later the experiment is over. David Lynch disconnects the electric current directly at the socket where the apparatus was plugged in. Acting quickly, he tilts the apparatus and places it flat on his table, carefully unscrews the circular dial so as to take out the trace. After unrolling the paper on his work-table, Lynch then contemplates – passionately – the revealing trace of the needle on the paper itself and imagines in these lines bespeaking tensions – these shock waves – some closer together than others, the image of a terrified body, convulsed and contorted at the moment of onset of a fit of hysteria.

We know that David Lynch does not simply make use of these measuring instruments in his workshop. They also manifest themselves time and time again in his films just as they do in his paintings and photographs. *Inland Empire* for example opens with recording / transmitting / tracing equipment that is just as similar. In the same way the catalogue of the exhibition *The Air is on Fire* includes many of these measuring instruments.[1] All these instruments have the special quality of being "captors" and "receivers" – all of them are endowed with the quality of being sensitive to invisible vibrations, latent waves and rhythmic modulations. They also take on, however, and David Lynch is surely not ignorant of the fact, a role and a quite special function as much for the artist as for the art historian, who thinks, lives and works with images. In fact, if David Lynch's instruments have as their aim to measure all movements and to reproduce them on a visual support, this is reminiscent of Aby Warburg's "seismograph." When, during the 1927 summer semester, the art historian, Aby Warburg, uses the technical drawing of a recording apparatus which transcribes and transmits invisible movements, it is to describe the activities of Nietzsche and of Burckhardt which he characterizes at that time as "being both [like] very sensitive seismographs whose bases tremble when they transmit and receive waves."[2] *The bases tremble* Warburg insists. All the creative work and process that Warburg, helped by his seismograph, picks up on and records here with regard to Burckhardt and Nietzsche seems to find an echo in the work of David Lynch. The waves, the shock waves and agitations which traverse and affect David Lynch's work are never fluid. But they do not stop registering fractures, tensions, resistances, ruptures, mutations and discontinuities, crises and catastrophes. Lynch's art is realized in this creative dissonance which has need of this chaos and this anarchy, as Burckhardt suggested, in order to be fully realized.[3] Lynch is a sort of cinematic seismograph – he is listening and recording but is not "just the describer of the visible movements that crop up here and there; he is, above all, the recorder and transmitter of the invisible movements that persist, [...] which are waiting for the moment – for us unexpected – to suddenly manifest themselves."[4] This trace, this revelatory line, David Lynch will reproduce as an image. This line drawn by impulse that twists, joins up to and passes through all the points of resistance, which jostles and ceaselessly bends is, as Étienne-Jules Marey described it in his seminal work on *La Méthode Graphique*, "the best way to represent phenomena."[5] But the bend, the curve in this line "freely disporting itself" – and we shall understand its importance for the cinema of David Lynch – is above all as Deleuze once wrote tellingly – pure Event. "It is not yet in the world: It is a world to itself [...] 'a place for cosmogenesis' Paul Klee used to say [...]. An event waiting for another event

[1] David Lynch, *The Air is on Fire* (London: Thames and Hudson, 2007).
[2] Aby Warburg, "Seminarübungen über Jacob Burckhardt" [1927], *Idea: Jahrbuch der Hamburger Kunsthalle*, ed. B. Roeck (Wiesbaden: Harrassowitz, 1991) 86.
[3] Maurizio Balsamo, "Création et paradoxalité," *Revue française de psychanalyse* 67 (2003/5): 1554.
[4] Georges Didi-Huberman, *L'image survivante: Histoire de l'art et temps des fantômes selon Aby Warburg* (Paris: Éditions de Minuit, 2002) 123.
[5] Etienne-Jules Marey, *La méthode graphique dans les sciences expérimentales et principalement en physiologie et en médecine* (Paris: Masson, 1878) 12.

to happen?"[6] The future event can only be *the moving image*. That is why Michel Chion in his seminal work *David Lynch* – placing himself more downstream, at the level of reception, than upstream, at the level of production, always wanted to be *listening* to the filmmaker and in this way "listen with your eyes, tuning in to what happens in the image, *its rhythmic modulations and vibrations*, and you will notice *variations, waves and movements* perceptible only by not looking."[7]

We must therefore pay attention to life, to that swarming, that ebb and flow, that survivance/survival, that wholly Warburgian *Nachleben* which underlies and is in the image, and finally listen out for its multiple rhythms. Perhaps too we will find in that clear admonishment to the accents of methodology according to Hugo von Hofmannsthal, all of the impulses and creative processes of every poet, or then again, of every artist in general, of every "total artist" to take up the expression used by *Les Cahiers du Cinéma* with regard to David Lynch. Thus the poet, the artist,

> is like a seismograph that vibrates from every quake, even if it is thousands of miles away. It's not that he thinks incessantly of all things in the world. But they think of him. They are in him and thus do they rule over him. Even his dull hours, his depressions, his confusions are impersonal states; they are like the spasms of the seismograph, and a deep enough gaze could read more mysterious things in them than in his poems.[8]

This book will be that of sensations as much as vibrations. Sensations, vibrations, emotions to which all the contributors to this book have been attentive. All of them offer, record and transmit a line, a wave of perception and reception: veritable shock waves, each one traces a story line, a place, an event in David Lynch's work. Each contribution is therefore a line both *active* and *creative* whose movements, bends, open and sinusoidal curves as well as their intersections, links and clashes will form analytical crucibles.

The first line/contribution rushes forward and traces in its wake a sort of route or journey. If a typically Lynchian film, however, implies a journey at the end of which the protagonist discovers a truth or *his/her* own truth, *Inland Empire* is the exception and seems to resist the idea of a journey, recording instead a dynamic, a series of comings and goings and curves. If, as we pointed out earlier, the line does not delineate the World, that is because it is already a World to itself. This is exactly the complex situation that *Inland Empire* gives us: the absence of another world to be found, and which the protagonist, Nikki (Laura Dern) nevertheless does not tire of seeking nor wanting to travel towards, physically or mentally. The leap into this *fantasmatic* world made by the subject is indicative of nothing other than the painful and traumatic *going back to oneself/meeting oneself* [TODD MCGOWAN]. As far as *Inland Empire* is concerned, it is not incumbent on us here to fail to recognize the system of closure with respect to the subject, but to understand that the condi-

6 Gilles Deleuze, *Le Pli, Leibniz et le Baroque* (Paris: Editions de Minuit, 1988) 21.
7 Michel Chion, *David Lynch*, 2nd ed. (London: British Film Institute, 2006) 160, *my emphasis*.
8 "David Lynch: Artiste Total," *Cahiers du Cinéma* 620 (Feb 2007); and Hugo von Hofmannsthal, *The Poet and the Present Time*, vol. I. (Frankfurt am Main: Fischer, 1979) 54.

tion of this closure, as Gilles Deleuze writes tellingly, "is valid for the infinite opening of the finite: it represents infinity finitely."[9] It offers to the world that chance to begin again, that possibility to repeat oneself made visible in *Inland Empire*. In other words, again those of Deleuze, Lynch puts "the world into the subject so that the subject can be for the world."[10]

But this operation is carried out at the cost of a *twist*, a sort of Möbius band which, in its turn, involves bent and curved lines and folds. And it is in the hollow itself of these inflections that particular moments stand out, fields of vision, areas of legibility wherein are offered to the gaze foci through which the artist seems to evoke an internal vision of special conflicting spaces where impulses, even drives towards death, sex and violence collide with one another to pour out into a veil, a mystic net in which the artist may be said to penetrate/immure himself just as much as the spectator. It is in these special and privileged geographical zones that together make up the Lynchian universe that the action of his films falls back on cinematic space itself. By way of these meta-cinematic or even über-cinematic considerations, these analyses permit a scrupulous examination of the *mise-en-scène* of these geographic zones in which figure and are deployed all the resources of the cinematic apparatus that chimes in with the complex narrative content of the film. It is in this sense – and in these special cinematic moments in which the text seems to resist all attempts at understanding, all narrative closure, that an ontology might be worked out and constituted in which the spectator would find himself phenomenologically involved in the experience of the gaze itself [GREG HAINGE]. It can, however, be noted that it is just this experience of involvement/insertion of the spectator into the heart of Lynch's work which invites us or constrains us, despite the warnings of Michel Chion, to the hermeneutic exercise of decrypting the text and the story [GARY BETTINSON].[11] Moreover, the films of David Lynch are undecipherable, unthinkable, but as Merleau-Ponty declared in a saying that has remained famous: "un film [...] se perçoit" ("a film [...] is perceived").[12] In fact, the transfer between the film and the spectator or the transfer to the spectator of an experience would not be available for normal mental articulation, an explicit narrative, but it becomes accessible, on the one hand, through the imaginative function of the film, and, on the other hand, through the cinematographic medium, *the cinematic apparatus* itself [DOMINIQUE DE COURCELLES].

If we can see in David Lynch's latest feature film *Inland Empire* a sort of re-articulation of the cinematic apparatus in which cinema becomes from that moment on visible in the film, it is precisely these ties, these correspondences, these movements between transitional and interstitial zones that are to be illuminated. In these precise moments-spaces in which cinema is reflected may also be detected the disturbing and arresting forces of sound images. Sounds and Images: *and* will have here the value of space and marks the both heterogeneous and combinatory mode

---

[9] Deleuze, *Le Pli*, 36.
[10] Deleuze, *Le Pli*, 37.
[11] See Michel Chion, *David Lynch*, trans. Robert Julian (London: British Film Institute, 1995) 20.
[12] Maurice Merleau-Ponty, "Le cinéma et la nouvelle psychologie," *Sens et non sens* (Paris: Gallimard, 1996 [1966]) 74.

of articulation of sounds and images [SCOTT WILSON]. It is indeed their discreet heterogeneity which will give rise in the screen of our brain ("the brain is the screen"[13]) to that place of desire which "proceeds along networks that are cultural and technical as well as neural." Lynch could then be said to direct a sort of "neuracinema" at the heart of which the Lacanian *a* designates the undefinable, mobile points of cultural anxiety, discordance and desire that articulate inner and outer worlds.

The art of Lynch could then be said to consist also in its *inter*-mediality [ALANNA THAIN]. This intermediality cannot only and simply be understood in the way of a system of transitions between media forms or genres, for in these transitional zones the body is involved in all its movements, in all its creative energy. In this *"in-between"* resonates then the question of the body. What about the body? In the interstices of these worlds, in these "mediated worlds," the body that throws itself into a crazy, even hysterical rhythmic dance – this is what is at stake in *Inland Empire* in the *loco*-motion scene – is then perceived as a veritable power in becoming, a potential renewed as a point of contact, of mutation and creativity, a veritable cinematic body in itself. With its free spirals, particularly intense, unfurling, animated and musical, the dancing body becomes predominant and itself occupies an interstitial-intermedial space.

A space for the emotions and sensations, the moving body in this choreography becomes erotic and then turns into a centering on woman, of a *feminocentrism*. In these arcanes of the feminine is to be found a locus *pregnant* with meaning. A place pregnant with conflicts where there is wrapped and woven in one and the same body, such is the case in *Blue Velvet*, a mixed semiotics of meanings tending to bring together opposite polarities, i.e. those of maternity and abortion [JASON T. CLEMENCE]. But woman in Lynch is declined as well in all her ambivalence, a carrier of strangeness and darkness, she is also the modern female body with Baudelairean features who, like "la mendiante rousse" ("the red-haired beggar girl"), even in her rags, "[...] shows us poverty/And beauty [...]" or she is even the body of a prostitute as shown in the poem "Allegory."[14] Whichever form she takes, woman knows the interplay of all transformations/deformations. She also circulates in Lynch's work with extreme fluidity to the point of displaying herself, *objectifying herself* as a sexual commodity within a socio-historical reality of sexual trafficking that does not cease to haunt the world of *Inland Empire* [JOSHUA D. GONSALVES].

At the precise moment of this fast track ebb and flow that constitutes sexual trafficking, we need to think of the very particular cinematographic movement Lynch makes in this particular case, with regard to this milieu, this industry. If we spoke earlier of *the impossibility of movement* (of travel) experienced by Nikki (Laura Dern) in *Inland Empire* (return/meeting of self with self), it is because this immobilism translates in Lynch's work a will towards, a power of fetishization. It is precisely in this way that Lacan will define the *image-fétiche* (image-fetish): in order to understand the fetish, we therefore need in the first place to think of cinema:

---

[13] Gilles Deleuze, *Two Regimes of Madness: Texts and Interviews 1975-1995*, trans. Ames Hodges and Mike Taormina (New York: Semiotexte, 2006) 283.
[14] Charles Baudelaire, *Les Fleurs du Mal, Œuvres Complètes*, vol. I. (Paris: Gallimard, 1975 [1861]) 83-85.

Pensez à la façon dont un mouvement cinématographique qui se déroulerait rapidement s'arrêterait tout d'un coup en un point, figeant tous les personnages. Cet instantané est caractéristique de la réduction de la scène pleine, signifiante articulée de sujet à sujet, à ce qui s'immobilise dans le fantasme.[15]

(Think of the way in which a cinematic movement taking place quickly might stop all of a sudden in one place, freezing all the characters. This snapshot is characteristic of the reduction of the full, meaningful scene, articulated from one subject to another, to what is then immobilized in fantasy.)

Lynch observes and *immobilizes* here (and elsewhere identically to it, and quite appropriately, in a series of frozen photographic images *Nude and Smoke*) with a sort of perverse power the whole sexual drama of a desire acted out as well as a reality captured on the female body in a "dream of strange desires wrapped inside a mystery story" [LOUIS ARMAND].[16] But in this female body of Nikki in which may be heard, read and written all tensions, breakdowns and violence there also arises an "American Gothic aesthetic" wherein, as David Punter emphasizes, "the worlds portrayed are ones infested with psychic and social decay, and colored with the heightened hues of putrescence. Violence, rape and breakdown are the key motifs."[17] This is just what *Blue Velvet*, *Mulholland Drive* and *Inland Empire* go to show. All of them stage a fantasmagory in which abject behavior does not cease to be declined under the sign of pleasure and eroticism [REBECCA BARR].

It is also this sickening fantasy of abjection that Lynch brings us into contact with that dominates Lynch's work [ERIC WILSON]. The repulsive image of that aqueous and putrid mass projected and exuded by, among other pictorial and cinematographic works, *Six Men Getting Sick*, corresponds quite accurately to the theoretical and decisive paradigm of the *formless* put forward by Georges Bataille. The formless, which also finds a place in the work of Francis Bacon, transgresses traditional notions of image and resemblance. From a sort of fantasmatic almost *sacred* phenomenology of the abject, the repulsive and the formless stems precisely a demeaning/defiling projection, i.e. the *sacrilege* and *sacrifice* of the image [FRANÇOIS-XAVIER GLEYZON].

*

On the screen of David Lynch's seismograph are traced, rolled up and clashing against each other lines of reading and analysis: sinusoidal and bent curves, points of tension, forces and fractures. It is in this space as frantic as it is hysterical that the *writing* of this book on David Lynch will be invented and created. Perhaps it is in this agitated and infinite trace that a true definition of writing with regard to the cinematographic and

[15] Jacques Lacan, *Séminaires IV: La Relation d'Objet*, ed. J.-A. Miller (Paris: Le Seuil, 1956/57) 119-20; 157.

[16] Lynch's description of *Blue Velvet* (1986) in *Lynch on Lynch*, ed. Chris Rodley (London: Faber, 2005) 138.

[17] David Punter, *The Literature of Terror: The Gothic Tradition*, vol.1. (London: Longman, 1980) 3.

artistic work of Lynch might be organized. In the scene/space that it de-limits the words of Deleuze are echoed: "to write is to struggle, to resist; to write is *to become*."[18] This *writing-becoming* is the book which follows – with the proviso that it not be taken as an aim or an end in itself, but as a perpetual work-in-progress, always in need of restarting, always in the process of being done, always *becoming*. Perhaps this is the ultimate aim of all writing and therefore of all art, i.e. that of creating and inventing and always renewing: "in other words a chance of life" or then again a creation, "the invention of a people."[19] But the people are missing, says Deleuze, the people are always missing. Already on the horizon a line is delineated and materializes: the promise of a change, the promise of an experience still to come. Perhaps better than anyone Jim Morrison was able to describe *avant la lettre* the cinema of David Lynch:

The movie will begin in five moments
The mindless voice announced
"All those unseated will await
the next show"

We filed slowly, languidly
into the hall. The auditorium
was vast & silent.
As we seated & were darkened
The voice continued:

The program for this evening
is not new. You have seen
this entertainment thru & thru
You've seen your birth, your
life & death; you might recall all
of the rest – (did you
have a good world when you
died?) – enough to base
a movie on?

I'm getting out of here
Where are you going?
To the other side of morning
Please don't chase the clouds, pagodas
[...]

It's alright, all your friends are here
When can I meet them?
After you've eaten I'm not hungry
Uh, we meant beaten

Silver stream, silvery scream
Oooooh, impossible concentration.[20]

Here the book begins...

18 Gilles Deleuze, *Foucault* (Paris: Les Editions de Minuit, 2004 [1984]) 51.
19 Gilles Deleuze, *Critique et Clinique* (Paris: Les Editions de Minuit, 1993) 15.
20 Jim Morrison, *The American Night*, vol 2. (New York: Vintage Books, 1991) 11.

TODD MCGOWAN
THE MATERIALITY OF FANTASY: THE ENCOUNTER WITH SOMETHING IN *INLAND EMPIRE*

LOCATING THE MATERIAL

What singles out David Lynch as a filmmaker is his exploration of filmic fantasy combined with his commitment to a materialist cinema. There are, of course, many filmmakers devoted to constructing escapist fantasies, and many others, though fewer and mostly working outside of Hollywood, who view the cinema as a tool for spotlighting the unnoticed material substratum of our existence. Lynch is perhaps the only filmmaker who brings these two cinematic approaches together. From his first film, *Eraserhead* (1977), he has not simply included fantasy and material images in the same film but has wedded them together inextricably. In *Eraserhead*, the controlling fantasy of the main character Henry (Jack Nance) involves a woman who emerges out of radiator in his bedroom where she sings and dances on a tiny stage, suggesting that the material object in some sense gives birth to the fantasy. In *Inland Empire* (2006), Lynch's speculation about the relationship between fantasy and material substance reaches its most profound point. Here, it is not that a material object inaugurates fantasy but that fantasy allows unprecedented access to the material real.

Just after the title credit, the opening of *Inland Empire* links fantasy to the concrete materiality that produces it through the close-up of an antiquated record playing and the static-filled announcement of a radio show, entitled "AXXoN N." Whereas modern production technology tends to hide the fact of production, the image and sound in this scene accentuate it. But Lynch doesn't forge this link in order to question the authenticity or importance of fantasy, as one might expect. *Inland Empire* shows instead that materiality is the key to the power that fantasy has.

This power becomes evident through the figure of the Lost Girl (Karolina Gruszka), who has sex with an anonymous man in a Polish hotel room at the beginning of the film. Subsequent to this traumatizing sexual encounter, she sits on a chair crying and watching the television, which unfolds a fantasmatic drama that ultimately transforms her situation and reunites her with her husband and son. The complex series of events that unfold in the fantasmatic world involves an actor, Nikki Grace (Laura Dern), who plays a role in a film that both transforms her own life and brings her into contact with the Lost Girl. While making the film, entitled *On High in Blue Tomorrows*, Nikki loses any sense of distinction between herself and her character Susan Blue, and she finds herself miraculously transported from Los Angeles to Poland, where her actions ultimately have the effect of freeing the Lost Girl from her situation. The film concludes with the reunion of the Lost Girl with her husband and son, followed by an epilogue during the closing credits of a group of women dancing in a large room while Nikki sits on a couch and watches.

In one sense, the narrative of *Inland Empire* shows fantasy functioning in a very traditional way. The Lost Girl's turn to fantasy through the television images removes her from a horrible situation and returns her to a blissful one. But typically fantasy does this only on the imaginary level, so that the fantasizing subject remains in the miserable situation, which is why political thinkers are often critical of the role that fantasy plays in culture. Throughout all of his films, Lynch goes beyond this idea of fantasy and grants it the capacity to create real change. Miracles occur in the Lynch film through the working out of fantasy, and these miracles are not imaginary. At the end of *Inland Empire*, the Lost Girl is not simply dreaming of a reunion with her family but rather achieves it, and she achieves it due to the fantasy that she experiences. By depicting fantasy as a real power for changing our circumstances, Lynch moves even further in the direction of rethinking its political bearing in this film than he has in his earlier ones.

Fantasy produces change by allowing us to accomplish what would be impossible within our social reality, and it does this by providing an opening to the material basis of subjectivity. What seems to belie this claim is fantasy's evident immateriality. Fantasies provide satisfaction for us to the extent that they defy material limitations, and even mass-produced fantasies that rely on a large material basis (studio equipment, thousands of workers providing technical support, and so on) constantly work to obscure this basis in order to create an effective fantasy. Nothing destroys the fantasy world that a film constructs more than a visible boom microphone or guide wires holding characters in place. The presence of obtrusive materiality is antithetic to the sustaining of a fantasy space. And yet, fantasy's rejection of the limitations of materiality allows it to access the material basis of subjectivity itself.

Perhaps the greatest difficulty for materialism as a philosophical and political position involves the problem that it has in creating the space for subjectivity. It is relatively easy for idealist thought to conceive of a subject acting freely through the realization of an idea, but materialism often devolves into a determinism that elides the subject. Marx confronts this problem directly in the opening of his *Theses on Feuerbach*, where he notes, "The chief defect of all hitherto existing materialism – that of Feuerbach included – is that the thing, reality, sensuousness, is conceived only in the form of the object or of *contemplation*, but not as *human sensuous activity*, *practice*, not subjectively. Hence, it happened that the *active* side, in contradistinction to materialism, was developed by idealism."[1] Marx goes on to argue for the possibility of a practical rather than a theoretical materialism that would allow for active subjectivity. But despite proposing a philosophy based on a materialist form of subjectivity, Marx himself continually falls back into an inescapable paradox: either the contradictions of historical development create revolutionary change, or the proletariat does so through a subjective agency that defies the ruling class. The twin heresies within Marxism – evolutionism and voluntarism –

---

[1] Karl Marx, "Theses on Feuerbach," *The Marx-Engels Reader*, 2nd ed., ed. Robert C. Tucker (New York: Norton, 1978) 143.

represent refusals to address the exigencies of this paradox. But even Marx himself tends to alternate between these two modes of explanation rather than genuinely linking together materialism and subjectivity. He thus falls victim to the same problem that he criticizes so aptly in the thought of Feuerbach. This is not simply a theoretical failing on the part of Marx himself but a problem inherent to materialist thought as such.

Through all of his analyses of the material structures of capitalism, Marx cannot find a place for subjectivity. The capitalist and the worker act like characters in a drama in which they play out the roles written for them in advance by their interests. Even revolution, according to this vision, follows from the exigencies of history that subjects simply align themselves with or not. Marx is unable to discover a materialist version of the subject because he operates with a materialist epistemology that assumes immediate access to the material real. Such a materialist epistemology necessarily figures the material in terms of what fits within the structure rather than one that disturbs it.

While discussing the unconscious in his *Seminar XI*, Jacques Lacan defines a cause not as what leads directly to an effect but as what registers a disturbance in the smooth structure of causes and effects. That is, a genuine cause occurs when the symbolic structure ceases to function automatically and begins to malfunction. The malfunction suggests that an event has taken place, that the structure has encountered something for which it cannot account. According to Lacan, "there is a cause only in something that doesn't work."[2] When an action simply leads to an expected result, we remain within the ideal terrain of the symbolic structure, even if the action is material. The fact that the material construction of a handgun leads to a murder does not challenge the ideal rules of sense that govern our society. It is not a material cause – or a cause at all in the strict sense – because it fails to violate our expectations concerning how events follow from each other.

A real material cause disturbs and disorients the symbolic structure. This cause is identical with subjectivity itself – the subject attached to its own mode of enjoyment rather than to the symbolic structure itself. The subject sticks out as the material that the social order continually stumbles over. The subject is akin to a log that can't be used in the construction of a house, and we notice it due to the disruption in utility that it occasions.[3] The problem is, however, that we tend not to pay attention to such logs, choosing instead to focus on those that can be used in building the house. Our lack of attention to what doesn't fit within the symbolic structure isn't simply a function of habit or inclination: the structure's survival depends on this failure of attention. We see the symbolic identities that hide the disruption of subjectivity, and these symbolic iden-

---

[2] Jacques Lacan, *The Four Fundamental Concepts of Psychoanalysis*, trans. Alan Sheridan (New York: Norton, 1978) 22. Slavoj Žižek notes, "a 'cause,' in the strict sense of the term, is precisely something which intervenes at the points where the network of causality (the chain of causes-and-effects) falters, where there is a cut, a gap, in the causal chain." Slavoj Žižek, *In Defense of Lost Causes* (New York: Verso, 2008) 288.

[3] The choice of the log is not an innocent example when discussing a Lynch film. In the *Twin Peaks* series (1990-1991), Lynch and co-creator Mark Frost use the figure of the Log Lady (Catherine E. Coulson), a woman who carries a log around with her and hears it speak to her, as an indication of how subjectivity manifests itself in the object that doesn't fit.

tities provide the assurance that everything is working out within this reality.[4]

But hiding the disruption also hides the enjoyment: a social reality without any disruptions would not only be impossible, but it would also be a stultifying enjoyment-free reality. The disruption energizes the symbolic structure at the same time that it threatens this structure. Fantasy provides a way of accessing the disruption and the enjoyment it provides while the imaginary status of fantasy minimizes the danger. The power of fantasy lies in its connection to what doesn't fit within the social reality – to the material real around which the reality is constructed.

This is the dimension of fantasy that *Inland Empire* is committed to revealing, and it attests to its singularity as a film. Many horror films document how a spiritual force haunts a material space. From Robert Wise's *The Haunting* (1963) to Stuart Rosenberg's *The Amityville Horror* (1979) to Mikael Håfström's *1408* (2007), cinema reveals that material places are not simply material, that they are suffused with a fantasmatic investment that appears in the form of a haunting. These types of films reveal that human dwelling doesn't simply occupy a place but also transforms it through an act of conferring meaning on the place. The meaning does not remain external to the place but leaves a residue in the material itself. Though horror films present this as a supernatural occurrence, its psychic resonance is nonetheless evident. Places do take on a fantasmatic significance based on the events that have occurred in them, which is why the idea of the haunted house has such psychic power even for non-believers in the supernatural. Materiality is the vehicle for our fantasies. But it is difficult to think of films that move in the other direction, showing materiality emerging from within the realm of fantasy. This is what Lynch attempts in *Inland Empire*.

SOMETHING IN *INLAND EMPIRE*
Most films, of course, follow a script, and the script provides order for the production and outlines the expectations of those involved. Even films that don't rely on scripts, however, depend on the controlling idea of the filmmaker or filmmakers. The improvised film does not escape the logic of the script and almost inevitably succumbs to it more fully than the scripted film, simply because the logic of this type of film is wider and more inclusive. Certain directors, like Alfred Hitchcock, are celebrated for scripting and storyboarding every detail, while others, such as Robert Altman, give actors a great deal of space for spontaneity. Altman's films are not all that more open to the depiction of what doesn't fit within the script than Hitchcock's. Every film remains scripted – which is to say, structured in a way that tries to account for everything, including the

---

[4] According to Martin Heidegger's well-known distinction, we live in a world in which things are ready-to-hand (*zuhanden*) or useful, and we notice them as things only when they lose their utility – like when a tool breaks – and thus become present-at-hand (*vorhanden*). For Heidegger, the encounter with the object as *vorhanden*, though it is derivative, is not uncommon and in fact represents the theoretical or scientific approach to being. Though this approach isolates the object from its use, it nonetheless continues to frame the object within a structure in which the object has a clearly defined place. What is *vorhanden* is not yet the material real in the sense that Lynch will conceive it in *Inland Empire*.

spontaneity of the actors. But within the scripted logic of the film there is something that doesn't fit.

The focus on *Inland Empire* is on the material that emerges from out of the script and yet doesn't fit in the world that the script constitutes. The film within *Inland Empire* – *On High in Blue Tomorrows* – has a script that director Kingsley Stewart (Jeremy Irons) apparently follows when he makes the film, but events occur that have no place within the script. The point is not that some unforeseen magic occurs when the cameras begin rolling that no script can anticipate, that the act of filming and making a movie has a creative power. Against this romanticism of the cinema, *Inland Empire* highlights a structural productivity. It is rather that script itself, understood as a fantasy, includes something that defies its own logic.

The first indication of a strange presence in the script for *On High in Blue Tomorrows* occurs when a neighbor, visitor #1 (Grace Zabriskie), arrives at Nikki's house early in the film. Her conversation with Nikki is awkward from the outset, but when she asks about Nikki's upcoming film, the awkwardness multiplies. When Nikki expresses doubt about whether or not she has the role, the visitor assures her that she does. As the visitor begins to question Nikki about the role, she stumbles, as if she encounters a word that she is physically unable to speak. She says, "It is a..." When the visitor tries to say the next word in the sentence, her head flinches, her eyes blink, and her mouth twitches. Lynch cuts to a close-up of Nikki looking puzzled at this bizarre interruption and then quickly back to the visitor who recovers herself and asks blandly, "It is an interesting role?" By registering this physical stumbling over a word concerning the film, Lynch provides a subtle hint about what the film contains, but this becomes more explicit as the conversation continues.

The dialogue between Nikki and the visitor becomes especially uncomfortable when she asks Nikki, "Is there a murder in your film?" Nikki replies, "Uh, no. It's not part of the story." The visitor continues, "No, I think you are wrong about that." Again, Nikki replies, "No." Finally, the visitor exclaims with a loud voice in a dramatic close-up, "Brutal fucking murder." The reverse shot of Nikki shows that this has disturbed her. She says, "I don't like this kind of talk, the things you've been saying. I think you should go now." What disturbs Nikki is not simply the language that the visitor uses but her insistence that the film contains an event that it isn't supposed to contain. Though the script, as Nikki indicates here, does not contain a murder, the film as we see it being filmed will. The murder doesn't belong in the film, and yet it appears in it. Lynch announces the presence of this piece that doesn't fit through a scene that doesn't seem to fit within the narrative of the film. Nothing prompts the visit to Nikki's house, and the visitor remains an eerie and unnamed figure. Though aspects of her conversation with Nikki appear normal, the overall strangeness of her visit foreshadows the material disruption in the film that she announces.[5]

---

[5] The Eastern European accent that actor Grace Zabriskie uses also announces the disturbance to come during the shooting of the film. Her voice foreshadows what Nikki will find in the film that doesn't belong there. Because the film is based on a Polish folk tale and an unfinished earlier European film, these earlier versions inject themselves into the current film and disturb the process of making it.

The clearest suggestion that materiality lurks within fantasy occurs during a discussion of *On High in Blue Tomorrows* at the studio. When the director Kingsley Stewart (Jeremy Irons) first goes over the script with Nikki and Devon, he tells them that the film is a remake of an original that was never finished. Nikki asks him why the film wasn't finished, and Kingsley replies with hesitation, "Well, after the characters had been film-ing for some time, they discovered something in... something... something inside the story." This prompts an outcry of disbelief from Devon, but Kingsley continues, "The two leads were murdered. It was based on a Polish gypsy folk tale. The title in German was *Vier Sieben*, *Four Seven*, and it was said to be cursed. So it turned out to be." Kingsley's manner of describing what happened during the filming of the original is crucial. Rather than simply saying that a tragedy occurred or that a strange event took place, he claims that "they discovered... some-thing inside the story." This formulation emphasizes that the filmic fantasy contains a material real that cannot be identified through any sort of symbolic designation, which is why Kingsley leaves it ambiguous while at the same time indicating its substantial status.

This material real lies at the center not just of *On High in Blue Tomor-rows* but also of *Inland Empire*. It inheres in Nikki's act of killing the Phantom (Krzysztof Majchrzak), the criminal figure who controls the Lost Girl. This act accomplishes something real, freeing the Lost Girl from her captivity, and it marks the emergence of the Lost Girl's own subjectivity. The Lost Girl's subjectivity, embodied in the act of killing the Phantom and freeing herself, does not fit within the structure of the fantasy, but it is only through the fantasmatic figure of Nikki Grace that it becomes ac-cessible.

Lynch makes this clear toward the end of the film when Nikki and the Lost Girl meet after the death of the Phantom. We see Nikki in the rabbit room – the point of transition between the social reality and the series of fantasies – where she is crying. A bright blue light begins to shine, and the song that began at the moment the Lost Girl experienced complete destitution starts again. As we hear the song, we see two women in a close-up, and then the film cuts to an image of the Lost Girl looking at the television but no longer crying. On the television screen, there are two women running down a hill, and it becomes clear that the Lost Girl is watching herself on television. When Nikki walks into the room, it is visi-ble on the television screen, and her shadow is simultaneously apparent in the actual room. But the next shot shows that Nikki is coming to the Lost Girl in the room itself, and when they kiss, the image is duplicated on the television screen. When Nikki slowly vanishes and leaves the Lost Girl alone, the film again underlines her fantasmatic status, though it is only through this fantasy that the Lost Girl accomplishes the reunion with her spouse and son that occurs in the next scene.

The materiality of fantasy derives from what fantasy tries to accom-plish for the subject. The function of fantasy for the subject is making the impossible possible. The subject confronts an impossible desire, a desire that cannot be realized, and fantasy constructs a scene where it is possi-ble to imagine the impossible happening. As Juan-David Nasio notes, "The function of the fantasy is to substitute for an impossible real satisfaction a possible fantasized satisfaction."[6] In order to envision the impossible, fantasy creates a world where the law of non-contradiction does not apply. Identities are doubled, while space and time fold over on themselves. Fantasy requires these violations of the law of non-contradiction because its ability to deliver enjoyment depends on the subject being removed from itself both spatially and temporally. Within a fantasy, one is at two places at the same time and in two temporalities at the same place.

Like the dream, film is a perfect fantasy space because it permits the spectator to be both involved in what's happening on the screen and removed from it. The spectator exists simultaneously in two different spaces and in two different temporalities. If the spectator identified completely with the actions and experiences of a character on the screen, the fantasy would be broken, and the film would lose its hold over the spectator. This explains the utter failure of Robert Montgomery's *Lady in the Lake* (1948), the film noir that attempts to place the spectator in the position of Montgomery's Philip Marlowe by confining the film to subjective shots from his point of view. This strategy allows for identification with Marlowe, but it doesn't allow for the spectator to develop a fantasmatic relation with the film. Without the contradictory experience of proximity and distance, fantasy cannot operate. It is this contradictory experience that permits fantasy to access the material real, a real that is at the source of all subjectivity.

In their groundbreaking exploration of fantasy, Jean Laplanche and Jean-Bertrand Pontalis locate fantasy around the question of origin.[7] Each of the fundamental fantasies they identify – the primal scene, castration, and seduction – attempt to envision the various moments at which subjectivity emerges. Fantasies privilege origins because the origin is what can't be explained from within a structure. No structure can account for its own emergence except retroactively in terms that presuppose what they intend to explain. The subject itself confronts the same problem. It originates in a loss of what it never had, so that any attempt to uncover its origin will necessarily falter when it comes to close to the truth. Fantasy, however, allows the subject to overcome this limitation and access the impossible origin.

Though not every fantasy directly concerns an origin, every fantasy is in a sense a fantasy of origins. Fantasy as such confronts what doesn't fit within the structure of subjectivity and imagines integrating it. Even the most banal fantasy – say, one involving a romantic attachment with a colleague at work – necessarily violates some sort of limit in order to envision the subject's satisfaction. No one fantasizes about what is smoothly integrated into her/his world, like one's spouse in marriage, simply because there is no enjoyment in such fantasies. If this part that doesn't fit is not specifically the origin, it is always a repetition of the origin – or a repetition of the disruptive power of the origin. The origin produces the symbolic structure through a violent act of negation that provides the ontological basis for the structure. And yet, the violence of

[6] Juan-David Nasio, *Le Fantasme: Le Plasir de Lire Lacan* (Paris: Petite Bibliothèque Payot, 2005) 13: "Le fantasme a pour fonction de substituer à une satisfaction reélle impossible, une satisfaction fantasmée possible."

[7] See Jean Laplanche and Jean-Bertrand Pontalis, *Fantasme originaire, fantasmes des origines, origines du fantasme* (Paris: Hachette, 1985).

the founding act (the beginning of a romance, the American Revolution, the overturning of Ptolemaic astronomy, the onset of Modernist art, and so on) has no place within the symbolic structure that it begets. Even the most secure relationship cannot sustain the disturbance of the initial experience of love and normalizes it through everyday rituals. But the disturbance of the origin continues to exist in the moments at which the symbolic structure fails, and these are the moments that attract fantasy, even when fantasy is not explicitly focused on origins. This disturbance is the real that fantasy allows us to access.

TOMORROW IS YESTERDAY

In order to access the material that doesn't fit, fantasy relies on a temporal dislocation. This dislocation is most clearly evident in the fantasy that directly focuses on the origin. In the fantasy of the primal scene, for instance, the subject views the parental coupling as it occurs before the birth of the subject who would be able to see it. What is impossible in a fantasy is not so much the event that takes place as the position from which the event is seen. Fantasy allows the subject to return to the past without losing the knowledge and perspective of the present.

The disruption of time in the fantasy world is apparent throughout *Inland Empire*, even very early in the film when we first see the rabbit room as the Lost Girl is watching television. The female rabbit sitting on the couch in the living room asks the other two, "What time is it?" This question occasions laughter from studio audience, suggesting that the rules of chronological time do not apply in this world. Soon after this scene, the first visitor tells Nikki, "I can't seem to remember if it's today, two days from now, or yesterday. I suppose if it was 9:45, I'd think it was after midnight." While the reaction to the rabbit's comment suggests that there is no objective chronological time, the first visitor's statement indicates her alienation from this version of time. In the film, characters experience time through their skewed relation to it. But it is this skewed relation to time in the fantasy structure of the film that renders visible subjectivity as such and the subject's capacity for intervention. This becomes most apparent after the sex scene between Nikki and Devon.

While they are still in bed together, Nikki describes what will be the next scene in the film. She tells him, "It is a story that happened yesterday, but I know it's tomorrow." Here, Nikki voices the split temporality of fantasy, its ability to show the future impinging on the past. She relates the story to Devon:

> It was that scene that we did yesterday when I'm getting groceries for you with your car, and it was in that alley. I parked the car. There's always parking there. So there I am... It's a scene we did yesterday. You weren't in it. That one when I'm in the alley. I'm going to get groceries for you with your car, and I parked there cause they're always parking. You know the one. I see this writing on metal, and I start remembering something. I'm remembering, this whole thing starts flooding in, this whole memory. I start to remember, and I don't know, I don't know what it is, it's me, Devon, it's me, Nikki.

The disturbing nature of this story manifests itself in Nikki's repetition of the initial details and in the panic she feels as she reaches the conclusion. It is also apparent in Devon's reaction. In the middle of the story, he interrupts, "Sue, damn," even though it is clear at this point that they are no longer making the film but are having sex as Nikki and Devon. Nikki herself recognizes her experience of a temporal loop in which she has returned to the past in order to encounter herself. This impossible encounter with oneself is how the subject experiences its subjectivity, but this encounter is necessarily traumatic in the way that it is for Nikki.

The film registers the trauma both visually and in the narrative. When Nikki first says, "It's me," while telling the story, she is referring to seeing herself in the earlier scene, but as she repeats it more urgently and with increasingly panic, it becomes evident that she wants Devon to affirm her identity. She says, "It's me, Devon, it's me Nikki. Look at me, you fucker." But Devon responds with laughter, and then a close-up of Nikki's face fades to black, which suggests her disappearance. The subsequent travelling shot of shadows moving through the empty halls of the house with a low menacing sound on the audio track underlines the disturbance.

The temporal disruption in fantasy is the mode through which fantasy depicts the subject as a material cause. Any attempt simply to describe the role of the subject inevitably has the effect of reducing subjectivity to a role within the symbolic structure. This is because descriptions follow the dictates of chronological time, and within chronological time, there is no room for what doesn't fit or doesn't work. Nothing sticks out in the forward and regular movement of time. But fantasy's disruption of time creates a space for subjectivity – or subjectivity is this disruption. The intervention of the subject creates a change from the future, a change that has causal antecedent in the past, and it is only fantasy, due to its ability to violate temporal laws, that can adequately represent this intervention.

Inland Empire depicts Nikki's encounter with herself that she describes in the sex scene with Devon in two scenes set apart from each other chronologically. In the first (well before Nikki's description), she is reading through the script on the set with Devon, Kingsley, and Kingsley's assistant Freddie (Harry Dean Stanton). During the reading, Freddie sees someone in the house constructed on the other side of the soundstage. Devon goes to investigate, and he hears someone running away but doesn't see anyone. He finds that the intruder escapes even though there seems to be no way out. As he reports back to the others, "They disappeared where it's real hard to disappear." Though the spectator doesn't know this at the time of this scene, Nikki is the intruder, and she is able to disappear because she moves not into another space but into another time. Through this seemingly unimportant scene, Lynch shows how subjectivity manifests itself: it is a disturbance that cannot be accounted for or explained in the objective world. He underlines this dimension of subjectivity by following Nikki's intrusion on the set with Kingsley's explanation that the original makers of their film found "something inside the story." This juxtaposition of Nikki's inexplicable appearance on the set from the future and the story of the discovery of something in the film aligns subjectivity with the material disturbance located at the center of fantasy.

When we later see this scene from Nikki's perspective in the future, the disturbance becomes more profound as the layers of the fantasy begin to multiply. After Nikki recounts the encounter with herself to Devon, the next scene in the film depicts that encounter. We see Nikki carrying a bag of groceries while walking down an alley toward Devon's parked car. She stops when she sees "AXXoN N." written on a metal door, and she enters through the open door adjacent to this one. The camera moves forward through a dark corridor, while a momentary flash of light illuminates Nikki. Finally, we see her emerge out of the darkness moving straight toward the camera. When she is first visible, she is blurry, but as she walks forward into a close-up, her face comes into focus. The blurriness of the image disguises the source of the voice that we hear, which sounds like Nikki. The reverse shot of Nikki, Devon, Kingsley, and Freddie reading through the script on the other side of the soundstage reveals that the voice did belong to Nikki, but not to the Nikki who was walking through the darkness. From Nikki's future perspective, we see the scene of the disturbance as it played out earlier. Devon comes to investigate, and Nikki, Kingsley, and Freddie stay behind. But in the final reverse shot, Nikki is absent from the image, even though she remained there throughout the earlier scene. After this disappearance, the Nikki of the future retreats and shuts herself in the house constructed at the back of the soundstage.

Once in the house, it is clear that Nikki has entered into a different fantasy world. Lynch emphasizes this through a series of shots in which she tries to make contact with Devon as he looks in from the outside. Lynch shows a panicked Nikki screaming "Billy" as she looks out the window of the house. A series of reverse shots show Devon looking at her but unable to see or hear. We see both Nikki and Devon in close-ups shot with a wide angle lens that distorts their faces and creates a sense of horror. The shots of Devon reveal the dirt and glare on the glass that obscures his vision, but the shots of Nikki show no similar obstacle. She has entered a space outside of the one they used to occupy, and the final shot of the failed interaction depicts Nikki in front of the window, which has become incredibly bright. The new fantasy space opens up in the next reverse shot, which doesn't show Devon (as the previous reverse shots had) but instead a driveway and gate leading out to a road.

In Lynch's earlier films, especially *Lost Highway* (1997) and *Mulholland Drive*, (2001) the collapse of a fantasy world would thrust the subject back into the social reality. In *Lost Highway*, the fantasy identity Peter Dayton (Balthazar Getty) disappears, and Fred Madison (Bill Pullman) reemerges as the moment when the fantasy concludes. In *Mulholland Drive*, Betty (Naomi Watts) finds herself returned to her mundane life as Diane after her fantasy loses its consistency. No such trajectory animates *Inland Empire*. Here, Nikki moves from one fantasy world into another at the moment of the first one's collapse – from the story of the film she is making in the present to the unfinished Polish original. The failure to confront the disturbance of subjectivity leads to yet another fantasy world that attempts to stage this confrontation again.

But at each point a fantasy collapses, we do see the relationship between fantasy and origins. *Inland Empire* shows how the temporal loop of fantasy permits an impossible return to the origin. The word that begins the film is "AXXoN N": we hear a recording that says, "AXXoN N, the longing radio play in history, tonight, continuing in the Baltic region, a gray winter day in an old hotel." This is the same word that Nikki finds on the metal door leading her back into the past. AXXoN N functions in the film as a master signifier, a signifier that begins the process of signification. Through it is nonsensical in itself, it inaugurates a world of sense by beginning a story.[8]

Fantasy gives this nonsensical beginning point a role in the narrative that it constructs, and in the process, it masks the nonsense of the master signifier. Rather than functioning as a nonsensical point of departure, the master signifier becomes a clue leading to the heart of the fantasy's mystery. AXXoN N points Nikki to an encounter with herself when she sees it on a door in the alley, and then later in the film its presence on another door directs her to the Phantom, whom she subsequently kills. Within the fantasy, the master signifier points toward subjectivity itself.

THE FREEDOM OF THE LOST GIRL

The various fantasy worlds that make up *Inland Empire* all emanate from the Lost Girl who appears at the beginning of the film. They represent her attempt to save herself from a situation in which she is reduced to sexual servitude by the Phantom. Here, fantasy has the opposite political valence from the one we typically associate with it. Rather than sustaining her bondage by blinding her to her oppressed situation, fantasy becomes the vehicle through which she can escape it. But the path through fantasy, as Lynch chronicles it in the film, is not an easy one. The freedom that fantasy provides demands an embrace of complete loss and destitution. Without this, fantasy can only function as an ideological supplement and leaves the subject within its oppressive situation. It is as if fantasy can free the subject only if it augments the trauma that the subject must endure.

After the initial image of the record playing, the film begins by exposing the situation of the Lost Girl, though Lynch leaves the situation much more ambiguous than one would expect. He shoots this world in black and white with very little lighting, making it impossible to have a sense of the setting, though the characters speak Polish. As the Lost Girl walks down a dark hotel hallway with a man, both her head and the head of the man are blurred beyond any recognition. This effect indicates the anonymity of both in this situation, where she is apparently a prostitute bringing her client to a room. She interacts without displaying any emotion concerning the sexual exchange. The image of the blurred heads continues throughout the scene, and when they have sex, the screen becomes so dark and blurry that they become indistinguishable. We hear the Lost Girl say (in Polish), "Where am I? I'm afraid. I'm afraid." Lynch initially depicts the Lost Girl as completely lost: she has no identity of her own; she is in the thrall of some man as his sex worker; she doesn't even have a distinct face or name. This is how Lynch envisions the zero point of the

---

[8] The choice of the term "AXXoN N" as the film's master signifier seems to make sense because it sounds similar to the director's call of "Action," which begins the construction of the filmic fantasy. But this is misleading: even the term "Action," when used to begin to create a fantasy structure, has a nonsensical status. One could begin with anything.

subject, lacking any substantial support for its identity or any network of signification to give it meaning. But out of this apparently hopeless situation, the power of fantasy emerges as a means of salvation.

Just as the Lost Girl expresses her fear a second time, music begins, and a woman sings, "From the other side, I see shining waves flowing." The song brings with it a change in the film's visuals: brighter light appears for the first time from what seems to be a window across the room, and then a shot of a movie camera introduces color for the first time in the film. The next shot depicts the Lost Girl sitting in a bright red dress on a green chair, and a reverse shot shows blue static on the television that she's watching. The movie camera and television screen bring color into the existence of the Lost Girl, and the tears that a subsequent close-up reveals are both tears of sorrow and tears of joy. The fantasy both makes her aware of her condition and imagines an exit from it.

The first images in the Lost Girl's fantasy are rabbits. The use of the rabbit room and the three rabbit characters seems to be just a moment of absurdity in *Inland Empire*. The rabbit often plays a privileged role in the world of fantasy, most obviously in *Alice in Wonderland*, but also in *Harvey* (Henry Koster, 1950), *The Matrix* (Andy and Larry Wachowski, 1999), and *Donnie Darko* (Richard Kelly, 2001). In most of these instances, the rabbit provides an introduction to the fantasy space, which is what the rabbits do for the Lost Girl in *Inland Empire*. The rabbits moving in fast forward represent the first image of the fantasy that she sees. Fantasy initially lures the subject with an image of respite from an impossible situation. This is why the first fantasmatic image in *Inland Empire* includes the pacifying figures of the rabbits. As the Lost Girl looks from her horrible situation to the television screen, the rabbits embody the possibility of a non-threatening escape.

The problem is that the rabbits do not represent the end point of the fantasy but just the beginning. From the destitute position of the Lost Girl, the flight to fantasy seems like a pure relief, but as the film goes on, it becomes clear that fantasy has its own traumatic dimension that the rabbit room serves to screen.[9] Past this screen, the fantasy offers the possibility of subjectivity and freedom, but these come with the cost of embracing an even greater destitution than the Lost Girl endures at the beginning of the film. Though we turn to fantasy to avoid the experience of loss, Lynch reveals in *Inland Empire* that the very structure of fantasy requires restaging the loss that we hope to avoid by turning to it. Rather than allowing us to elude castration, fantasy demands that we come to embrace it.

Castration is the debt that the subject pays to the social order in which it exists. A subject sacrifices a part of itself – the possibility of the ultimate enjoyment – in order to co-exist with other subjects who have

---

[9] The clown functions in *Inland Empire* in the same way as the rabbit. We seek relief from the everyday in the exaggerated features of the clown, but they can quickly become the source of terror. The figure of the clown becomes horrifying at two crucial points in *Inland Empire*. Toward the end of the film, a long shot shows Nikki walking across a clown face painting on the floor. The scene is dimly lit and a spotlight follows Nikki, as she moves in slow motion. As the scene ends, the camera moves to a close-up of her face, which looks like a terrifying clown face. A quick reverse shot shows her normal face as if it was looking at the clown version of herself, and she appears horrified by the image. When Nikki kills the Phantom at the end of the film, he has the face of a clown, with the large red lips actually created by blood.

made a similar sacrifice. This sacrificed enjoyment is then embodied by the phallic signifier, to which no one has access though many try to possess. But trouble that castration causes does not begin with the struggle over the phallic signifier; instead, it stems from the illusion that castration creates. The subject of castration believes that it has lost something substantial, that it has sacrificed a possibility for enjoyment that really existed rather than a possibility that came into existence through the act of being sacrificed. Though castration involves sacrificing what one doesn't have for an entity (the social group) that doesn't exist, it nonetheless creates the illusion of the substantiality of what was lost and of what was gained. This is what leads to fantasy.

Faced with the loss of an imaginary part of themselves, subjects turn to fantasy as a way of eluding castration. Through its return to the origin of subjectivity, fantasy promises to restore the enjoyment that the subject has lost through castration. Through fantasy, neurotics attempt to cheat the law of castration while outwardly obeying it. Fantasy makes it possible for the subject to bypass the sacrifice of enjoyment without any real-life consequences. This is crucial to fantasy's appeal.

But within the fantasy structure of *Inland Empire*, the idea of consequences recurs through the form of the two strange visitors that Nikki receives. Toward the beginning of the film, the first visitor tells her, "if today was tomorrow, you wouldn't even remember that you owed on an unpaid bill. Actions do have consequences." The second visitor repeats this idea much later, "I come about an unpaid bill that needs paying." These two interventions point toward the idea that fantasy tries to elude a payment that cannot be eluded. Though fantasy initially promises a way of cheating castration, the enjoyment that it provides depends on the experience of loss. Nikki submits to loss as she is stabbed and dies on Hollywood Boulevard. This experience, in which she is playing the part of Sue in the film, allows Nikki to shoot the Phantom and free the Lost Girl.

THE OTHER SIDE OF MATERIALISM

Nikki's death scene shows her experience of absolute loss and the insignificance of that loss for those around her. Not only does she die an anonymous death amid street people on Hollywood Boulevard, but even those surrounding her at the time of her death are focused on the question of whether or not the bus goes to Pomona rather than her demise. This testifies not to the cruel indifference of the three people next to Nikki – they seem sympathetic to her, in fact – but to the predominance of their own suffering. As the first (Helena Chase) and second (Nae) street person talk about the bus, Lynch intersperses shots of Nikki as she lies dying on the ground. She is situated between them, but her death doesn't register within their conversation.

As Nikki is dying, the second street person relates a story about her friend Niko in Pomona that forges again the connection between Hollywood fantasy and the experience of loss. Niko has a beautiful blonde wig that makes everyone fall for her. According to the woman:

My friend Niko who lives in Pomona was a blonde wig. She wears it at parties, but she is on hard drugs and turning tricks now. She looks very good in her blonde wig just like a movie star. Even girls fall in love with her when she's looking so good in her blonde star wig. She blows kisses and laughs but she has got a hole in her vagina wall. She has torn a hole into her intestine from her vagina... She has seen a doctor, but it is too expensive. And now she knows her time has run out.

The woman narrating this story combines the fantasmatic glamour of Hollywood with the material destruction of the body. After she completes her story, Nikki vomits blood onto the sidewalk, and in a long shot, we see the blood flow over one of the stars on Hollywood Boulevard. The first street woman comforts Nikki at the moment of her death, lighting her lighter in front of Nikki's eyes and telling her, "no more blue tomorrows, you're on high now, love." The lengthy close-up on Nikki's face after her death registers this moment of absolute loss, but what follows situates this experience of loss within the world of filmic fantasy.

As the camera pulls back from Nikki's dead body lying on Hollywood Boulevard, eerie music begins and another camera becomes visible, revealing that we have been seeing the death of Sue, not Nikki, who is playing Sue in the film. Here, Lynch makes reference to the common method for alluding to the material dimension of cinematic production: rendering the filmmaking apparatus itself visible. Typically, showing the camera works to block the power of the filmic fantasy, but what occurs in the death scene in *Inland Empire* immediately after the camera becomes visible indicates Lynch's continued commitment to the fantasy. The visible camera pulls back so that it once again disappears from the frame, and it is at this point that the film's director yells, "Cut it." By first showing the camera and then moving it out of sight, Lynch prioritizes the perspective of the fantasy. We do not see the material apparatus directly but from within the structure of the fantasy, which allows us access to it. It is the film that renders visible not just the experience of death but also the destitution that exists on Hollywood Boulevard.

By plunging the spectator back into the fantasy and eliminating the possibility of inhabiting a position outside the fantasy, Lynch takes up a relationship to Hollywood that one would not expect in a film like *Inland Empire*. The narrative and visual structure of the film represents a direct challenge to the conventions that dominate Hollywood, and the story reveals the horrors of the studio productions. One can thus understand why Jonathan Rosenbaum sees the film as a full-fledged critique of Hollywood. He notes, "In *Inland Empire*, after 30 years of struggling with studios, he goes further, recording some of his own visceral recoil from Hollywood in general and its meat market in particular – which makes me wonder if his art has been permanently changed for the better."[10] Lynch no doubt shares Rosenbaum's contempt for studio control and for Hollywood's exploitation of powerless women and men, but *Inland Empire* is not for all that a critique of Hollywood. Lynch's decision to pull back the camera and transport the spectator back into the fantasy offers the indication that, despite whatever contempt he might feel, he finally takes the side of Hollywood and the fantasies that it produces. Hollywood's retreat from reality represents our path to materiality.

[10] Jonathan Rosembaum, "Hollywood from the Fringes," *Chicago Reader* (26 January 2007): http://www.chicagoreader.com/features/stories/moviereviews/2007/070126/.

The link between the specific fantasies of Hollywood and materiality becomes clear when Doris Side stabs Sue/Nikki toward the end of the film. After the stabbing, Sue pulls the screwdriver out of her stomach and drops it to the ground, where it lands next to one of the stars on Hollywood Boulevard. Lynch's use of lighting is pivotal in the shot that depicts the screwdriver on the ground. The well-lit left side of the image clearly reveals the screwdriver and the first name on the star – "Dorothy" – but the last name is almost impossible to make out in this brief shot on a single viewing (which is why some early reviewers of the film speculated incorrectly concerning Dorothy's last name).[11] By leaving the name "L'Amour" in shadow, Lynch visually suggests a reference not to an actor named "Dorothy" but to a character. The reference to *The Wizard of Oz* (Victor Fleming, 1939) appears at this point in the film because it represents the ultimate Hollywood fantasy, and Lynch juxtaposes the allusion to this fantasy with what seems to be an ordinary screwdriver (albeit one used as a murder weapon). Here, *Inland Empire* reveals the power of Hollywood fantasy to affect our way of seeing. Through its lens, we are able to see the material object not as a simple tool to be used but as something taken out of the world of functionality where a smooth relationship exists between causes and effects.

It is important that the primary weapon in *Inland Empire* is not a knife or a gun but a screwdriver. Knives and guns are, of course, designed to function as weapons while screwdrivers, though they can certainly maim and even kill, are not. The use to which Doris Side puts the screwdriver sticks out in the way that subjectivity itself sticks out.[12] There is no direct through-line leading from the production of the screwdriver to its use as a weapon. As a result, *Inland Empire* allows us to see the screwdriver in its materiality, especially when it falls to the ground next to the Hollywood star. The filmic fantasy exposes the object in a way that no other form might.

This privilege of the filmic fantasy receives its ultimate affirmation in the epilogue of *Inland Empire*, which plays over the closing credits. Before the credits begin, a woman with one leg and an odd stick in place of the other walks across a parlor, stops, looks around, and says, "Sweet."[13] The camera then travels around the room and locates other characters alluded to in the film or from other films, such as Laura Harring from *Mulholland Drive* or Nastassja Kinski from Wim Wenders' *Paris, Texas* (1984),

---

11 For instance, Barry Paris suggests that it is the star of Dorothy Stratten, and Scott Marks claims that the star belongs to Dorothy Malone. See Barry Paris, "*Inland Empire*: David Lynch Crafts a Baffling Visual Delight," *Pittsburgh Post-Gazette* (5 April 2007): http://www.post-gazette.com/pg/07095/775205-120.stm; and Scott Marks, "*Inland Empire*," *Emulsion Compulsion* (29 August 2007): http://www.emulsioncompulsion.com/2007/08/29/reviews/dvd-reviews/inland-empire-david-lynch-2007.

12 When we first see Doris Side early in the film, the screwdriver is literally sticking out of her side. She arrives at a police station to confess that she has been hypnotized to kill someone "with a screwdriver." When she says these words, the camera pans down her chest to a bandage underneath her shirt. As she unwraps the bandage, we see the screwdriver stabbed into her side, which adds a level of irony to her name.

13 This woman appears to be the sister of the Phantom. In her interview with Mr. K, Nikki alludes to her while describing the Phantom. She says, "He was a marine from North Carolina. He had a sister with one leg. She had a sort of car stick for the other one. She killed three kids in the first grade. This is the kind of shit. Fucking funny, people. They all got their own peculiarities, their own way of living."

who is sitting on a couch next to Nikki.[14] During this survey of the room, Lynch cuts to a close-up of a saw cutting a log, after which a group of women walks to the center of the room and begin to dance to Nina Simone's "Sinner Man." Though the epilogue focuses on the women (and especially the one woman lip-synching the song), we do continue to see the lumberjack sawing the log first in a separate shot and then at the edge of the image of the women. Of course, the lumberjack cutting a log has no place in an elegant room full of women dancing. Without his presence, this would be a scene straight from a Fellini film, a phantasmagoria that leaves the material world completely behind. But his presence is what places this scene within Lynch's universe. Rather than just an odd juxtaposition or weirdness for the sake of weirdness, the lumberjack amid the dancing women stands out as the material real that fantasy allows us to access. It is only within fantasies, such as the kind that Hollywood produces, that the work of the subject itself – not work that creates a useful or saleable commodity, but work that no calculus can account for – stands out.

---

[14] The presence of Nastassja Kinski in the epilogue, along with the casting of Harry Dean Stanton as Freddie, serves as a clear allusion to *Paris, Texas,* a film in which they play the two principal roles. *Inland Empire* alludes specifically to this film because it also shows the productive power of fantasy. It is only through the fantasy space of a peep show that Harry Dean Stanton's character Travis is able to reveal the truth to Nastassja Kinski's Jane, his former spouse. For an analysis of this dynamic in *Paris, Texas,* see Todd McGowan, *The Real Gaze: Film Theory After Lacan* (Albany: SUNY Press, 2007).

GREG HAINGE
RED VELVET: LYNCH'S CINEMAT(OGRAPH)IC ONTOLOGY

Since Michel Chion's early monograph from 1992 (and which first appeared in English translation in 1995), much ink has been spilled on the
work of David Lynch. Books have appeared by Martha Nochimson (1997),
Paul A. Woods (1997), Slavoj Žižek (2000), David Hughes (2001), Jeff
Johnson (2004), Todd McGowan (2007), Michelle Le Blanc and Colin
Odell (2007), Eric G Wilson (2007), Mark Stewart (2008) and, most recently, the mammoth and completist tome by Greg Olson, *David Lynch:
Beautiful Dark* (2008).[1] All of these books in different ways and to differ-
ing degrees perform a narrativization of Lynch's films, re-recounting them
from a specific, situated positionality so as to render the particular interpretative strategy they employ all the more persuasive for the reader. This
is the case even in Michel Chion's early work, in spite of his own take on
Lynch's cinema. Indeed, in his analysis of Lynch's early work *The Grandmother*, Chion begins with a scene by scene re-narration of the short film,
all the while drawing attention to the apparent inconsistency of his own
method, writing:

> I have asked the reader to bear with this laborious effort to recount in detail
> an unnarratable film which is, first of all, a series of images, sounds, ges-
> tures, bodies and actions which must be grasped literally before any
> attempt at interpretation, because I wanted to start the evocation of David
> Lynch's cinema by illustrating what this disconcerting world is based upon:
> a very peculiar logic requiring us to renounce all *a priori* interpretations of
> behavior and facts, whether taken separately or in succession.[2]

Chion's comments here indicate very clearly that he is on the side of
those critics (like myself[3]) who contend that Lynch is a director who in
some way refuses to make sense, and yet, even as he asserts this he
cannot but re-narrate the films, which is to say insert them into a framework which would appear to obey an external logic, a set in which there
would be some relation of cause and effect between the individual elements. This is perhaps a more general tendency of cinema criticism, but it
is certainly the dominant approach in Lynch studies, nearly all of the

* With thanks to Tony Thwaites, my favourite Lacanian, Matthew Campora for sharing his
excellent work on a similar topic, and the Centre for Critical and Cultural Studies at the University of Queensland for providing the author with a Faculty Fellowship without which this paper
could not have been written.

1 Note that this list includes only those works that deal with Lynch's entire *œuvre* and does not
therefore include studies of single films, nor edited collections such as Sheen and Davidson
(2004), nor the essential book of interviews *Lynch on Lynch*, edited by Chris Rodley.
2 Michel Chion, *David Lynch*, trans. Robert Julian (London: British Film Institute, 1995) 20.
3 Greg Hainge, "Weird or Loopy? Specular Spaces, Feedback and Artifice in Lost Highway's
Aesthetics of Sensation," *The Cinema of David Lynch: American Dreams, Nightmare Visions*,
ed. Erica Sheen and Annette Davison (London: Wallflower Press, 2004) 137.

monographs cited wishing to make the films conform to an overarching narrative not only as individual filmic texts but also as a body of work in which each limb would conform, to a greater or lesser degree, to the whole mapped out by a kind of genetic blueprint.

The narrative structures to which Lynch's work is made to conform are, more often than not, psychoanalytic ones, often invoking dream theories be they Jungian, Freudian or Lacanian. One of the most impressive such works to my mind is Todd McGowan's *The Impossible David Lynch*, which manages to find a common thread running through even those parts of Lynch's *œuvre* that, for most critics, need to be considered separately due to the particularities of the industrial circumstances and collaborative modes through which they were made, namely *Dune* and *The Straight Story*. Whilst I am sure he did not intend his title to serve as an ironic commentary on his own methodology *à la Chion*, McGowan's text ultimately performs the impossible and rids Lynch's work of the apparent impossibility it presents by inserting every aspect of it into a pre-established interpretative framework, a narrative structure that, I would argue, is not its own. So whilst I find McGowan's arguments utterly compelling in their own right, I find ultimately that their potential to serve as critiques of Lynch's films hangs not so much on their applicability to an immanent reading of the cinematic text such as that proposed by Chion but, rather, on the reader's own investment in and adherence to the psychoanalytic narrative being proposed. This is to say, then, that McGowan, like so many others, *refuses* to let Lynch's films not make sense. This can be seen very clearly at the start of the following passage which goes on to give a prime example of one of those psychoanalytic narratives whose credibility as a valid analytic strategy may well depend solely on the reader's own ideological and critical sympathies. McGowan writes:

> The bizarre nature of MIKE's rant suggests that Lynch obscures what he's saying with engine noise in order to hide the fact that he isn't saying anything – that MIKE speaks nonsense. But psychoanalysis renders this seemingly incoherent statement sensible. MIKE indicates that Leland's incestuous activity is a theft of enjoyment – a stealing of the corn – and that it cannot continue because "the thread will be torn." Phallic authority's effort to enjoy without the tearing of the thread, without loss, inevitably fails. The phallus never successfully possesses the privileged object, but merely engages in an endless pursuit of this object, a pursuit that results in the satisfaction of the drive. [4]

Whether through an incessant re-narration of the plot elements of Lynch's films – such that these individual elements are imbued with a coherence that is often not as present in the filmic texts themselves – or the kind of re-narrativization undertaken by McGowan here and in which every aspect of the Lynchian *œuvre* is seen to obey the exigencies of an externally imposed (often psychoanalytic) narrative, we might then say of the critical responses to Lynch's work something similar to what Tom Gunning has suggested in regards to scholarship in the history of cinema. Gunning comments: "the history of early cinema, like the history of cinema gener-

---

[4] Todd McGowan, *The Impossible David Lynch* (New York: Columbia University Press, 2007) 148.

ally, has been written and theorized under the hegemony of narrative films."[5] For Gunning, pre-1906 cinema cannot be viewed in the same way as cinema post-1906 when, in the period running from 1907-1913, there comes about a period of *"narrativization* of the cinema, culminating in the appearance of feature films which radically revised the variety format."[6] Cinema pre-1906 is characterized not by its adherence to a narrative structure, but is what Gunning terms (adapting Sergei Eisenstein's notion of the attraction, which "aggressively subject[s] the spectator to sensual or psychological impact") a "cinema of attractions."[7] This is a conception of the cinema that sees it "less as a way of talking stories than as a way of presenting a series of views to an audience, fascinating because of their illusory power... and exoticism."[8] It is a cinema that delights in "its ability to *show* something... an exhibitionist cinema" that "directly solicits spectator attention, inciting visual curiosity, and supplying pleasure through an exciting spectacle."[9] In the cinema of attractions, furthermore, "theatrical display dominates over narrative absorption, emphasizing the direct simulation of shock or surprise at the expense of unfolding a story or creating a diegetic universe."[10] This, then, is a cinema which constitutes the polar opposite of classical narrative cinema in which "the various components of cinema expression [are] mobilized around, and subjected to, strict narrative ends."[11] Rather, as for Méliès, "the scenario, the 'fable,' or 'tale'" is considered only "at the end" since it has *"no importance,"* surviving "merely as a pretext for the 'stage effects,' the 'tricks,' or for a nicely arranged tableau."[12]

To suggest that Lynch's cinema is just such a cinema of attractions may seem somewhat counter-intuitive given the apparent periodization and supplanting of this cinematic form that Gunning's account would seem to imply. However, whilst certain aspects of the cinema of attractions were indeed consigned to history books by successive developments – and this is the case particularly with the material conditions of exhibition, the variety format and fairground spectacle of vaudeville and the nickelodeon[13] – post-1906, as Gunning notes, "the cinema of attractions does not disappear with the dominance of narrative, but rather goes underground, both into certain avant-garde practices and as a component of narrative films."[14] This is to say – as Malte Hagener notes in his chapter of a book which both reappraises the early work on the cinema of attractions by Gunning and others and then proves the ahistorical usefulness of this term through a series of analyses of contemporary films that turn around this concept of "attractions" – that whilst the "cinema of attrac-

[5] Tom Gunning, "The Cinema of Attractions: Early film, its Spectator and the Avant-Garde," *The Cinema of Attractions Reloaded*, ed. Wanda Strauven (Amsterdam: Amsterdam University Press, 2006) 56.

[6] Gunning, "The Cinema of Attractions," 60.

[7] Gunning, "The Cinema of Attractions," 59.

[8] Gunning, "The Cinema of Attractions," 57.

[9] Gunning, "The Cinema of Attractions," 57, 58.

[10] Gunning, "The Cinema of Attractions," 59.

[11] Andre Gaudreault, "From 'Primitive Cinema' to 'Kine-Attractography,'" *The Cinema of Attractions Reloaded*, ed. Wanda Strauven (Amsterdam: Amsterdam University Press, 2006) 98.

[12] Méliès qtd in Gunning, "The Cinema of Attractions," 57.

[13] See Gunning, "The Cinema of Attractions," 59-60.

[14] Gunning, "The Cinema of Attractions," 57.

tions" is wrongly understood in most applications of it "as the opposite to narrative integration," Gunning in fact uses the two terms "as dialectical recto-and-verso which coexisted (and continue to do so) ever since the first films encountered an audience."[15] Thus, for Hagener, these categories must not be thought of in terms of a neat periodization but, rather, as "a continuum in which the dominance of one term over the other imperceptibly gave way."[16] Ultimately, then, "where one can find attractions, one can also find integration on another level – and the other way around."[17] For Wanda Strauven, the editor of this collection of essays, the cinema of attractions is similarly imbricated in all cinema forms to such an extent that she provocatively wonders whether "the cinema of attractions is the true nature of cinema and that we have to consider classical cinema as a detour or 'intermezzo'?"[18]

In what remains of this paper I want to take up this provocation and ask whether we might in fact better understand Lynch's cinema if we do not subject it to the kind of integrative approaches favored by the two types of narratival analysis we started off by examining. This is not to say, as should be clear by now, that Lynch entirely rejects all kinds of narrative structure, for this is obviously not the case. Rather, I want to suggest that his cinema is situated on this continuum between narrative integration and attractions, that there are moments throughout his work when the text seems explicitly to resist full narrative closure. What is more, this often happens at moments when the films seem either to delight in their own trickery, at moments of great monstration, or when we enter an über-cinematic space, suggesting, perhaps, that attractions do indeed constitute one of the essential poles of the cinema for Lynch, a constituent part of its ontology as a relational event, which is to say an ontology in which the spectator would also be imbricated in the phenomenological scene of cinema as viewing experience.

As befits the content of this paper, the following sections will not be inserted into a fully integrated framework, every aspect pulled back and tied down to the narrative woven up until this point. Rather, like Méliès, this narrative will stand as the pretext to present, as in a variety format, some of Lynch's own stage effects and it will do so, in its own self-reflexive way, in a number of acts.

ACT I. WHAT LYNCH SAID

Even though Lynch has himself been involved with transcendental meditation since the very early days of his career, his own book on the subject, in which this practice is explicitly articulated to his artistic activity, did not appear until the very end of 2006. It is no doubt in part because of this that, with the notable exception of Olson, the authors of the monographs cited have never really explored the links between Lynch's filmic output and transcendental meditation. For the purposes of the present study,

---

[15] Malte Hagener, "Programming Attractions: Avant-Garde Exhibition Practice in the 1920s and 1930s," *The Cinema of Attractions Reloaded*, ed. Wanda Strauven (Amsterdam: Amsterdam University Press, 2006) 265.

[16] Hagener, "Programming Attractions," 265.

[17] Hagener, "Programming Attractions," 266.

[18] *The Cinema of Attractions Reloaded*, ed. Wanda Strauven (Amsterdam: Amsterdam University Press, 2006) 24.

what is interesting about this book is not so much its commentary on the practice of transcendental meditation but rather the insight it provides into Lynch's opinions on the cinema as an event whose relational ontology is created both in the cinematographic space of the cinema as a technologically-specific medium and in the cinematic space of the theater (to use the US nomenclature). Indeed, in *Catching the Big Fish: Meditation, Consciousness, and Creativity*, we find Lynch proclaiming:

> It's so magical – I don't know why – to go into a theater and have the lights go down. It's very quiet, and then the curtains start to open. Maybe they're red. And you go into a world.[19]
>
> Cinema is a language. It can say things – big, abstract things. And I love that about it. [...]
>
> For me, it's so beautiful to think about these pictures and sounds flowing together in time and in sequence, making something that can be done only through cinema. It's not just words or music – it's a whole range of elements coming together and making something that didn't exist before. It's telling stories, it's devising a world, an experience, that people cannot have unless they see that film.
>
> When I catch an idea for a film, I fall in love with the way cinema can express it. I like a story that holds abstractions, and that's what cinema can do.[20]
>
> A film should stand on its own. It's absurd if a filmmaker needs to say what a film means in words. The world in the film is a created one, and people sometimes love going into that world. For them that world is real. And if people find out certain things about how something was done, or how this means this or that means that, the next time they see the film, these things enter into the experience. And then the film becomes different. I think it's so precious and important to maintain that world and not say certain things that could break the experience.
>
> You don't need anything outside of the work.[21]
>
> Cinema is a lot like music. It can be very abstract, but people have a yearning to make intellectual sense of it, to put it right into words. And when they can't do that, it feels frustrating.[22]

A similar reflection on the specificity of the cinematic medium and the importance of the cinematic experience can be found in a section called "True experience" on the extras disc that comes with some of the DVD versions of *Inland Empire*. Lynch explains:

> Then comes a sound that's quite loud, and if you can hear that wind, then probably that next sound will be loud enough to feel the feeling. Now if you're playing the music on a telephone or on your computer, you will never in a trillion years experience the film. You'll think you have experienced it, but you'll be cheated, it will be a weak, you'll be experiencing weakness, an extreme petrification of a potential experience in another world. So don't let your friends or some television advertisement trick you into accepting weakness. It's such a sadness. Power in that world is critical. Everything has been worked on to be a certain way, and if you don't

---

[19] David Lynch, *Catching the Big Fish: Meditation, Consciousness, and Creativity* (New York: Tarcher, 2006) 15.
[20] Lynch, *Catching the Big Fish*, 17.
[21] Lynch, *Catching the Big Fish*, 19.
[22] Lynch, *Catching the Big Fish*, 20.

have a set-up for your film, it's just a joke, a sickening, horrifying joke, and this world is so troubled, and it's such a sadness that you think you've seen a film on your fucking telephone. Get real.

ACT II. MONSTERS

Monsters of one kind or another populate all of David Lynch's films. The most obvious examples can be found, of course, in *Eraserhead*, *Dune* and *The Elephant Man*, whilst a different kind of, let us say, psychopathic monster can be found in *Blue Velvet*, *Twin Peaks* and *Wild at Heart*. These are not Lynch's only monsters, however, for a monster is not only a being that deviates from the natural or conventional order, be this physiological or moral, but also, via an alternative etymology, a monstrative being, a being who exists to be seen or shown. For whilst the Oxford English Dictionary prefers the Latin cognate *monere*, to warn, many (including McKenzie whose article is of direct relevance to this paper) trace the term back to the Medieval Latin *monstrare*, to show – or show forth, as Shildrick specifies.[23] Marie Hélène Huet suggests that this is a matter of different traditions and traces this signification of the word monster back to Augustine's *City of God*, through to the Renaissance when Fortunio Liceti wrote in 1616,

> monsters are thus named, not because they are signs of things to come, as Cicero and the Vulgate believed... but because they are such that their new and incredible appearance stirs admiration and surprise in the Beholders, and startles them so much that everyone wants to show them to others [se les *monstre* réciproquement].[24]

Yet perhaps, as with our previous account of divergent early cinema forms, it is once again the case here that these two alternative etymologies are not in fact mutually exclusive, one supplanting the other at a certain point in time but, rather, that they always already inhabit each other. Margrit Shildrick writes:

> Monstrously embodied selves are, then, fundamentally disturbing in that they cannot be accounted for within the binary parameters of sameness and difference, in which the latter is measured in terms of the former. Instead, they transgress boundaries in being simultaneously too close, too recognizable (threatening merging, indifference), and in being excessive, in being irreducibly other to the binary itself.[25]

"Fundamentally disturbing" and "irreducibly other;" is the monstrous body that is defined according to its deviation from a norm not then necessarily also a monstrative body, a body which constitutes an appeal to vision, a hypervisible body? If so, then the cast of monsters in Lynch's films grows exponentially.

---

[23] Margrit Shildrick, "Monstrous Reflections on the Mirror of the Self-Same," *Belief, Bodies and Being: Feminist Reflections on Embodiment*, ed. Deborah Orr, et al. (Lanham: Rowman and Littlefield, 2006) 38.

[24] Qtd in Marie Hélène Huet, *Monstrous Imagination* (Cambridge: Harvard University Press, 1993) 6.

[25] Margrit Shildrick, "Becoming Vulnerable: Contagious Encounters and the Ethics of Risk," *Journal of Medical Humanities* 21.4 (2000): 220.

ACT II, SCENE I

The Elephant Man constitutes the most obvious example of a convergence of this dual etymology, for the freak show is a monstrative space for the display of monsters. The climax of *Eraserhead*, meanwhile, comes as Henry cuts away his baby's swaddling-clothes, not only or perhaps not even primarily as an escape from a situation he can no longer bear but precisely in order for us to be able to *see*. This shot of Henry's baby constitutes a hiatus in the film's syntax, one of those moments of monstration found by Gaudreault and Gunning where the shot "is implicitly understood as an autonomous and autarkic unity,"[26] the film's punctum if you will. And can we not say the same of *Blue Velvet's* most famous scene when Frank becomes doubly monstrous as he is *seen* in a spectacle that is then explicitly figured on screen for yet another viewer?

The excessive monstration of certain characters and scenes in Lynch's films, though, makes monsters also of less obvious targets. The über-monstrative scenes in *Lost Highway*, for instance, come at the start of the film with the arrival of the video tapes which figure the entire filmic and diegetic space as a panopticon where everything is always on show. This theme is continued with the appearances of the Mystery Man with the video camera who shows himself to Fred, and Fred to himself in scenes which, significantly, always confound the possibility of total narrative integration.

ACT II, SCENE II

It is perhaps in *Mulholland Drive* more than in any other of Lynch's films, however, that the entire space of the film turns around this central problematic of a desire to *see* and concomitant inability to make that which is seen cohere in an enclosed, containable and therefore safe structure. This is figured explicitly, of course, in the film's very title which is articulated to the film's thematics not only because of its Hollywood connections, but also because the road that lends its name to the film contains a particularly acute blind corner, which is to say a point at which one strains to see, an appeal to vision. This monstrative site, as the film's opening scene shows us in graphic detail, is hostile to narrative, for it is at this bend that the woman who will become Rita's own personal narrative is erased from her memory. More than this, however, the crash scene itself is shot not only or primarily to serve the film's narrative ends but, rather, as an end in itself, as a spectacle or attraction to be watched for a pleasure that has nothing to do with narrative progression or closure and more to do with a pure sensation and erotics akin to that found in JG Ballard's work dealing with this kind of event.

ACT II, SCENE III

This same spatial configuration recurs at other key moments in the film, the monstrative scene that is presented in each case presenting what we might well term an erotics of the image or shot insofar as these scenes are staged precisely in order to seduce the viewer, to arouse in her a

---

[26] Andre Gaudreault and Tom Gunning, "Early Cinema as a Challenge to Film History," *The Cinema of Attractions Reloaded*, ed. Wanda Strauven (Amsterdam: Amsterdam University Press, 2006) 375.

sense of expectation that, when the reveal finally comes, is dissipated not in the *jouissance* of intellectual integration but, rather, the very opposite, the confounding of narrative that requires us to invent new modes of apprehension, a mere acceptance of that which appears to us as irreconcilably other, of the monstrous. Indeed, at key moments in *Mulholland Drive*, the camera follows the same spatial trajectory as the car heading down Mulholland Drive, a tracking shot heading towards a point beyond which we cannot see but where we know something to be seen awaits.

The first of these moments comes once Rita, after the car crash, has stumbled down the hill and hidden herself in Betty's Aunt's apartment. We cut to a scene where Dan tells Herb of a recurring dream he has been having about the Winkie's restaurant where they are sitting. Dan explains that in his dream he has seen a monstrous looking man out the back of the restaurant, a man with a face he hopes he will never see outside a dream. The two men thus go to see if the man is there so that Dan can "get rid of this goddawful feeling," which is to say to achieve narrative closure by confirming that this figure is just a figment of his imagination, existing only in his dreams. So they leave the restaurant and walk towards the wall behind which there may be a monster waiting to be seen. A tracking shot presents us Dan's perspective as we get closer so that when the monster does as is its wont and shows itself, the shock is as great for us as for Dan who falls in a faint. This monster (in reality a particularly dirty and dreadlocked bum played by Bonnie Aarons) seems to have no function in relation to plot progression – indeed, this entire scene seems to be merely incidental if not entirely superfluous if the film is analyzed under the hegemony of narrative. What is more, the Bum does not only resist integration into narrative structure, when he returns in the final section of the film (to be analyzed later) he seems increasingly to take on the role of an active destroyer of narrative at the very moment when some semblance of narrative coherence attempts to struggle into existence.

The Bum or monster behind the wall then must not, cannot be integrated into a coherent structure (nor perhaps even a fixed gender since attributed a male gender by Dan yet played by a female actor); he stands precisely as that which frustrates all attempts to do so and yet is mockingly held up by Lynch as that which might allow us to unlock the film's mysteries. When the film was first released, the promotional website for the film offered Lynch aficionados an interactive game in which players were invited to solve a series of puzzles that would provide them with an extension number to punch into an animated version of one of the telephones found in the film. The carrot to entice the player to advance through all of the game's levels was the promise that upon successful completion, the code to interpret the film would be given to the player. When the game was completed, however, the player was presented only with the very same scene as Dan in the film as, out of nowhere, the Bum emerged from behind a wall.

The second instance of this spatial trajectory figured by a tracking shot heading towards a point beyond which we cannot initially see and that becomes, as the camera turns a corner, incomprehensible as opposed to invisible comes after the scene in Club Silencio. Having witnessed Rebekah del Rio collapse to the ground, Betty, crying, reaches into her handbag to find a tissue but discovers a mysterious small blue metallic box with a triangular key hole. Betty and Rita rush home; Betty places the box on the bed then inexplicably disappears as Rita pulls down a hat box from the top of a wardrobe, out of which she pulls another handbag. Rita reaches inside this bag and, from underneath the wads of dollar bills it contains, pulls a blue metallic triangular key that she uses to open the box. The viewer, again expecting *something* to be revealed as this box is opened, is presented only with a shot that zooms into the box's empty black interior until the entire frame is black. This shot then serves as a cut after which we see the box fall onto the ground. The camera pans up from the box to a doorway and a right-angled corridor, meaning, of course, that we cannot see what lies around the corner. When someone does enter the frame, it is not the Bum or any other such monstrous creature, but merely Betty's Aunt Ruth who looks around with a puzzled expression on her face. A reverse shot shows her point of view as she surveys the apartment's bedroom, perhaps wondering what she had heard falling – and yet when the camera pans to the carpet where we saw the box fall, it is no longer there. She turns and leaves, having failed to solve the mystery, leaving us contemplating the corridor's blind spot once again. A series of two rapid dissolves suddenly shift us into a tracking shot that seems to be heading back the way that Betty's Aunt has gone, which is to say towards the bedroom, but at a different time to previously as the bright oranges and yellows of a daylight flooded apartment have been replaced by the dark hues of a shot operating at the threshold of visibility. As we turn the corner, whilst we do not see an empty room, our ability to understand what we are seeing is no greater than Aunt Ruth's, for we see a woman lying on the (now unmade) bed with her back turned towards us. We cut to a shot of the Cowboy who says "hey pretty girl, time to wake up." We fade to black then fade back to an image of this same female form lying on the bed, but this time the woman's legs have taken on the cyanotic hue of a week-old corpse. Although we appear to be in an entirely different time frame, therefore, we cut back to the same shot of the Cowboy standing in the doorway, the editing of this shot/reverse-shot sequence seeming to imply continuity. We fade to black as the Cowboy shuts the door, then hear a knock at a door and fade back in on this same female form lying on this same bed, except that this time the woman, whose hair seems to have changed color, gets up to answer the door.

This woman, it turns out, is Betty, or rather it isn't because she is now called Diane Selwyn, has a very different relationship with Rita (now called Camilla Rhodes) to previously, lives not in Aunt Ruth's apartment but in the house that Betty and Rita snuck into in the first part of the film and is not a successful starlet but a wannabe struggling to get bit parts. These two seemingly incommensurable parts of the film have been perfectly sutured together by many critics in a kind of critical continuity commentary, in spite of the fact that in this last thirty minutes of the film Lynch consistently subverts the viewer's expectation of continuity editing, shot/reverse-shot sequences linked by continuous movements or sounds thrusting us into an entirely different space and scenario across the cut. What is more, in the film's final sequence we are presented with a different metallic blue key that appears and disappears at random and that would appear to hold some importance in terms of narrative progression, for Diane's hired gun holds it up in Winkie's and tells her that "when it's finished you'll find this where I told you." Glancing over at Dan, who is back at Winkie's where this meeting is taking place, Diane asks, "what's it open?," but the only response she gets is laughter that continues across a dissolve to a tracking shot heading towards the wall in the car park behind the diner. This time the camera actually turns the blind corner and reveals, at least partly, what we expected to find there: the Bum. Only this time he is holding the metallic blue box that he puts inside a crumpled brown paper bag which he then places on the ground. At this point, as the film's two greatest sites of monstration come together, the film's narrative finally stops trying to make sense at all and abandons all hope of pulling all of its strands together into a coherent whole: the kindly elderly couple who had helped Betty at the airport emerge from the bag, now one-inch tall, their movements taking place in double time. We cut to a shot of the new blue key on a coffee table next to Diane who stares at it intently. She turns upon hearing a knock at the door and when we cut to the door, of which we see only the bottom in close-up, we see the miniaturized elderly couple scrambling underneath it. Against a sonic background of screams, the old couple, returned to full size again, chase Diane through the house. Backing away from them whilst screaming hysterically herself, she falls onto her bed, reaches into her bedside drawer, pulls out a revolver and shoots herself in the mouth. The sound of the gunshot does not accompany a shot of the discharge of the gun's load, however, but triggers a cloud of smoke that rises from behind the bed and fills the entire screen, obscuring vision. From out of this haze that serves as a dissolve emerges the Bum who looks directly into camera, perhaps challenging us to make sense of what we have just seen.

ACT III. SMOKE AND MIRRORS

The smoke that fills the screen at the end of the diegesis (if such a term can still apply to Lynch in light of the argument herein) returns us, of course, to a space of attractions, to a vaudeville scene where magicians disguise the deception at work with clouds of smoke and flourishes of capes and reveal, to their wondrous audience, nothing but the mastery of their own craft. Following Gunning's assertions concerning early cinema as a cinema of attractions, we might also say, of course, that this scene returns us to a specifically cinematic space. Indeed, throughout this entire last nightmarish scene, there is a flickering, strobing light issuing from somewhere, a recurrent trope in Lynch that seems to occur at moments precisely like this, which is to say moments when narrative falls away and the spectator is required to entertain a different relation to the cinematic object on display. Greg Olson has suggested that this strobing light is linked to the more general theme of electricity in Lynch's universe, writing that the director "loves to stress the power of electricity by flashing it on and off in a strobing effect, which simultaneously emphasizes his own power, since his hand is always on the effect-controlling light switch."[27] I would like to suggest, however, that these flickering lights that reoccur

[27] Greg Olson, *David Lynch: Beautiful Dark* (Lanham: The Scarecrow Press, 2008) 546.

throughout Lynch's films might in fact signify the light of the cinema projector, that they are then a sign that the trickery on display – non-
sequential cuts, miniaturization, time manipulation, etc., to name but
those seen in the final sequence of *Mulholland Drive* – arises precisely
through the specificities of the cinematic apparatus. That this is a particularly cinematic space is suggested also by what we see once the smoke
clears, for the dissolve that shows us the Bum one last time leads into a
composite shot in which the Bum is figured on a backdrop of red velvet.
As in *Twin Peaks'* red room where a strobing light and red velvet curtains
meet and where cinematic trickery is often on full display, whether they
appear individually or in combination these monstrative elements – the
projector's light being what makes the cinematic image visible and the
theatre's opulent red velvet curtain being a sign of exhibition, what both
promises and delays cinematic spectacle – seem to pull us back to that
original ontological condition of cinema as an attraction, to an era before
the hegemony of narrative when audiences were captivated by the possi-
bilities of cinema itself as opposed to the stories that it told. The most
obvious site in which these elements can be found in Lynch's work, of
course, is in the theatre itself.

ENTR'ACTE

If in Lynch's work the cinema is foregrounded as spectacle or attraction
at certain privileged moments during which, what is more, the artifice and
trickery through which the cinema achieves its enchanting effects are
themselves put on display, then it is perhaps unsurprising that this should
happen, oftentimes, in the theatres that figure in his films. Club Silencio,
of course, is called a club but is in reality a theatre with the requisite red
curtains, and it is in this space that triggers a dissolution of narrative that
the illusion of the spectacle is broken also. "No hay banda," we are told,
and yet we hear a band, thanks, of course, to the technology deployed
within the architecture of the cinema.

But we would be mistaken in thinking that it is only the technology of
the cinematic apparatus that is involved in this mobilization of cinematic
space as a space of monstration, for the theatres used by Lynch are in-
variably older theatres from the golden age of the movie palace whose
architecture was itself intended to enthral the cinemagoer. Indeed, the
very architectural design of movie palaces, not only in the auditorium but
also in the foyer, powder rooms and even the exteriors of the theatre,
was itself a space of multiple attractions. As Valentine notes:

> the experience of the film – that is, the reality for the observer – was
> largely influenced by the surroundings. The experience of "going to the
> movies" equaled, and often surpassed, what was seen on the screen. The
> theater was central to the experience and, therefore, to the memory –
> which is, in fact, what movies were selling.[28]

Nor was it only the architecture of the building that converted the entire
space of these movie palaces into a sphere of attractions. As Melnick and

[28] Maggie Valentine, *The Show Starts on the Sidewalk: An Architectural History of the Movie Theatre, Starring S. Charles Lee* (New Haven: Yale University Press, 1994) xii.

Fuchs comment: "elaborate movie palaces, with their stage shows, large orchestras, and other forms of entertainment, became destinations in and of themselves, not just venues for films."[29] If Lynch's films signal a return of sorts to an early conception of the cinema, then, they also return repeatedly to its architectural past, its pre-multiplex days when the spectator was drawn into the action more. As Valentine again suggests:

> the movie palaces, which dominated motion picture exhibition from the late 1910s through the 1920s, glorified the monumentality of the film experience. The surroundings created a palpable emotional atmosphere for the movies, extending the fantasy of the film to include the physical environment in which it was viewed.[30]

The importance of the space of the theatre both as a recurrent diegetic site in Lynch's work and the privileged space it occupies in his vision of the phenomenological experience of the cinema for the moviegoer – which is lost entirely in some of the other formats he riles against so fiercely (such as mobile phones)[31] – surely springs from a similar conception of the cinema as an *experience*. What is more, if the implications of Valentine's analysis are that the cinematic spectacle witnessed by the viewer extends beyond the limits of the screen and into the auditorium itself – or even further, as the old movie palace adage that she uses as the title of her book indicates: *The Show Starts on the Sidewalk* – then this is precisely what the confounding of narrative in the moments of attraction that appear in Lynch's films does too. Breaking the hermeneutic circle that would make of the diegesis presented on screen an autonomous, self-sufficient and hence distant entity, these moments interpolate the spectator and draw her into the action, mystery and spectacle as an active participant.

Again, this breakdown of the boundary of cinematic spectacle is explicitly figured in various key scenes, such as the scenes of video monstration in *Lost Highway* already mentioned. It is when these scenes move into the architecture of an old movie theatre that the point is made even more explicitly, however. Apart from the scene in Club Silencio already examined, one of the most striking examples comes towards the end of *Inland Empire* as Nikki Grace / Susan Blue (Laura Dern) enters (through a red velvet curtain, even though she seems to enter from the *rear* of the auditorium) an old theatre on Hollywood Boulevard on whose screen she is confronted by an image of herself, seemingly shot in real time, as though it were a magnified mirror image of herself. (And let us note that rather than *starting* on the sidewalk, the spectacle of her broken narrative subsequently moves outside the theatre to continue and end on the sidewalk.)

But this privileging of cinematic space as a site in which narrative is confounded in order to instigate a direct relation with the viewer – to implicate her in the film's mystery and enigma by disavowing the possibility of narrative closure that would create and maintain a distance between on

---

[29] Ross Melnick and Andreas Fuchs, *Cinema treasures: A New Look at Classic Movie Theaters* (St. Paul: MBI, 2004) 62.
[30] Valentine, *The Show Starts on the Sidewalk*, 34.
[31] See the final quotation in Act I above.

screen action and viewer – is rendered clearer still in the short, two-minute film that Lynch made for the 2007 Cannes film festival – these projects subsequently being collated into the portmanteau project *Chacun son cinéma ou ce petit coup au coeur quand la lumière s'éteint et que le film commence*. Indeed, in this short we can see in condensed form very many if not all of the phenomena examined thus far.

ACT IV. ABSURDA

The short is called *Absurda*, a title that encapsulates the essence of what has been said here in regards to Lynch's disregard for reason and narrative coherence at the same time as it sends us into a metacinematic space, Absurda being the name that he gave to his own production company, this indicating perhaps that Lynch is signalling this as a text through which he will explicitly talk about his own art. The film opens with a shot of a movie theatre auditorium. Filmed from a fixed point at the rear of the auditorium and off to one side, as though we had just come in through one of the rear entrances, we see rows of empty seats, cloister-like elaborately decorated passages running besides the aisles – signalling this as a movie palace – and a cinema screen (henceforth the screen as opposed to the frame, the latter serving here to designate the whole image seen by the viewer of *Absurda*). A beam of light enters from the top left of the frame, a light which resembles the light of the film projector but behaves in reality like a spotlight, which is to say a beam of light whose function it is to highlight specific attractions. On the screen, we see a black and white image (whilst the auditorium is shot in color) showing a door at the back of an empty room, this door being positioned in such a way in regards to the viewing position of the camera that we might imagine it to be a mirror image of the doorway in which we, the phantasmagorical spectator, stand. Most significantly, however, we see a giant pair of scissors that extend from the screen at a perpendicular angle out into the auditorium itself, quite literally cutting through the division between onscreen cinematic space and the architectural space of the cinema. Offscreen (or, to be consistent, out of frame) voices comment on the scissors before a man's voice (Tom, we later find out) asks, "where is this guy, he's supposed to show us something?," at which point a figure (wearing Lynch's own preferred uniform, a white buttoned-up shirt and black jacket) walks into the room on the screen and stands in the doorway. The onscreen character and the out of frame voices start a conversation made up of linked non-sequiturs that are the aural equivalent of Lynch's false continuity editing:

> *Tom*: Hey, what's with the scissors?
> *Man on screen*: They're what was used.
> *Tom*: Whatever.
> *Man on screen*: I can't hear you.
> *Tom*: What the hell.
> *Cindy*: He said he can't hear you.
> *Tom*: Give me that megaphone. [through megaphone] I thought you were going to show us a dance.
> *Man on screen*: She was a dancer.

At this point the scissors open up, pulling back before snipping shut violently as they are pulled out of the auditorium and back into the screen. At the point in the onscreen space where the scissors cut, a red dress appears on the floor and from it a digitally manipulated female figure rises up, rotating in a two-dimensional plane, her head seeming to separate from her body and float freely, this spectacle being highlighted by the spotlight that pans to her. Meanwhile the conversation continues.

> Cindy: What?
> Woman: I'm sort of afraid.
> Man: It's just a gag.
> Cindy: Who is he?
> Man on screen: This is what she looked like when she was younger.
> Woman: Hey, that looks like you Cindy.
> Tom: Yeah!
> Cindy: What's going on?

The dancer seems to jump back and forth as a series of rapid cuts between different degrees of close-up shots slam her up against the boundary of the screen before she finally breaks through it and flies into the auditorium, through and beyond the point at which we and (we suppose) the owners of the voices we hear stand. Cindy declares: "It *is* me" and, as a blood-spattered face enters the top of the screen in close-up, the man on screen states: "This is the one who did it."

> Cindy: I've had this dream.
> Man: That's Tom.
> Woman: Yeah!
> Tom: No, no, no, that ain't me.
> Man: What? Tom, that was you.
> [scream]
> Cindy: Weird.
> Tom: I'm not feeling so good.

The dancer's disembodied head returns and floats in the onscreen space and disappears as the scissors return, stabbing violently at the space that was occupied by the dancer.

> Cindy: Wait a minute.
> Tom: What's wrong.
> Cindy: Tommy, what are you looking at me like that for?
> Tom: So I feel a little strange, that's what.
> Cindy: What are you looking at me like that for?

The onscreen screen goes blank as the auditorium fills with smoke and a flickering light more dispersed than the spotlight of before. Cindy screams, the woman screams, the man begs Tom to stop. The screams fade out with an echo and sustain, seeming to pass into another space as the smoke in the auditorium is sucked into the screen until it is nothing but a haze from which emerges, *en pointe*, a pirouetting ballet dancer. Cindy's voice returns, this time as a voice-over narrator, saying, "So I went dancing, I've always loved to dance," before the screen image of the dancer gradually dissipates into the smoke around her as the camera is pulled more and more out of focus, enacting a figural process on her body that confounds the clear delineation of background and foreground as the entire frame fades to black.

LOOSE ENDS

In the final analysis, then, like Michel Chion, I wish to contend that Lynch's films contain privileged, moments that deploy, "a very peculiar logic requiring us to renounce all *a priori* interpretations of behavior and facts, whether taken separately or in succession."[32] However, I would contend that this does not make of him quite the maverick and hyper-idiosyncratic filmmaker that such a statement might seem to imply. Rather, by explicitly signalling these moments as über-cinematic, I suggest that Lynch expresses through his work a conception of a cinematographic and cinematic ontology that can be traced back to the very origins of cinema, pre-narrative integration. Like the early cinema of attractions, then, Lynch's cinema cannot be analyzed (only) according to analytic paradigms that tie every aspect of the filmic object back to a guiding central narrative; rather, Lynch's films leave many loose ends flapping in the wind.

If this is the case, then this has profound implications for the way in which Lynch's films need to be apprehended. More than this, however, it has profound implications for those very psychoanalytic strategies that I critiqued at the start of the paper, not only in regards to Lynch's work but also their applicability to any cinematic form in which can be found attractions and sites of monstration. For if we trace the (implicit) Lacanian concept of suture back to the article that first articulated it as a central element of Lacan's thought, Jacques-Alain Miller's "Suture (Elements of the Logic of the Signifier)," we can see that when this concept is imported into film theory it is primarily a narratival device. Miller suggests that the logic of the signifier is, precisely, "a minimal logic in that within it are given those pieces only which are necessary to assure it a progression reduced to a linear movement, uniformally [sic] generated at each point of its necessary sequence."[33] When this is extrapolated out into a theory of suture for cinematic spectatorship by Jean-Pierre Oudart, suture comes to represent, "the closure of the cinematic *énoncé* in line with its relationship with its subject (the filmic subject or rather the cinematic subject), which is recognized, and then put in its place as the spectator."[34] The necessity of closure that arises in this scenario can be traced back, of course, to the process of subject or identity formation for Lacan, meticulously unpicked by Miller. In this scenario, the child enters into the symbolic realm under the coercion of the paternal Other. Once there, the child now imagines that its earlier indifferentiation was an ideal fusional-identity with the mother, and longs for a return to that imaginary pre-Œdipal wholeness. It is this imaginary wholeness on which the ego is now modelled and against which it will now be measured as the child attempts to recreate a

---

[32] Chion, *David Lynch*, 20. Like Chion also, in order to do this I have had to follow the seemingly contradictory operation by which some of Lynch's narratives are retold in order to show the extent to which they resist narrative integration.

[33] Jacques-Alain Miller, "Suture (Elements of the Logic of the Signifier)," *Screen* 18.4 (Winter 1977-78): 25.

[34] Jean-Pierre Oudart, "Cinema and Suture," *Screen* 18.4 (1977-78): 35.

complete identity that is now sensed to be lacking. When this scenario is transplanted into film theory, suture of course similarly refers to the process whereby the cinematic subject is inserted into the film's system of meaning as the element able to provide a sense of unity or logic to a formal system which would seem to be lacking coherence, stitching together the logic of, for instance, a shot/reverse-shot sequence so that the film's syntax becomes comprehensible as a unified, coherent whole. Does this then account for what we find in Lynch? Not really, for not only does Lynch repeatedly present his audiences with identities that are mobile and incapable of being contained within the bounds of a single, socialized ego, his own cinematic syntax, as shown herein, consistently resists such a process of suture, of total integration into a symbolic whole. And in light of this suggestion, could it be that *Mulholland Drive*'s last line of dialogue, spoken by a monstrative blue-haired woman seated before a red-velvet curtain, is addressed as a salutary warning to any viewer who would attempt to integrate this, or any other of Lynch's moments of attraction, into a coherent narrative?

It ain't over...

"Silencio."

GARY BETTINSON
ERASERHEAD: COMPREHENSION, COMPLEXITY,
& THE MIDNIGHT MOVIE

In a film career studded with recondite narratives, *Eraserhead* (1977) remains David Lynch's most systematically difficult film. From the outset it
ambiguates the story-world's reality status, parades a host of impossible
agents, and distresses narrative causality. Obscure paraphernalia mystifies
the *mise-en-scène*; space and time become perplexingly labile. In the light
of so much obscurity, critical writing has tended to invoke experiential
dream states to characterize the film's effects. Some critics state the
point strongly: "*Eraserhead*...is the dream experience itself;"[1] "[*Eraserhead*] actually *is* a dream."[2] Accordingly, the film "takes control of the
viewer's mind"[3] to the degree that "the viewer becomes the dreamer."[4]
Such overheated claims are pure fantasy in a literal sense, but they exemplify a more general supposition about the film's form and effects –
Eraserhead, it is assumed, rejects canonical storytelling norms and in-
duces some sort of disorienting viewing state, overwhelming the
spectator's powers of comprehension. We gain a better purchase on
Eraserhead's difficulties, however, by recognizing a formal play between
standard and nonstandard devices, and between tactics of orientation and
disorientation. For all the challenges it poses, Lynch's narration lays out
orienting cues that shape the spectator's comprehension in strategic
ways. Rather than envisage a spectator position of cognitive surrender,
we might consider how the spectator's cue-driven activity guides her
through seemingly impenetrable narrative terrain. From another angle, we
can ask how Lynch organizes his narration so as to encourage particular
kinds of complex viewer response.[5]

As a point of departure, this chapter traces the orienting structures
built into *Eraserhead*'s large-scale form. Often these structures spring
from canonic storytelling principles, cueing the spectator's body of
knowledge about well-told narratives. This analysis leads us toward a
consideration of the film's engagement with style and affect. Lynch co-
ordinates stylistic and emotion cues to steer comprehension along particular paths, yielding responses both visceral and complex. The latter part of
the chapter extends this account of cue-perception, comprehension, and
emotion specifically to the context of *Eraserhead*'s original exhibition –

---

[1] K. George Godwin, "Eraserhead," *Film Quarterly* 39.1 (1985): 38.
[2] Paul A. Woods, *Weirdsville USA: The Obsessive Universe of David Lynch* (London: Plexus, 1997) 33, italics in original.
[3] K. George Godwin, "David Lynch Retrospect: *Eraserhead*," *Cinefantastique* 14:4-5 (1984): 50.
[4] Godwin, "Eraserhead," 39. For Godwin, "Lynch has managed to capture the processes of dream consciousness with remarkable precision" ("Eraserhead" 38), while Woods is convinced by *Eraserhead*'s "faithfulness to dream logic" (*Weirdsville* 33).
[5] For a cue-based theory of cinematic narration, see David Bordwell, *Narration in the Fiction Film* (London: Routledge, 1985).

the 1970s "midnight movie." As a specialized context prizing ritualized audience experience, the midnight movie venue promoted a distinctive array of viewing practices, all of which have implications for cue-attention, narrative uptake, emotional experience, and the implicit intentions of the filmmaker. We might suppose, for instance, that Lynch's carefully-prepared narrational cues would be disregarded by spectators whose collective concerns pivot around appropriation. All this allusion to viewer activity, of course, differs sharply from the dream analogy's implications of passive spectatorship. On the cue-based model of comprehension, the spectator searches out cues and acts on them. Of relevance to this chapter is how Lynch orchestrates – and the spectator processes – an intricate and involving procession of cues.

WEIRD AT HEART?

"There are a host of movies," George M. Wilson points out, "in which it is not expected that the audience make detailed sense of the narrative action in conventional psychological terms."[6] Though determinate meanings are stymied by such films (Wilson cites as an example Lynch's *Mulholland Drive* (2001)), story comprehension remains at the core of the spectator's activity. One reason for this rests in standard viewing procedures, molded by innate dispositions. A set of deep-grained proclivities inclines the spectator toward particular tasks: spectators tend to (1) focus attention and prime curiosity; (2) recognize pattern and notice novelty; (3) launch empathetic engagement and imaginative "play;" and (4) enlist knowledge structures and standard heuristics. All these activities are put into the service of story construction, and are applied even to films that demote intelligible "meaning."

To the spectator's habits of mind can be added the work's strategic cues, devised to engage and shape those comprehension-driven propensities. Cues for story construction not only nourish viewers' appetite for comprehension; they provide spectators cognitive orientation, a steady foothold in the action's unfolding. Such cues – embedded in causal events, agential activity, narrative obstacles, and the like – acquire special significance in films that stress lyrical, diffuse, or disorienting experience.[7] *Eraserhead* looks bent on distressing comprehension, but Lynch supplies ballast by arraying story-based cues across the work, hinting that a determinate meaning is harbored among the story enigmas.

Critics have generally slighted Lynch's orienting techniques, preferring to alight on his films' more outré devices. Intriguing as his plot scenarios are, Lynch is "basically a non-narrative filmmaker."[8] Yet to thus summarize Lynch is to overlook his mastery of the canonical story format. Critical writing has tended to marginalize Lynch's debt to canonic norms –

[6] George M. Wilson, "Interpretation," *The Routledge Companion to Philosophy and Film*, ed. Paisley Livingston and Carl Plantinga (London: Routledge, 2009) 171.

[7] It should be noted that disorientation does not automatically imply negative experience. Some avant-garde films, for instance, seek to disdain real-world phenomena and experience, yet elicit pleasure through an abstract play with form. However, such works are typically non-narrative and thus needn't furnish orienting cues to assist in the construction of a story.

[8] Jim Hoberman, *Vulgar Modernism: Writing on Movies and Other Media* (Philadelphia: Temple University Press, 1991) 234.

thus *Eraserhead* is "completely *sui generis*,"[9] and evokes "art cut off from its sources."[10] Recently, however, some film scholars, without downgrading Lynch's innovations, have indicated the ways that Lynch derives or departs from various traditions, e.g. the art cinema,[11] classical narration[12], and popular genre.[13] Traditional norms serve partly as navigational cues in *Eraserhead*, helping spectators negotiate the work. Some prevalent norms allow Lynch to ensure spectator orientation. Canonic plot architecture governs initial phases of action, accreting digressions only once plot concerns are crystallized. A web of compositional norms (motifs, foreshadowing, character arcs, symmetry) calls attention to pattern, repetition, and other trackable regularities. Communicative shifts in the narration boost the spectator's grasp of story action. And semi-familiar elements tap into knowledge schemas, equipping spectators with provisional roadmaps to comprehension.

To notice *Eraserhead*'s orienting structures is not to downplay its evident difficulties. Rather, by doing so we better perceive Lynch's interplay of transparent and abstruse elements, of canonical and nonstandard devices. Orientation comes forward as a prime concern of both text and spectator, reminding us that *Eraserhead* is not a wholly impenetrable work. That the film contains orienting cues, moreover, testifies to Lynch's dedication to narrative. Puzzling though it is, *Eraserhead* furnishes a discriminable story, and orienting tactics solicit the spectator's effort toward constructing it.

Eraserhead's early segments present a cluster of difficulties. The narration vacillates on the reality-status of the action, withholds expositional information, parades a host of elements that defy classification, and flaunts a sparse and languid pace (thereby deferring the delineation of a clear plotline). It furnishes Henry (Jack Nance) no personal history, no circumscribed goals, no go-getting motivation. The laws, logistics, and boundaries of the diegetic world go undefined. And spatio-temporal connections become confusingly indeterminate, hinting at temporal causality while keeping spatial relations ambiguous (consider the crosscutting that links Henry's floating head to the scabrous figure who manipulates levers). All these uncertainties are made flagrant by an overt, defamiliarizing narration. Against these evident difficulties, however, Lynch sets tacit aids to comprehension. Social stereotypes (e.g. the austere mother-in-law) are easily assimilated to the spectator's prefilmic knowledge. Characters are effortlessly identified and reidentified, thanks to perspicuous staging and salient bodily traits. A light-hearted mood renders story action accessible and engaging. All such devices are employed strategically, as orienting cues lubricating the spectator's comprehension. Once estab-

9 Godwin, "Eraserhead," 43.
10 Jim Hoberman and Jonathan Rosenbaum, *Midnight Movies* (Cambridge: DaCapo Press, 1991) 309.
11 Kristin Thompson, *Storytelling in Film and Television* (Cambridge: Harvard University Press, 2003); J. J. Murphy, *Me and You and Memento and Fargo: How Independent Screenplays Work* (New York: Continuum, 2007).
12 Warren Buckland, "Making Sense of *Lost Highway*," *Puzzle Films: Complex Storytelling in Contemporary Cinema* (London: Wiley-Blackwell, 2009).
13 Steven J. Schneider, "The Essential Evil in/of *Eraserhead* (or, Lynch to the Contrary)," *The Cinema of David Lynch: American Dreams, Nightmare Visions*, ed. Erica Sheen and Annette Davison. (New York: Wallflower Press, 2004).

lished, the orienting device may itself be assigned a problematizing function. Hence the "austere matriarch" schema initially orients spectators to
Mrs X (Jeanne Bates) – but when Mrs X displays incompatible traits such
as aggressive sexuality, the orienting schema becomes a root source of
complexity. Accustomed to the Hollywood norm of gradual character
change, spectators are here confronted with abrupt and unmotivated
shifts in character behavior. In such cases, an initial orientation gives way
to cognitive dissonance and narrative incongruity.

Lynch repeats this formula (orientation supplanted by dissonance)
across the film's large-scale form. Perhaps surprisingly, the early phases
of *Eraserhead* hew closely to conventional story architecture. A concise
prologue, an itinerary through the narrative's principal locales, and a for-
ward-pointing incident (the news of the infant's birth) here comprise what
Kristin Thompson terms "The Setup," the first of four constitutive parts
composing American feature film narratives.[14] Typically, Thompson argues, each major segment hinges on progressions or hindrances in the
protagonist's goal-oriented activity. Most often, the purposeful hero formulates self-directed goals, but *Eraserhead*'s protagonist – kin to the
passive character of art cinema – has loosely-defined goals "thrust upon"
him.[15] Pressed into twin domestic roles, Henry's implicit objective is to
fulfill his duty-bound, familial obligations; another objective is inferably
organized around his covert romantic desires. The Setup concludes at the
30-minute mark: following the X family rendezvous, the narration
launches the "Complicating Action," a major plot phase in which the protagonist encounters "a whole new situation with which [he] must cope."[16]
Henry's domestic travails – enforced cohabitation, spousal discord, and
inhibited agency – fill out this portion of plot which culminates, as per
convention, near the film's midway point.

From this phase onward, mapping the action onto Thompson's tem-
plate becomes progressively difficult. The causal machinery by which
Lynch motivates early action becomes attenuated. Goals lacking specificity grow still more opaque. In what would usually comprise the
"Development" block of action, *Eraserhead* abandons standard structural
lynchpins to a string of obscure, apparently disconnected incidents – all of
which seem detached from even fuzzy character goals. At the level of
macrostructure, *Eraserhead* maximizes a schema also employed at a local
level: initial orientation slides into palpable disorientation as cues for story
construction grow diffuse, ambiguous, or contradictory. Yet, erratic as it
looks, *Eraserhead*'s inexplicable Development does not fully abandon orienting structures. Formal integrity is built into the film's most arcane
sequences, rewarding the spectator's search for patterned structure. The
camera's plunge into a yawning chasm reinstates a motif from the film's
prologue. A topos of technological failure finds elaboration when a factory
clerk presses a faulty bell. Cohesion devices such as these cultivate spectator orientation and nourish an alertness for pattern. (By lending
structural fulcrum to the action, moreover, motivic elements distinguish

---

[14] Kristin Thompson, *Storytelling in the New Hollywood: Understanding Classical Narrative Technique* (Cambridge: Harvard University Press, 1999).
[15] Thompson, *Storytelling in the New Hollywood*, 14.
[16] Thompson, *Storytelling in the New Hollywood*, 28.

Eraserhead further from the shapeless progression of dreamstates.) *Eraserhead*'s midpoint launches a prolonged challenge to comprehension, but the events it sets forth are neither purely non-narrative nor completely inscrutable.

Lynch adverts to a canonical plot armature at the film's "Climax." Formal symmetry, a mainstay of classical construction, revives elements introduced in the prologue portion of the Setup – the encrusted planet, the character working levers, a gaping void, airborne shavings, and so on. Plot symmetry not only orients the spectator by appealing to her preference for pattern; it also adumbrates narrative closure and fosters an impression of structural rigor. This apparent formal rigor – at odds with the wayward preceding action – is further consolidated by a brief epilogue depicting Henry's union with The Lady in the Radiator (Laurel Near). Critics assimilate *Eraserhead* to the horror genre, but this epilogue reminds us that a romance story integrally structures the narrative (and provides one more index of the film's classical moorings). Henry's fraught romance with Mary (Charlotte Stewart), their de rigueur marriage and subsequent estrangement, is established in the first two story phases. From the Setup, as in conventional romance plots, the narration parades a string of potential lovers for the protagonist – Mary, Mrs X, The Lady in the Radiator, and the vampish neighbour.[17] The epilogue resolves Henry's romantic decision-making (and announces the film's end) by uniting him obliquely with the "correct" partner. In all, *Eraserhead* evinces a deceptive degree of structural unity, swerving from and reverting to the canonical format at strategic junctures – a stratagem coordinated to the upkeep of the spectator's orientation, attention, and narrative comprehension.

The principle of orientation permeates other narrational tactics as well. First, Lynch posits an intrinsic norm of sporadic demystification, clarifying obscure details of the diegesis periodically. (Notably this tactic inverts the narration's habit of disarraying an initial orientation.) The spectator is baffled when Mary writhes inexplicably against a bedframe, but when a suitcase pops into view the gesture is at last disambiguated. Unspecified sonic textures may eventually be supplied a source, as when mysterious squeaking sounds are attributed to suckling pups. Such disambiguating tactics not only abet orientation; they foster the assumption that cryptic elements will at some stage be made perspicuous. Consequently, the tactic solicits and shapes the spectator's heuristic procedures. Tacitly aware of the disambiguating norm, spectators tolerate enigmatic elements and anticipate intelligible explanations; they sustain attention and curiosity, warding off the "stopping routines" that dissipate interest;[18] and they continue to construct inferences and hypotheses, mindful that a dilatory narration will parcel out confirming instances only intermittently. Given that hypotheses are validated in piecemeal fashion, the spectator formulates tentative, provisional guesses and assumptions. Nonetheless,

---

[17] A likely intertext here is Orson Welles' *The Trial* (1962). Like K (Anthony Perkins), Henry is a blighted protagonist, absurdly thrust into a situation from which he cannot escape, and situated as the unlikely object of desire for a host of more or less predatory or virginal females. Lynch acknowledges the influence of Kafka's fiction upon his storytelling in Chris Rodley, *Lynch on Lynch* (London: Faber and Faber, 1997) 56.

[18] Brian Boyd, *On the Origin of Stories: Evolution, Cognition, and Fiction* (Cambridge: The Belknap Press of Harvard University Press, 2009) 93.

disambiguation fitfully encourages the spectator to undertake further hermeneutic and story-making routines.

To further ensure orientation, Lynch exploits the spectator's prior knowledge. On the one hand, *Eraserhead* calls upon competencies of cinematic traditions: audiences tutored in art cinema narration or German Expressionist cinema will cope better with *Eraserhead*'s ellipses and eccentricities than will viewers unschooled in those traditions. On the other hand, the spectator's real-world knowledge is targeted as a stabilizing force. The most communicative segments of *Eraserhead* organize action around paradigm scenarios, situation prototypes familiar from everyday experience. These scenarios in turn cue the spectator's "scripts," or standard expectations of ordinary events and situations. Scripts provide spectators not only with a set of mental compass points, but a stock of expectations against which the anomalous moment stands out. A paradigm scenario crystallizes when Henry attends a dinner with his prospective parents-in-law. The script for such encounters encompasses polite ritual and social etiquette, but Lynch violates these expectations by flaunting various sorts of impropriety (as when Mrs X nuzzles Henry's neck, or when the roasted chicken performs lewd leg thrusts). The strangeness of this sequence gains much of its force by reference to real-world schemata, the store of prior knowledge explicitly activated by the narrative situation. Again, these schemata furnish an orienting ground of familiarity. Not surprisingly, moreover, the ensuing Development section of the plot – an especially recondite stretch of action – will tactically winnow out paradigm scenarios and deplete script activation, diminishing a crucial crutch for comprehension.

A still more localized fund of prior knowledge is the person schema.[19] Spectators ascribe person-like traits to characters, presupposing a fundamental correspondence with human conspecifics. *Eraserhead*'s putrid infant appears monstrous chiefly because it travesties this default assumption. Though the infant elicits ontological doubt, however, it does not wholly negate assumptions of personhood; as we'll see, the infant generates ambivalent reactions that impact upon the spectator's emotions. More generally, *Eraserhead* arrays its characters on a hierarchy of relative strangeness, tacitly ranking agents by reference to the extra-filmic person schema. Thus Henry – a "strange" protagonist by the schema's criteria – is apt to appear relatively normal compared to the vile offspring (which violates categoric norms), the vaudevillian (who is horribly deformed), and the X family (whose bodies, like the story world's technology, are prone to arbitrary malfunction). Like other knowledge frameworks, the person schema functions as both a baseline of familiarity and a barometer for difference.

Canonical plot construction, cohesion devices, narrational communicativeness, schema activation – by all such means Lynch strategically modulates the spectator's orientation and uptake of story. Of course, not every aspect of *Eraserhead* can be assimilated exactly to prior knowledge structures. The tiny theater tucked inside Henry's radiator defies schemata for spatial reality. At a denotative level, some imagery remains epistemologically opaque, defeating a priori frames of reference. Yet it is

[19] David Bordwell, *Poetics of Cinema* (New York: Routledge, 2008) 113.

only partially true that "our own experience proves constantly to be inappropriate for [*Eraserhead*'s] world, and no guide is provided within the film itself."[20] Instead, our prior experience (in the form of scripts and general knowledge sets) interfaces directly with stimuli set out in the film (e.g. paradigm scenarios) to enable our grasp of the diegetic world. Even cognitively opaque items do not retard the spectator's effort toward understanding – they may harbor hidden meanings, and thus stimulate the spectator toward hermeneutic inquiry. In general, by flaunting difficult phenomena, complex films such as *Eraserhead* increase mental effort and expand the viewer's cognitive repertoire – all the while recruiting orienting tactics to sustain attention and reward curiosity.

AROUSING STYLE

My discussion has so far stressed mental processing – attention, knowledge, inferences, hypotheses – but Lynch also engages the mind's emotional faculties to modify and sharpen comprehension. Emotion is exploited not only for its facility to cue narrative judgments, predictions, and desires. It also becomes a key source of complexity, matched to the work's quandaries of comprehension and meaning. Several tactics nurture this quality. Cues for emotional arousal confront prompts for affective distance. Mixed emotions are evoked, and breed equivocal judgments. "Excessive" stylistic cues squander emotional arousal, coaxing spectators down affective cul-de-sacs. *Eraserhead* generates complex emotional experience, but such experience remains inseparable from the thought processes that drive comprehension.[21]

Spectator emotions provide a flight path for narrative judgments and desires. Consider the repugnant infant in *Eraserhead*, whose arousal of affect molds the spectator's narrative concerns. At a fundamental level, Lynch exploits both the spectator's automaticity (i.e. mandatory responses, such as the startle reflex) and basic emotions (i.e. universal "macro"-emotions, such as disgust) to establish the baby as monstrous (as opposed to, say, merely pathetic). More intricately, Lynch capitalizes on the "higher emotions" to assert the infant's fiendishness. Henry's reactions to the infant, for instance, are typified by relatively complex emotion states. He registers resentment at the newborn's attention-getting cries, which conspire to curb his agency. He also betrays a state of humiliation, provoked by the infant's apparently mocking behavior – a throaty cackle let loose when Henry's romantic hopes are dashed.[22] Similarly, the *spectator's* response to the infant is informed by higher-order emotions shaped and steered by the narration. Antipathetic emotions are most primary, summoned up not only by direct aversion, but also by a string of mental judgments that include allegiance with Henry. Necessarily, both low-level and complex arousal states impinge on the spectator's narrative concerns. Take *Eraserhead*'s climax. Disgust for the infant and sympathy with Henry clinches the general desirability of the final outcome (the infant's extermi-

---

[20] Godwin, "David Lynch Retrospect," 52.

[21] For a cue-based approach to filmic emotion see Greg M. Smith, *Film Structure and the Emotion System* (Cambridge and New York: Cambridge University Press, 2003).

[22] Its relentless wailing, gargling, and cackling ensure that the infant is as much an object of aural displeasure as of bodily disgust. Moreover, Henry's humiliation is exacerbated by the wretched state of his tormentor – even this pitiful creature finds Henry's situation risible.

nation). Yet the bare premise of this outcome – an act of infanticide – is one that irrepressibly stirs the moral and social emotions, eliciting the spectator's negative appraisal. Lynch orchestrates emotional response such that the climax gains broad acceptance and approbation. But by tapping and transgressing deep-seated moral schemas, he laces affirmative emotion with negative feeling.

Crucial to the spectator's concern-based emotions is Lynch's occasionally "excessive" play with film style. Cinematic excess comes forward when style splinters from story, achieving a perceptual salience unbound to narrative meaning.[23] Excess need not engage the emotions, but Lynch's perceptual play will often stir arousal. When a drifter in *Wild at Heart* (1990) enters the town of Big Tuna, nondiegetic music swerves sharply into an obtrusive crescendo, whipping gymnastic horns into a dissonant welter. Stylistic convention marks the music cue as both foreboding and fear-invoking; it floods the soundscape in disjunctive fashion, signaling imminent threat. Yet the image track is wholly innocuous – blazing sunlight dissipates dread, while a long-shot setup registers aesthetic distance, not affective saturation. Even so, the frantic music cue works upon the spectator's perceptual capacities. Its sudden increase in dynamics and tempo, its discordant bassline and lurching horns, all supply physiological stimuli that prime emotional response. That an emotion proper does not coalesce reflects the lack of an object fit to orient and harness emotion. With Godardian discomfiture, Lynch augurs a narrative threat that doesn't materialize, and achieves this threat purely by stylistic devices. Style outstrips story, cueing attention toward excess, and arousing diffuse physiological response.

Excess manifests narrative and stylistic disunity, but it doesn't block the spectator from customarily relating style to narrative concerns. Even unmotivated uses of style encroach on the spectator's story construction. The musical stinger in *Wild at Heart* generates felt bodily states (e.g. anxiety), and these affects naturally orient themselves toward the narrative image, however incongruous that image is to sound. Cued by excess, the spectator's affect in turn galvanizes story-centered activities. Inferences brace the spectator for unpleasant action. Hypotheses evolve concern for the drifter's wellbeing. The musical stinger might seem utterly divorced from story concerns, but it combines with affect to prod spectators toward particular lines of *narrative* inference. *Wild at Heart*'s excess complicates the spectator's construction of story. It splits attention, deflecting concentration from story toward the text's materiality. It tantalizes emotion by baiting spectators into affective dead ends, putting emotion on red alert and flaunting false alarms. And it makes spectators leery of a narration that has lodged spurious appeals to inference and emotion, and which may continue to mislead as the film progresses. Excess may be "counternarrative,"[24] but Lynch recruits it to shape the spectator's uptake of narrative, all the while engaging the spectator in

[23] Kristin Thompson, "The Concept of Cinematic Excess," *Film Theory and Criticism: Introductory Readings*, ed. Leo Braudy and Marshall Cohen (Oxford University Press, 2004) 131.
[24] Thompson, "Cinematic Excess," 134.

perceptual play, sustaining a concern with tonal disturbance, and asserting the influence of a sometimes devious narration.[25]

Eraserhead is at first blush shot through with "excessive" arousal. As often in Lynch's work, the sound track claims attention and cues affect by various strategies of abstraction. Loud, persistent, and unpleasant diegetic noise – an intensification of what Lynch calls "room tone," "the sound that you hear when there's silence"[26]– exceeds its ambient function to dredge up the spectator's "existential emotions," such as anxiety, dread, or "self-conscious unease."[27] Sonic excess also catches attention by straining the spectator's perception, as when "probient" room tone smothers character dialogue, stifling intelligibility.[28] Conversely, Lynch abruptly siphons off probient sound, refreshing perceptual awareness and launching suspense. In all such ways, comprehension gains focus as style and affect mesh. *Eraserhead*, however, differs from prototypical excess, in that its most palpable elements appear strongly motivated. Oppressive sound design, low-key lighting, "planimetric" framing,[29] way-out décor – each source of excess functions integrally to specify *Eraserhead*'s narrative world, and each vividly demonstrates its capacity to seize attention, stimulate affect, and shape understanding.

The extent to which affect-laden style guides story uptake can be seen in the way that audiovisual combinations cue narrative closure. The infant's gory demise pushes Lynch's stylistic design to a high pitch. Shot juxtapositions rapidly shuttle the infant about the visual field, refusing steady purchase on the creature's spatial position, and forcing the spectator's eye to track the discontinuous movement. A discordant jumble of sounds swells the auditory field, pressing loudness and dissonance to a kind of limit. Looming close-ups render the heinous infant with disconcerting intimacy. Light fixtures in Henry's apartment inexplicably short-circuit, mobilizing a perverse form of pathetic fallacy – apt for a story world

25   Lynch's cinema may also be considered counternarrative in the sense evoked by Paul Schrader. Describing what he sees as an "exhaustion of narrative" in contemporary culture, Schrader notes the rise of "recent 'counter-narrative' entertainments" such as reality TV, anecdotal narrative (Schrader gives as an example Richard Linklater's *Slacker* (1991)), reenactment drama, videogames, mini-mini dramas, and documentaries ("Beyond the Silver Screen," *The Guardian* [Friday 19 June]). These genres, allied to particular media forms (cinema, television, streaming video, cartoons, and so on), are at once reactions to narrative over-saturation and efforts to achieve novelty when it seems that all the original stories have been told. Lynch's films supply one species of counternarrative in Schrader's sense. *Eraserhead*, *Inland Empire* (2006), *Lost Highway* (1997), and other complex films in Lynch's oeuvre don't dispense with narrative altogether, but discover fresh ways to exhume formulaic stories, situations, and genres.

26   Rodley, *Lynch on Lynch*, 72.

27   Carl Plantinga, *Moving Viewers: American Film and the Spectator's Experience* (Berkeley: University of California Press, 2009) 158; Schneider, "The Essential Evil in/of *Eraserhead*," 9.

28   It should be stressed that *Eraserhead* submerges dialogue only rarely and at strategic junctures. Typically in the film, probient sound makes way for character dialogue, ceding primacy to dramatic clarity. This tendency betrays the ground of conventions underwriting Lynch's stylistic engagement and narrative construction; in sum, it gives evidence of what Michel Chion calls Lynch's "classic side." See Chion, *David Lynch* (London: British Film Institute, 1995) 43.

29   See David Bordwell, *Figures Traced in Light: On Cinematic Staging* (Berkeley; Los Angeles; London: University of California Press, 2005). In planimetric shots, the camera is stationed perpendicular to a background surface, encouraging lateral as well as depth staging. Henry's dogged trek across the full width of the frame early in *Eraserhead* provides an instance, his diminutive stature diminished further by an imposing rear surface. Lynch employs the planimetric image early on in the film, exploiting its capacity to enrich deadpan performance, while establishing the comic flavour of the opening stretches of action.

where technology overwhelms the natural landscape.[30] In all, Lynch syncretizes image and sound to create an affectively-charged apogee. Consequently he is able to foster an impression of narrative, cognitive, and emotional closure. To see how crucial style is to this effect, we need only note that at all other levels, irresolution reigns. At the film's close, open-endedness governs different sets of response: narrative (is Henry mired in a dream?), emotional (what constitutes the correct affective response at the film's end: elation, relief, sadness, estrangement?), moral (is Henry a child-killer, or a slayer of monsters? should the sympathy he elicits be revoked?), and hermeneutic (how can the film's events be explicated? how to nail down "meaning"?). Stylistic devices converge upon a superficial closure, alerting the spectator to expect the film soon to end, and eliciting strong but diffuse affect (what Torben Grodal calls "saturated" emotion).[31] That affective response remains equivocal owes much to a narration that withholds crucial information. The spectator's knowledge radically incomplete, Lynch's denouement can spur arousal that is emotionally ambivalent and open-ended.

Linked to ambivalent arousal is another hallmark of art cinema narration – critical detachment. *Eraserhead*, it has been argued, "relentlessly appl[ies] alienation devices"[32] so as to "evoke feelings of 'estrangement' in the viewer." [33] Like art films generally, Lynch's cinema is taken to traffic in a remote, reflective, viewing perspective. This entails blocking off emotions in toto, or more plausibly, evoking "distanced" feeling states, such as admiration or irony. *Eraserhead* effects distanciation through various devices. Hieratic character traits – Henry's diffidence, say, or Mr X's frozen smirk – teeter on opacity, disturbing the spectator's inferential and identificatory practices. A progressively loose architecture, fraught with digressions and dislocations, derails spectator hypotheses. Tonal inconsistency flouts predictions of dramatic unity. Narrative inconclusiveness tames univocal emotion. And the realism afforded impossible objects (e.g. the infant) evokes "artifact emotions"[34] – a kind of fascination directed at the constructedness and artifice of the representation (as distinct from absorption in the representation itself). All these tactics prima facie relegate emotion, urging on the spectator's sense-making and interpretive activities.

Yet just as accounts of art cinema tend to downplay the role of emotion, so it goes with *Eraserhead* and Lynch's cinema generally. Cognitive engagement need not imply affective estrangement. To *Eraserhead*'s distancing effects can be contrasted its arousal of affects and emotions, some complex (embarrassment, resentment), others autonomic (surprise, disgust). More specifically, Lynch's narration sets up a play between affective estrangement and arousal. Sometimes Lynch alternates cues for

[30] Beyond *Eraserhead*, Lynch turns the malfunctioning light topos into a favourite authorial motif – note its appearance, for instance, in *Blue Velvet* and *Mulholland Drive*.

[31] Torben Grodal, *Embodied Visions: Evolution, Emotion, Culture, and Film* (Clarendon: Oxford University Press, 2009) 149.

[32] Godwin, "Eraserhead," 37.

[33] Torben Grodal, *Moving Pictures: A New Theory of Film Genres, Feelings, and Cognition* (Clarendon: Oxford University Press, 1997) 127. For a contrasting view, see Todd McGowan, *The Impossible David Lynch* (New York: Columbia University Press, 2007).

[34] *Emotion and the Structure of Narrative Film: Film as an Emotion Machine*, Ed S. Tan (Mahwah: Lawrence Erlbaum, 1996).

arousal and distance, causing spectators to oscillate between binary levels of involvement. Most typically, and more elaborately, the dual perspectives are imbricated. Consider *Eraserhead*'s brief epilogue. By showing a pair of agents embracing, Lynch supplies a prototypical hook for affective involvement. Close-ups redundantly cue engagement. Facial expressions radiate serenity (Henry) and happiness (the Lady in the Radiator), and furnish a prime site for emotional contagion. From this angle, the epilogue evokes strong affirmative feeling, or "emotional flooding."[35] Yet against these systematic cues to arousal, Lynch pits alienating devices. An incongruous din punctures the harmony we perceive in the characters. (It also foregoes the kind of sensuous score we expect of conventional romantic closure.) In addition, Lynch whites-out the image, steeping the visual field in obfuscating light, and melting the characters into a wispy vapor (an authorial motif revived at the Climax of *Blue Velvet* (1986)). From all these cues springs contradictory arousal. Both gross detachment and determinate emotion fail to crystallize, reconfirming the closure's indeterminacy. In the final analysis, *Eraserhead* remains thoroughly enigmatic, and it correlates ambiguous arousal to the uncertainties of story comprehension and interpretation.

MIDNIGHT MIMICRY

So far, we have assumed that Lynch's spectator constructs story action, mounts interpretations, and experiences emotion, all in response to a patterned network of cues. *Eraserhead*, though, is identified with a specialized screening context that values in-group sociality as much as attentiveness to the screen. Of what relevance, then, is a cue-based model of spectator activity to a theatrical situation in which attention is frequently deflected from the film and its array of cues?

Like much cult film exhibition, the 1970s midnight movie fostered a theatrical environment apt for extroverted forms of reception. Late-night screenings of *Pink Flamingos* (1972) and *The Rocky Horror Picture Show* (1975) yielded unforeseen displays of chanting, dance, and "exhibitionist" behaviour.[36] Favorite stretches of dialogue were fired back at the screen by ebullient spectators. And audience members synchronized overt responses among themselves, affirming the bonding effects of communal viewing experience. *Eraserhead* – apparently fit to arouse strong reactions – was launched on the midnight circuit by Lynch and distributor Ben Barenholtz in September 1977. It played initially at the Cinema Village on 12th Street, and in carefully nominated urban districts thereafter. According to some reports, audience members were stirred to an interactive engagement with both the film and one another.[37] More so than in ordinary theatrical contexts, it seems, the attention of viewers at midnight shows must shuttle between auditorium and screen.

If the viewer is not held rapt to the fiction, then it might be countered that I have sketched an implausibly attentive and susceptible spectator.

[35] Grodal, *Moving Pictures*, 135.
[36] Godwin, "Eraserhead," 37.
[37] Hoberman and Rosenbaum, *Midnight Movies*, 302; Stuart Samuels, *Midnight Movies* (New York: Collier Macmillan, 1983) 159; Josh Frank and Charlie Buckholtz, *In Heaven Everything Is Fine: The Unsolved Life of Peter Ivers and the Lost History of New Wave Theatre* (New York: Free Press, 2008) 131.

The counterargument might go like this: in midnight movie viewing (1) attention routinely strays from the phenomenal film, thereby (2) diminishing pickup of cues and (3) leading to divergent responses unintended by the filmmaker. Consequently, the viewer's activity differs sharply from the patterns of perception and comprehension proposed above. A cue-based model of spectatorship presupposes viewer attention, but the midnight audience fixates *Eraserhead* only sporadically – the premium on group identification outdraws the primacy of the artwork.

We can offer a rebuttal of these concerns. First, arrested attention is not a necessary requisite for cue-driven perception. That our eyes sometimes drift from the artwork is a given in any viewing situation, yet this tends not to diminish our capacity to notice cues – some of which make especially vivid appeals to our attention. Redundancy is built into films partly to compensate for such occasional slips in concentration. Granted, the midnight experience goes beyond attentional lapses; it places compelling and dispersed demands on the spectator's mental awareness. According to some eyewitnesses, however, the 1970s midnight audience greeted *Eraserhead* not with boisterous enthusiasm, but with "silence and bewilderment" – there was, Barenholtz notes, "very little interaction of the *Rocky Horror* and *Pink Flamingos* kind."[38] At the Nuart theatre, chants of "Eraserhead" had to be instigated by a dutiful employee.[39] Even those commentators reporting crowd participation have noted the subduing effects of Lynch's film.[40] *Eraserhead* might not hook attention at every step, but it seems to have compelled viewers more systematically than certain other midnight movies – a result, perhaps, of its comprehensive challenge to meaning and intelligibility.[41]

In any event, it seems improbable that midnight viewers are wholly or chiefly neglectful of textual cues. On the contrary, at least some parts of the work – typically its most salient and idiosyncratic cues – are *over*-learned and internalized by devoted spectators who know the film intimately. Midnight viewing rituals (e.g. singing, clapping, masquerade) are elaborated and refined upon repeat exposure, and competencies of group practice are passed on to new initiates. Textual cues are hardly marginal to these customs. Shared patterns of response harness particular stimuli as points of departure. When repeat audiences laugh ahead of a gag in *Harold and Maude* (1971), they do so in anticipation of cues designed to produce laughter.[42] Similarly, group applause at the climax of *Eraserhead* feeds off textual stimuli – audience approval here converges on the infant's destruction.[43] "Expressive" spectatorship, therefore, need not signify a radical decline in cue attention. Indeed, the spectator's ex-

---

[38] Personal communication with Barenholtz, 15 June 2009. "The *Eraserhead* base audience," Barenholtz adds, "consisted of serious, adventurous filmgoers."

[39] Frank and Buckholtz, *In Heaven Everything Is Fine*, 131.

[40] E.g. Godwin, "David Lynch Retrospect," 51.

[41] Nor, evidently, was *Eraserhead*'s original audience as "reefer happy" as the late-night audience of, say, *The Harder They Come* (1972) or *Reefer Madness* (1936). Deep intoxication inevitably depletes the spectator's cue pickup, and at some stage the intoxicated viewer ceases to "view" the film in a meaningful sense. If the notion of the "film spectator" has utility, it has to presuppose some measure of engagement between spectator and film (and in the case of midnight movie viewing, some degree of mutual attention among audience members too).

[42] Samuels, *Midnight Movies*, 182.

[43] Hoberman and Rosenbaum, *Midnight Movies*, 302.

pressivity is precisely launched upon the pickup and processing of stimuli perceived in the work. Furthermore, the meaningful features of a midnight movie will be evident to those who view the film habitually, since repeat viewings provide multiple opportunities for cue recognition. Even if we grant that *Eraserhead* spurs interactive engagement, there is little to suggest that the audience's cue awareness tapers off drastically.

Subsequently, the third premise of the counterargument looks fragile. Recall its basic outline: apparently liberated from cue detection, spectators repurpose the film to fit their own agendas, elaborating diverse and personalized reactions, and flouting "perversely" the intentions of the author.[44] Emancipation from cues thus enables the midnight viewer to forge largely self-determined activities. Plainly, however, this supposition flies in the face of the empirical midnight audience, whose ethos affirms joint attention and studied synchronicity – in short, an overwhelming homogeneity of response. Communal film viewing promotes group convergence, not variegation.[45]

Nor is it necessary to postulate an unbridgeable gap between what the filmmaker intended and the activity of the midnight moviegoer. To the extent that midnight viewers appropriate movies to various ends, some aspects of their activity probably outrun the makers' intentions – George Romero might not have anticipated the cries of "Eat them!" that attended *Night of the Living Dead* (1968).[46] One might argue, however, that audiences isolate what will become the work's "cult" elements only because the film has worked on them in the intended ways. Cheering the demise of a deformed baby seems callous, but this reaction at *Eraserhead*'s climax attests to the successful arousal of disgust toward the creature, as well as a general approbation toward Henry – cognitive-affective outcomes desired and designed by Lynch. Of course, viewers may wittingly cut against the "proper" response, as when Romero's flesh-eaters are willed by viewers to devour the unfortunate townsfolk. But in such cases, spectators recognize that their reactions deform the cues presented. These spectators do not naively misconstrue story events. Having first grasped the action, they determine to resist the film's operations in ways that accord with group sensibilities (say, an underground antibourgeois ethic). Even "perverse" spectatorship entails that narrational cues be successfully grasped.

Midnight movie consumption relies on standard viewing skills, but it also mobilizes a distinctive set of exhibition practices. These practices supplement rather than supplant the spectator's ordinary viewing processes. As such, they exert a modifying influence on the spectator's cognition and emotion. One cluster of activities is context-specific and specialized, drawing on prior knowledge about midnight shows, their norms of interactivity, imperatives of mutual attention, and so forth. Other practices are film-specific, motivated by group-derived goals. Late-night viewers in the 1970s plumbed the midnight movie for cult potential,

---

44 Janet Staiger, *Perverse Spectators: The Practices of Film Reception* (New York: New York University Press, 2000).

45 This is not to claim that the activity of midnight audiences follows a lockstep rigor. Certainly, the midnight experience is kept fresh by spectators creatively recasting favourite display reactions, and testing the popularity of new ones.

46 Samuels, *Midnight Movies*, 66.

appropriating and enlarging its most outrageous elements. By a process of piecemeal selection, spectators isolated those filmic features most ripe for group esteem. Not every midnight film was appropriated for cult veneration. For Umberto Eco, ascribing cult value to an art object entails that the perceiver "break [the object] up or take it apart so that one then may remember only parts of it, regardless of their original relationship to the whole."[47] I'm skeptical that spectators dissect the work quite in the way Eco suggests – it seems more plausible to posit pre-focused attention, testing of data against criteria (e.g. standards of "bad taste"), and mental construction of extractable items, each process running simultaneous with the encoding of incoming stimuli. Nonrandom appropriation is a process of construction, not of dismantling into parts.

Nevertheless, the bracketing of some features and not others holds good for midnight cult viewing. Moreover, audience engagement is naturally modified by these goal-directed practices. By biasing attention toward nonstandard phenomena, viewers not only neglect but actively downplay the normative underpinnings of midnight movies. Like its late-night bedfellows, *Eraserhead* rests on a body of canonic norms, but cult-viewing practices explicitly work to subdue these norms in favor of more outré elements.

More so than standard theatrical experience, midnight moviegoing impacts on the spectator's faculties of emotion. Most broadly, the accent on overt sociality and convergent response may intensify emotional contagion among audience members. All things being equal, individuals "respond more intensely if [they] form part of a large audience that listens, claps, sings, sways, dances, laughs, or cries together."[48] Group contagion reinforces and renews emotional experience, generally in concert with affectively saturated cues present in the film (say, the strong triggers for disgust in *Eraserhead*). Contagion also patterns emotional response for repeat encounters. Individuals discover what the group considers the work's emotional peaks, and they predispose certain emotions to attach to those peaks on repeat viewings. In addition, the revivifying force of group contagion supplies longevity to emotional reactions that might otherwise decay through habituation.[49]

The midnight audience coveted particular types of affective experience. Most salient is what might be called dysphoric pleasure, a kind of cognitive delight derived from the collective experience of unpleasant affect. Apparently, the 1970s audience meshed dysphoric emotion with appropriation. As "seekers of the grotesque,"[50] they gauged a film's cult potential partly by assessing its capacity to arouse negative emotion. Correspondingly, most canonized midnight movies are those which assign

[47] Umberto Eco, "*Casablanca*: Cult Movies and Intertextual Collage," *SubStance* 14:2/47 (1985): 4.

[48] Boyd, *On the Origin of Stories*, 105.

[49] More interesting, perhaps, is the possibility of collective emotion that defiantly clashes with the affective stimulus set forth in the film, yielding ambivalent emotion states. If this occurs, audience reaction may differ radically from that anticipated by the filmmaker. Again, though, this is a case of spectators working consciously against the inferred "correct" response, rather than simply misjudging affective meaning.

[50] The description comes from Ben Barenholtz, personal communication, 15 June 2009.

dysphoric pleasure a central role, as evinced by *The Texas Chain Saw Massacre* (1974), *El Topo* (1970), and *Eraserhead*.[51]

Midnight movies embrace a wide range of unpleasant emotions and affects, but one aversive state in particular – physical disgust – endures among midnight features and Lynch's cinema in general. Physical disgust is sought (by midnight viewers) and showcased (by midnight movies) – it exemplifies a spectatorial as well as an aesthetic concern. *Eraserhead*'s original audience was thus highly receptive to disgusting subject matter and dysphoric experience.[52] Given the spectator's appetite for disgust, midnight movie viewing often animates the "paradox of negative emotion," a contradictory desire to experience undesirable emotions. Carl Plantinga suggests that mainstream Hollywood films resolve the paradox by forecasting euphoric outcomes, weighting the gains of painful events, and harnessing the physiological residue of negative emotions in ways that enhance positive emotional experience.[53] Viewers of mainstream films submit to unpleasant emotions thanks in part to the promise of "affective compensation," emotional relief delivered by happy endings or by "some other fortuitous outcome" built into the narrative.[54]

Spectators of mainstream films tolerate dysphoric emotion, but the midnight movie viewer embraces it. Negative affect often engenders the sort of extroverted reactions prized by the midnight audience. Disgust, for instance, provokes behaviors that are uninhibited, cognitively impenetrable, and overt, while also being predictable and essentially uniform among group members. So unrestrained are the action tendencies triggered by disgust that they supply one source of dysphoric pleasure for midnight movie viewers, compounding group convergence and reciprocity. Furthermore, what counts as disgusting also frequently violates polite social mores, and hence offers further appeal to the midnight spectator. Thus disgust not only strengthens emotional bonds among the group, e.g. by spurring emotionally gregarious reactions; it also dovetails with a broadly countercultural ideology, generating group approval by upsetting traditional standards of good taste.

Yet midnight movies do not shun tactics that ameliorate negative affect. *Eraserhead*, along with other films in Lynch's oeuvre, takes the edge off unpleasant arousal, though not necessarily with the goal of affective compensation. One tactic exploits character reactions so as to cue the spectator's response to the object of disgust. Plantinga[55] observes this

---

[51] Even the ostensibly euphoric midnight movies exploit negative experience. Consider the grotesque faux suicides staged by the morbid teen in *Harold and Maude*, and the putative "gross-out" connotations springing from that film's central romance. Or note the way Perry Henzell punctures the feel-good vibe of *The Harder They Come* with spikes of brutal violence.

[52] Even so, distributor Barenholtz "tried very hard to discourage pregnant women from seeing [*Eraserhead*]." Personal communication, 8 June 2009.

[53] Plantinga, *Moving Viewers*, 184.

[54] Carl Plantinga, "Trauma, Pleasure, and Emotion in the Viewing of *Titanic*: A Cognitive Approach." *Film Theory and Contemporary Hollywood Movies*. Ed. Warren Buckland (New York and London: Routledge, 2009) 240. An overlapping argument is put forth by Torben Grodal, who suggests that certain fictions present negative emotional experiences as necessary components in the protagonist's pursuit of positive goals: "Just as mountain climbers suffer hardships and a very high risk of death to climb to the top of Mount Everest, so viewers should, to some degree, be motivated to be exposed to aversive stimuli" (*Embodied Visions*, 124).

[55] Plantinga, *Moving Viewers*.

manoeuvre at work in *Blue Velvet*, in which Jeffrey (Kyle MacLachlan) casually handles a gruesomely vagrant human ear, and in *The Elephant Man* (1980), where Dr Treves (Anthony Hopkins) shows compassion to John Merrick (John Hurt) in spite of Merrick's appalling physique. These displays of composure cue spectators to inhibit their own feelings of disgust.[56]

Often in Lynch, however, the characters' reactions and nonreactions to disgusting phenomena flout the action tendencies we know to be appropriate (e.g. flinching or flight). Ghastly spots erupt on the oily head of *Eraserhead*'s infant, but Henry's facial reaction is alarmingly muted. In *Wild at Heart*, a gunshot blast reduces a storekeeper's arm to an awful stump, yet his colleague's words of comfort are offhandedly matter-of-fact. By throwing weight onto characters' incongruous reactions, Lynch attenuates the emotional force of the disgusting object or event – not so as to permit spectators dysphoric relief, but rather to amplify the characters' off-kilter traits and idiosyncratic behavior. In addition, Lynch again sets up ambivalent arousal, combining saturated emotion cues with prompts for affective detachment.

Alleviation of disgust also arises from the mixing of affects. *Eraserhead* yokes disgust with euphoric emotion, piercing negative affect with stabs of wry humor. It also blends disgust with still different sorts of dysphoric affect. Unpleasant social emotions, such as embarrassment, mingle with the disgusting and the comic, and may dilute somewhat the palpability of disgusted affect. Often *Eraserhead* shades disgust into other emotions. Queasy imagery and "illbient" sound[57] render the X family dinner repellent, but the scene's blend of satiric humor and painful embarrassment yields a complex mix of affective states. This synthesis of pleasant and unpleasant affect tempers pure disgust, and contributes to the narration's tonal uncertainty – a device that Kristin Thompson and others identify in Lynch's film and television work.[58] It's a blend also ingredient to other midnight movies – consider the scatological humor in *Pink Flamingos*.[59] Arguably, moreover, the norms of midnight movie viewing – mutual attention, synchronized reactions, "exhibitionist" feedback – provide a kind of emotional relief valve for disgust, allaying dysphoric experience through means of shared and outgoing expression. It's not, therefore, that midnight movies disdain affective compensation or dysphoric relief. But such effects are often only byproducts of other concerns (e.g. character delineation, creation of tone, mode of film reception and so

---

[56] Plantinga, *Moving Viewers*, 211.

[57] On the use of illbient sound in Lynch's cinema, see Murray Smith, "A Reasonable Guide to Horrible Noise (Part 2): Listening to *Lost Highway*," in Lennard Hojbjerg and Peter Schepelern (eds), *Film Style and Story: A Tribute to Torben* (Museum Tusculaneum Press, 2003).

[58] Thompson, *Storytelling in Film and Television*, 116.

[59] Plantinga notes the vogue for comic renderings of disgusting subject-matter in contemporary Hollywood gross-out comedies such as *Dumb & Dumber* (1994), *There's Something About Mary* (1998), and *Shallow Hal* (2001) – evidence, perhaps, of the domestication of midnight movie concerns, as discussed by Hoberman and Rosenbaum (Plantinga, *Moving Viewers* 67-8; 204; Hoberman and Rosenbaum 321-22). One might also adduce *Meet the Parents* (2000), which stages its own variation on the paradigm scenario invoked by the X family dinner in *Eraserhead*.

forth). Unlike its mainstream counterpart, the midnight audience harbors small expectation of affective payoffs or happy ends.[60]

Put in its original context, *Eraserhead* is revealed as both satisfying and exceeding the propensities of its audience. A mordant and grotesque fiction is entirely apt for viewers favorably disposed to dysphoric pleasure. Moreover, if we suppose that *Eraserhead* stirs outwardly expressed emotions, its items of disgust serve as one sort of affective trigger. Strong stimuli for unpleasant emotions cue overt action tendencies, and the display rules governing midnight events not only permit but roundly endorse conspicuous reactions. An audience which so responds exhibits focused attention to the cues on screen. In addition, affective response may be reinforced and extended through group harmonization. In all this, *Eraserhead* repays the attention of midnight viewers, but it also transcends midnight movie criteria. It goes beyond powerful arousal of basic emotions to tap the higher emotions. Most strikingly, as we have seen, it launches a bold challenge to the spectator's comprehension at both denotative and hermeneutic levels. The sheer complexity of this challenge makes *Eraserhead* an atypical midnight movie but an irreducibly Lynchian film.

The difficulties posed by *Eraserhead*, I've tried to suggest, spring partly from canonical storytelling principles and ordinary viewing practices. At the level of constructional design, orthodox devices at once tacitly orient the spectator and underline the story action's strangeness. The knowing orchestration of canonic norms, sprinkled among or fused with defamiliarizing cues, reveals a confident grasp of the traditional story format. From this angle, Lynch's transition to films such as *The Straight Story* (1999), *The Elephant Man*, and *Dune* (1984), and even to indie-mainstream hybrids like *Twin Peaks: Fire Walk with Me* (1992) and *Blue Velvet*, seems a less drastic departure than is often claimed. Furthermore, Lynch's use of canonic story devices gives the lie to the dream analogy – on the whole, classical devices ensure that *Eraserhead* bears more pattern and order than do dreams.

Nor does the dream analogy successfully illuminate viewing practices. To postulate a dreamlike spectator position is to confuse reception and representation. Dreamlike images do not engender dreamlike mental states. Whether attention is intensely focused or divided (as in midnight movie viewing), spectators engage in cue-bound procedures that are participatory and active. The dream experience is best conceived as one more knowledge schema cued by the text, encouraging expectations of attenuated logic, spatiotemporal plasticity, impossible beings, and the like. Finally, *Eraserhead*'s difficulties of comprehension work to expand the spectator's affective and cognitive repertoire. By launching a refusal of

[60] I'm not claiming that all midnight movies eschew happy endings. Some midnight movies evidently do target uplifting closure (though what seems to be an affirmative ending – say, in *Eraserhead* or *The Texas Chain Saw Massacre* – is often just an ambivalent or ambiguous one; moreover, such climaxes are wont to look upbeat in the light of the often apocalyptic action that precedes them). More important is the set of affective expectations that attend different modes or types of film. Plantinga argues that viewers of mainstream movies will brook negative emotions in anticipation of positive emotional payoffs (see also Grodal, *Embodied Visions*, 124). Midnight moviegoers, by contrast, enter into dysphoric experience for its own sake, not for some prospective euphoric reward. Negative arousal might be leavened in various ways, but the midnight viewer is indifferent: dysphoric experience is revelled in, not tolerated.

the prior knowledge it triggers, the film sharpens spectators' sense-making strategies, affective responses (e.g. expressions of disgust), social schemas (e.g. standards of propriety), and evaluation of reality status. It also refreshes scripts for paradigmatic events, pressing viewers to imagine unforeseeable permutations of familiar situations. Films like those by David Lynch, which challenge and stretch knowledge structures, yield rich evolutionary uses. In ways both obvious and oblique, *Eraserhead* persists in the spectator's mind.

DOMINIQUE DE COURCELLES
"WAKING DREAMS ARE THE ONES THAT ARE IMPORTANT"
NOT BELONGING TO EITHER, SOUND & IMAGE, & TIME

How could we risk giving an interpretation of the cinematographic work of David Lynch if we take into account what he himself was able to say about his films? Does he not in fact affirm: "What I could say about what I wanted to relate in my films would not have any importance. It's as if you dug up someone who has been dead for four hundred years and asked him to talk about his book."[1]

Not wanting in any case "to dig up someone who has been dead for four hundred years" and to disturb, even to fill up his rest or his emptiness, I will be content nevertheless to let my gaze roam over the table from whence emerge figures, David Lynch's figures, and to apply to myself that other affirmation by this artist: "Waking dreams are the ones that are important, the ones that come when I'm quietly sitting in a chair, gently letting my mind wander."[2] I will give myself over therefore to the occupation of the "waking dream," of the "gentle diversion of the spirit" and try to elucidate the thrill that David Lynch admits he is in search of: "Cinema for me is a very strong desire to marry image with sound. When I manage it I feel a real thrill. I'm not sure I'm looking for anything else apart from that thrill."[3] David Lynch, a trained painter, came to cinema because in cinema "there are sound and image and time."[4]

I notice that over the table where I am preparing to write about David Lynch, emerging from the flat surface, there are Fred Madison and a woman straight out of *Lost Highway* (1997) accompanied by a character dressed in black with broad ears. These will be the figures of my waking dream of David Lynch's work in its entirety, that work that makes me think and affirm that after scores of hours spent in viewing different films and drawings and paintings as well, I no longer have the capability and even less the need to entertain my own nocturnal dreams as I only have to abandon myself to the waking dreams of David Lynch – I have truly entered into the waking dreams of David Lynch which are mine as well. Now I can totally take on board that remark of Samuel Beckett in *The Unnamable*:

> C'est peut-être ça que je sens, qu'il y a un dehors et un dedans et moi au milieu, c'est peut-être ça que je suis, la chose qui divise le monde en deux, d'une part le dehors, de l'autre le dedans, ça peut être mince comme une lame, je ne suis ni d'un côté ni de l'autre, je suis au milieu, je suis la cloi-

---

[1] Interview in *La Revue du Cinéma* 424 (February 1987): 26.
[2] Interview in *Max* (November 1990).
[3] Interview in *Studio Magazine* 63 (June 1992).
[4] Interview in *Les Cahiers du Cinéma* 482 (July-Aug 1994): 14-17.

son, j'ai deux faces et pas d'épaisseur, c'est peut-être ça que je sens, je me sens qui vibre, je suis le tympan, d'un côté c'est le crâne, de l'autre le monde, je ne suis ni de l'un ni de l'autre...

(Perhaps that's what I feel, an outside and an inside and me in the middle, perhaps that's what I am, the thing that divides the world in two, on the one side the outside, on the other the inside, that can be as thin as foil, I'm neither one side nor the other, I'm in the middle, I'm the partition, I've two surfaces and no thickness, perhaps that's what I feel, myself vibrating, I'm the tympanum, on the one hand the mind, on the other the world, I don't belong to either...)[5]

The idea for the screenplay for *Lost Highway* supposedly came to David Lynch on the last night on location of his film *Fire Walk with Me*, as a prematuration or claim of incompletion of what he was in the process of completing. *Lost Highway* would allow him then to bring to light elements which failed to find expression, which were relegated to obscurity or silence in *Fire Walk with Me*, and to help to assimilate them thanks to the new potential space of a shared filmic reality still to come. It's about the idea of a couple who live in a house and a video cassette arrives for them in the mail. When they watch it, they discover the front of their house on it. But the film also has another source, viz. a scene that David Lynch tells of as having been actually experienced by him in real life. He woke up one morning, heard his intercom ringing and a man's voice over the intercom calling him "Dave." Michel Chion reports Lynch's own words:

I said: "yes!" and the man said: "Dick Laurant (with an a) is dead." And I said: "what?," and then there was nobody there. I couldn't see the entrance to the house unless I went to the other end of it and looked out of the big window, and there there was no-one. And I don't know who Dick Laurant was... I swear it's a true story.[6]

The making of the film *Lost Highway*, neither true nor false, in the sense that speculative or scientific knowledge is true or false, but based on this "true story" is therefore destined to permit communication or the sharing of a certain type of experience – "the true story," the transfer to a member of the audience of an experience which would not be available for normal mental articulation but which becomes accessible through the imaginative function of film. "A film is not thought out, it is perceived," declared Merleau-Ponty in 1945.[7] Listening allows us to imagine, it is the basis for images. We have heard someone or something and that provokes visions; shots come then like images dictated by a narrative even when there is no explicit narrative. William Blake remarked:

The Imagination is not a State:
It is the Human Existence itself

[5]   *The Unnamable. Three Novels by Samuel Beckett – Molloy, Malone Dies, The Unnamable* (New York: Grove Press, 1955) 383.
[6]   Michel Chion, *David Lynch* (Paris: Cahiers du Cinéma, collection "Auteurs," 2007) 247.
[7]   Such was the conclusion of a lecture given in 1945 at the Institute of Advanced Cinematographic Studies: "Le cinéma et la nouvelle psychologie" ("Cinema and the new psychology"), *Sens et non sens (Sense and nonsense)* (Paris: Gallimard, 1966) 74.

Can we not consider that the imaginative function of David Lynch's film consists in actualizing aspects of the self that introspection or dreams would perhaps never be able to mobilize? Right away, by telling us that scene as a source of *Lost Highway* – the lost highway -, David Lynch posits that the lost highway – the film – will act as an operator to make a passage from visions or a transmutation between experience, all "genuine" experience and the plasticity of film as psychic workload, perhaps as a "mysterious" or "mystic" workload offered to a member of the audience.

Lost Highway: the title alone draws attention to itself by reason of its enigmatic character, with the first image of a road sliding away to infinity, the road of travelling by night, the road that tends towards a point at an indefinable infinity that does not fail to evoke the mortal road that leads to paradise of Hieronymus Bosch or the journey of the Tibetan dead through impenetrable darkness and flashes of light. Baudelaire spoke of sleep as *"ce voyage aventureux de tous les soirs* (that adventurous journey of every night,)" a rendezvous with the past in what we call the future and which is just the present of the moment in which the encounter takes place. Right away we breathe in the night air, we feel the force of the wind that brushes the mythic and the archaic nature of lost childhood. We feel the intimate emotions of our early years and the infinity of the cosmos, we are brought back to the familiar, to the already experienced: such is our installation in the "waking dream" state while we are "quietly sitting on a chair" in order to watch the film. *Lost Highway* is indeed that still recognizable "lost highway" where the distinction between the outside and the inside, internal and external reality, is not necessarily relevant. Present both in the opening credits and in the closing frame of the film, this highway of the title frames and wraps round the film: the simple figure of a spatio-temporal ribbon which is always turning round on itself in a perpetual loop like a Möbius band and which cinema, more than any other art, is capable of showing. Indefinite voluntary suspension of linear reasoning is then felt in that frenzied pulsing of the David Bowie song *I'm Deranged*, so suited to the yellow line slipping away under the wheels of a car in which is located the camera and which rolls through the night at an inordinate speed, anticipating the beginning and the end. These credit images mark out in this way the suspension of reasoning and the limited presence of the subject so that representation can come out of it as an unlimited object, a plastic and dreamlike transcendence which denies all interpretation and all demarcation of depth by its horizontal evidence of freedom.

The first scene is as follows: a man, Fred Madison, the actor Bill Pullman, is in his house, unshaven, in the early hours of morning. Someone rings him and a man's voice pronounces over the intercom the phrase "Dick Laurent is dead." So it is that the film comes into existence, through this listening without seeing as its opening scene, exercised in a horizontal and minimalist interior like a primitive and mythic ghost. We know that myth is the relating of an event which has taken place in a primeval time, the fabled epoch when everything started, the time when, through the action of supernatural beings, reality came into existence. This overheard voice makes such a strong impression by being deprived of a visible body that it invades all that is real and constructs reality on the basis of its own self. Through this voice is effected the plastic creation of a reality which is a veritable visual and filmic body. It is in this plastic creation that the eye has been able to play its part. This primordial voice, produced by a metal intercom with a slightly displaced echo, sounds in English like a dry crackling, and we will hear it again at the end of the film, different, deformed, other and the same. For the film finishes in the same way it started, with the same siren sound that is heard immediately after the phrase "Dick Laurent is dead," with this one difference that the first view we have of it is from inside the house and from the receiver's viewpoint, whereas the second is from the outside with the transmitter that rings on the intercom. The film is therefore situated in that interval which is not one, between inside and outside, since everything starts with a death which is not a death, given that Dick Laurent, who is also a certain Mr. Eddy, only dies at the end of the film way out in the desert. Besides, the same man receives the information as the one who then gives it, rendering unreal the former and making him appear in retrospect like a deforming perspective without consistency of the same event. But what event? This event, cropping up twice, similar but not identical, indicates that there is perhaps an infinity of possible perspectives impossible to total like a vanishing point such as the road whose band we have just seen unravelling to infinity in a perpetual loop on itself.

David Lynch has often stated explicitly that he likes to work by association of ideas without rationalizing. We are particularly struck in *Lost Highway* by the open, ambiguous, undecided nature of the dialogues. We immediately experience this undecidedness subjectively when we hear Renee Madison, the actress Patricia Arquette, declare to her husband, a jazz saxophonist, that she is going to stay at home to read. "Read what?" asks Fred, and she doesn't answer. It is absolutely impossible to know what she is going to read, if she is going to read, if this dialogue is hinting at something, if we are to read between the lines, and the art of the director consists in having it said in such a way by the actors that even their delivery of the lines digs a huge hole which is not normal reading-between-the-lines, which is emptiness, nothing. So it is that the film, this body of a film, is perhaps an empty body, designated as all or nothing, pure coincidence and pure emptiness, palpable emptiness and nothing, even before being language and sense, perhaps the space of a waking dream, but what dream? Whose dream? The emphasis changes then from: What is the film about? What is the film going to be about? to: What is it like to see and hear emptiness and nothing? Does it come down to a mystical experience, the space of a mystic dream? When Fred telephones his wife from his jazz club, nobody answers him: the mystery of "Read what?" by she who is not accountable for what she reads is thus celebrated. André Breton in *La clé des champs* (*The Key to the Fields*) wrote: "There is a way of going to the cinema like other people go to church and I think that, from a certain angle, quite independently of what is being shown there, it is there that the only absolutely modern mystery is being celebrated." This "absolutely modern mystery," independent of all content, is it not emptiness? So it is that the emptiness of David Lynch's film could quite easily be an analogy for, if not a continuation of, the definitive emptiness of the tomb abandoned by the body of a divine dead Word in the same way that the fine house of Fred and Renee is empty.

The following morning, in front of their house, Renee finds a cassette in an envelope. They watch it together in a stupor: the cassette merely shows a panoramic view of the front of their house. At night, after making love wordlessly in the dark and lugubrious house, Fred recounts a dream to Renee in which he summoned her without being able to find her, and when he looks at her, after relating his dream, he has a terrifying and fleeting vision of her with a man's face. Is it Renee or is it her double? Is Fred dreaming, in a waking state or not? Another morning, another cassette. This time the camera has gone over the interior of their house and discovered them as a couple stretched out in bed. Two policemen, called by a terrified Renee, arrive and do not notice any signs of breaking and entering. Evening again, at a friend of Renee's, Andy. It is then that a man dressed in black, with big ears, first of all glimpsed by special effect through the black hair of Renee, introduces himself to Fred. Lynch then chooses to totally isolate the two characters erasing all the sounds of a party and dubbing their dialogue with a muffled and continuous rumbling that gets louder: "As a matter of fact I'm there right now... At your house..." this Mystery Man says to Fred while giving him a cell phone. "Call me." Fred composes his own number and immediately someone answers him: "I told you I was here." And the Mystery Man's laugh is both near and far, an alien presence that leaves Fred restless and threatens his existence. There is one person too many in the house, but is it the Mystery Man? Is it Fred or is it a double of Fred who is sharing his house? Silences and muffled noises punctuate the whole of the first part of the film like a starting dough from which sounds ought to emerge. The whispers and words on the edge of exclamation give us the feeling of living in a dream, while the laughter brutally echoed and displaced by the Mystery Man's telephone earpiece makes everything tip over into nightmare. So it is that this tone both mythic and mysterious allows us to situate the film as if watched by a primitive witness who is perhaps merely the Mystery Man or one of his alter egos or even himself a member of the audience like someone else.

Hans Belting speaks of a "filmic illusion operating under the seal of the real": "It is the technical animation activating the film that creates in the spectator the impression that, in their succession, these fleeting images are nothing other than his own images, those he experiences in his dream and imagination."[8] And he adds: "The experience of cinema, while affecting to suggest an experience of the real, is close to a dream state in which we are exposed to images we cannot control though we can have the impression that we ourselves are productive of them."[9] But the art historian would not be able like the filmmaker David Lynch to "know" so well, i.e. to savor, taste, feel modulations of the voice, changes in sound colors which give the feeling of living in a dream, one's own dream and which charge space with wonders and terrifying threats. The waking dream of David Lynch is reality and reality is his waking dream. For the spectator this dream that we do not control is someone else's dream, David Lynch's, one in which we risk being caught.

[8] Hans Belting, *Pour une anthropologie des images* (Paris: Gallimard, 2004) 103.
[9] Belting, *Pour une anthropologie des images*, 104.

In *Lost Highway* the nightmare heralded by the laughter of the Mystery Man is very quickly delineated. Another cassette arrives showing a horrible scene of carnage. Fred finds himself in prison because of an image. He is the only one to receive the third video cassette, to put it in the cassette drive and to watch it – he sees himself killing his own wife in a black and white picture of poor quality immediately followed by a very short shot of the murder in color because this is the reality with red being the predominant color and we know that red is the color of mystery or enigma for Lynch; reality proceeds here from the picture and it is also mystery and enigma. Renee does indeed look as if she has been killed and Fred is arrested and imprisoned as her murderer even though he has no memory of this murder and it is this arrest which, for Lynch as director, is the most surprising thing in the story. Fred Madison is henceforth merely a human shape devoid of memory and he is condemned to the electric chair. In this corridor of death he suffers atrocious headaches and nightmares about mysterious images of places and people unknown to him. Has a double got hold of him and assumed his appearance trying to eliminate him in order to take his place? And we know that the phenomenon of split personality borders on manifestations of occultism and possession as Otto Rank has shown.[10] Can we not detect above all in the hallucinatory double a desire for annihilation? This refers to a time punctuated by repetition, suspended by a constant return of the same thing. Here it is in fact that there is an eclipse of Fred Madison's temporal existence: his execution lasts the length of an eclipse which constitutes the second part of the film. Does not David Lynch give us in this negated time insight into the absolutely unstageable?

One morning the prison warden is surprised to see someone else in Fred's cell, a young man called Pete Dayton who is identified as someone quite innocuous, who cannot remember what he has been doing for the last two days and who is taken back to his parents. It is indeed another person, Pete Dayton, who can be neither a deformed version or a visual scrambling of Fred Madison. Pete goes back to the garage where he works and is reunited with his friends and his girlfriend. The only point in common between Fred Madison, jazz saxophonist, and Pete Dayton, young car mechanic, is that both of them use their ear: the first as a musician, the second as an expert in the art of locating by sound what is wrong with the engine in a car as Mr. Eddy says to Pete when he asks him to find a solution to a mysterious noise he can hear in his luxurious car and which disturbs him. So it is that the two become one, through their ear: but is it one and the same character played by two different actors or a character who changes his identity during the course of the film? And we mentioned earlier that the Mystery Man dressed in black has a face remarkable for its wide ears. In the "blank" of Fred Madison's conscience is revealed a "spirit of depth" to take up Anton Ehrenzweig's expression,[11] capable of accomplishing integrative tasks; there is something positive in emptiness, in nothingness, there is potential in the empty shape and this potential turns out to be Pete Dayton by displacement, associative contiguousness, substitution: "A divinity that shapes our

[10] Otto Rank, *Don Juan et le double* (Paris: Petite bibliothèque Payot, 1932).
[11] Anton Ehrenzweig, *L'Ordre caché de l'art* (Paris: Gallimard, 1974).

ends, rough hew them how we will," wrote Shakespeare.[12] Fred Madison has disappeared. Two have become one.

The second part of the film is a veritable storm zone marked musically by brass instruments and roars, catching at words that sound dictated or coming out of nowhere with deviant human behavior, for example when Mr. Eddy, a rich crook, who has taken Pete "for a ride" in his top-of-the-range car, rains down bloody and murderous blows on a driver who was driving just a tad too close to him, or when the crook's mistress, a beautiful young woman called Alice, comes to seduce the car mechanic and to take him to do a "blagging" at the home of a director of porno films, Andy, who falls head first onto a glass table which cuts him through the forehead and leaves him dead. This is what Bergson called *l'absurdité comique* ("comic absurdity") in which the maddest and most dangerous irrationality takes on the appearance of the most rigorous reasoning like when we dream.[13] He calls it *la logique de l'imagination* ("the logic of the imagination") which opposes itself to the logic of reason by "raising the crust of well-formed judgments and solidly founded ideas" (*en soulevant la croûte de jugements bien tassés et d'idées solidement assises*).[14] I laugh when I hear Mr. Eddy beating the driver half to death to "teach him a lesson;" Andy's death does not arouse in me any particular feeling of compassion, in the same way that Renee's death on screen did not particularly affect me. At the same time a whole system of poetics is developed in the analogy, equivalent to a splitting in half: in Mr. Eddy's mistress we recognize Renee, but a blonde Renee, still played by Patricia Arquette; but is the actress playing two different characters or a character who has split in half? Alice claims that Mr. Eddy is holding her captive; Pete watches a porno film projected like a loop in which Alice plays a seemingly consenting adult; Pete receives by telephone threats from the man dressed in black who talks to him about the situation of death row prisoners left waiting; the policemen who conducted an inquiry into Renee's death conduct an inquiry into the death of Andy who was Renee's friend; Alice, who has picked up money and jewelry in Andy's house, invites Pete, who is becoming more and more suspicious and is himself subject to hallucinations, to take her to a receiver of stolen goods whose cabin is situated way out in the desert. So it is that the story of *Lost Highway* is always reversible, its storyline is recommencement and recreation, transfer. What happened originally has not been swallowed up in a once-and-for-all story, the basic events are not abolished by time, the story can still be remade and repeated, even reinterpreted,[15] even though the characters really have nothing to say to each other and often do not speak to each other. The two ends of the film because they are similar without being identical, because they do not coincide even though they play at creating coincidence, refer us back to the same impossible present, which implies that time has not passed in the meantime, in the interval, in the duration of the film; certainly there has been a progression

---

[12] *Hamlet* 5.2.10-11.
[13] Henri Bergson, *Le Rire* (Paris: Œuvres, 1970) 475, 477.
[14] Henri Bergson, *Le Rire*, 407-08.
[15] Certain interpreters have not stopped themselves from going down this route like Slavoj Žižek who gives a Lacanian analysis of the film: *Lacrimae Rerum, Essays on Kieslowski, Hitchcock, Tarkovsky, Lynch and a few others* (Paris: Ed. Amsterdam, 2005).

because we have gone from an initial situation to a final situation, time has elapsed, but not a linear time, rather a broken, fragmented and dislocated time.

So it is that we can hear all this film, its modulating and vibrating rhythms, its shouts, its rumors and its roars, the multiplicity or possible infinity of senses in tune with the rustling of words and sounds, the never-to-be-achieved rearrangement of the past, an order thrown up in the present and the immediate future: all this comes under the jurisdiction of the paradoxes of a non-linear time, of its succeeding or intermingled virtualities. What does it mean to see at the end of the day? Is it having access to reality or to make-believe? Is the visual reducible to the visible if, in what is visible, it is what is invisible or what has disappeared which attracts us? In *Lost Highway* the night drives destinies and people drive at night and people are in the night as in a dark room in which all ways remain possible, open, in the image of the lost highway. It is a well-known fact that in black light certain configurations and certain physical structures that are otherwise not obvious can be rendered perceptible. Seeing would then consist of grasping the correspondences and links that allow us to form a unique context, immediately contradicted, so that the totality of fragments form an impossible whole like pieces taken from different puzzles that defy the laws of representation whose unintelligibility is always in suspense or potential. So it is that the film is framed by two nocturnal sex acts: it develops from the first sex act in their empty, dark and lugubrious house between Fred and Renee, a couple as childless as they are unable to communicate, up to the second between Pete and Alice illuminated by the headlights of their car in front of an empty cabin way out in the desert. "I want you" repeats Pete to Alice, while the whore speaks coldly into his ear: "You will never have me" and goes off, vertical and naked, towards the cabin. That's it. The night is feminine – blurring the outlines of distinct objects, it reconstitutes a lost whole, from Renee dead and cut up to Alice with her perfect body, the ultimate container, out of synch and spectral, a smooth and empty container on which and in which there is no possible handle: she solders back and re-forms what the day has plundered and loosened. She brings together and fuses what light separates. The story can be "filmed" without linearity. The night at the beginning and the end is indeed the place where everything converges, is tied up or disperses, it is always the night revelatory of destinies. A "spectral" night in which opposites appear to coincide, a "spectral" and paradoxical night?

In this way resonating nodes are produced which establish a status of specific truth and contribute to giving a feeling of truth and reality but detached from contingent events. Everything holds together because there is a paradoxical coincidence like a bridge between worlds, between scales, between violence and apathy, silences and words, between unnatural words and dismembered words. Woman and night are here communicators, they form the bridge. Unexpected combinations, reconciliations between people and things remote and foreign allow all the givens to apparently free themselves up, to escape from their meanings and the evidence for their existence: when Pete gets up after having made love, he has the facial features of Bill Pullman and Fred Madison; and the Mystery Man is standing in front of him with his video camera filming him; Dick Laurent and Mr. Eddy are one and the same person; Fred flees in his car, stops off at a mysterious Lost Highway Hotel and takes a room next to the one where Renee and Dick Laurent/Mr Eddy are. He hears them and recognizes them and decides to kill Mr. Eddy. Through this strange and spectral cohesion we enter a world in a constant state of flux for which we do not have, can never have, an access code. It's a truly active chaos in which enlightenment alternates with the most grave opacity, a chaos of images which meet and organize themselves into a world before dispersing. What function is then filling the film, this body without language? Does it establish an organization of desires and defenses? The question of content, of latent thought, could have no relevance at all. The film progresses without interpretation from Renee to Alice, from Fred to Pete and back to Fred again as *déjà vu*. There is no progression indicated by desire or reality; trapped sensitivity falls flat. The identity of the Mystery Man, neither named nor neutral, is that given to him in the credits. There is nothing left to do but to try and grasp – the only grasping possible – this film corpus literally, without manipulation or complicity. The singular and the unusual are no longer henceforth anecdotal, but run the gamut of all that is human. No-one dies in a David Lynch film, as the critics are of one voice to emphasize. Someone can be excluded from a certain visual plan, but only so as to better reappear in another.[16]

So it is that it seems that deliverance from a burdensome past is never as liberating as when the non-present is held in the indiscreet discretion of a latency where it makes itself to be less forgotten so that it is not always permissible to hope for new norms. It seems that it is necessary to have at one's disposition a second life which can serve as a reserve for one's own posterity, i.e. where the possibility of letting the transformation of the undesirable be reanimated so as to satisfy the new norms of desire, the possibility of making the present more dense by means of repetition or, on the contrary, the emergence of the new.

We can quote here the strange and muddled experience lived through by the philosopher Jacques Derrida led to evoke the spectral nature of cinema in a film of Ken McKullen, *Ghost Dance*, in which he plays himself:

Et à la fin de mon improvisation, je devais lui dire à la comédienne: Et vous alors, est-ce que vous croyez aux fantômes?" Et en la répétant de nouveau au moins trente fois, à la demande du cinéaste, elle dit : "Oui, maintenant, oui. " Déjà, dans la prise de vue, elle l'a répété au moins trente fois. Déjà, ce fut un peu étrange, spectral, décalé, hors de soi, cela arrivait plusieurs fois en une fois. Mais imaginez quelle a pu être mon expérience quand, trois ans après, alors que Pascale Ogier, dans l'intervalle, était morte, j'ai revu le film aux Etats-Unis... J'ai vu tout à coup arriver sur l'écran le visage de Pascale, que je savais être le visage d'une morte. Elle répondait à ma question : "Croyez-vous aux fantômes ? " En me regardant quasiment dans les yeux, elle me disait encore sur grand écran : "Oui, maintenant, oui "... Maintenant, maintenant, c'est-à-dire dans cette salle obscure d'un autre continent, dans un autre monde, maintenant oui, crois-moi, je crois aux fantômes

[16] Eric Dufour, *David Lynch: matière, temps et image* (Paris: Vrin, 2008) 109.

(And at the end of my part I had to say to the actress: "And do <u>you</u> believe in ghosts ?" And repeating it again and again at least thirty times at the director's request she said: "Yes, I do now, yes..." Already in the shot she repeated it at least thirty times. Already it was a little bit strange, spectral, off-the-wall, beside itself, it happened several times at once. But imagine what my experience must have been when, three years later, while Pascale Ogier in the meantime had died, I saw the film again in the USA... I saw the face of Pascale suddenly come onto the screen and knew it to be the face of a dead woman. She answered my question: "Do you believe in ghosts?" Looking at me almost straight in the eye she told me yet again on the big screen: "Yes, now I do, yes..." Now, now, that's to say in this dark cinema on another continent, in another world, now yes, believe me, I believe in ghosts.)[17]

And I will limit myself to quoting here as a counterpoint to Derrida's text the necessarily unanswerable question of Michel Chion, a theorist and historian of sound, but also a composer of music and a film director, addressed to "David Lynch, the real one" on the occasion of an exhibition of his paintings at the Cartier Foundation: "On this canvas you have written the name of what we can see and sometimes you have stuck on the real object. There is the word 'money' written above real coins and here it says 'blood' under a red blob. Is it real blood?" So it is that David Lynch's cinema like life obliges us to journey between several worlds and to survive in them by mastering the transitions from one world to the next. Film like myth is a true story which has to do with the realities of the world of the senses and which is made up of recurring characters. We can believe in Fred and Pete, Renee and Alice, in Pascale and ghosts as we believe in coins and in blood, in the discontinuous and the fragmented, thanks to words, the words/plans of David Lynch which are so many muddled representations called into being by the verbal and acoustic evocation of something which one has never really seen. The philosopher Jacques Derrida and the actress Pascale Ogier are already isolated and separated in their picture since the larger picture only shows on screen the face of Pascale while the philosopher sits in the dark cinema to watch her and hear her, but they could stay together and they do stay together in another type of organized image which would be like a special time zone which we gain entrance to as if by breaking into it by chance, which is precisely the experience of the philosopher seeing the film again in the United States. This chance is in *Lost Highway* the information that passes through an intercom.

Is the Mystery Man a phantom? But, as we have said, what good does it do to ask ourselves that question if all we have to do is to take the filmic body, the image and the film, literally? Carrier of the video camera, pure externalness, the Mystery Man has joined Fred whose house he claimed at first to share as his double, as an alter ego, and he goes with him from now on, he veritably haunts him. He participates in the action since he it is who takes it upon himself to finish off Dick Laurent, beaten till he bleeds by Fred who also cuts his throat and since he allows the crook to deliver a final "message," the legacy of a word emanating from a dislocated body: "<u>You and me, mister, we can really outugly them some</u>

[17] Jacques Derrida, *Echographies de la télévision* (Paris: Galilée, 1996) 134-35.

bit, can't we?" Is it through this complex and composite activity of the Mystery Man, a purely unidentifiable point of view, that images and sounds, all these fragments of reality, are brought together as a filmic whole to allow the spectator to enter there? The embarrassing presence of the Mystery Man fills in, like a haunting, the emptiness that Fred carries inside him. For Fred his meeting with the Mystery Man reveals to him the hollow space that he has within him, his fundamental incompleteness prior to any story, and it allows him to survive under the fascination of that sardonic gaze, under the fascination of a person who cannot be portrayed and is unidentifiable. But what kind of survival and what kind of entrance, in what kind of strange world are we talking about here? Fred drives through the desert, stops in front of his house, throws into the intercom the phrase at the beginning of the film: "Dick Laurent is dead," then runs away. The last frames show him in his nocturnal and fantastic flight, his face deformed and convulsed no doubt by the force of that last acoustic impression, alone as if the Mystery Man who has now disappeared had been a figment of his imagination, on the point of being caught up by the police before the endless road starts to fly past again at a dizzying speed. The black of the image is transformed into an image of the face of Fred Madison which contains within it a whole world. The image in its gushing forth is and remains a mystery in the way that Fred Madison's face has come out of total darkness. An apparition, spatial or temporal, a ribbon lit by headlights with black and total emptiness on both sides, the negative black hole for daylight and for all hope. In this emptiness great shouts of distress are lost, but this emptiness is also what separates and isolates and defends against dissolution by wholeness, by fusion. The impression of eternity: What? Eternity? is there because we are waiting for the end of this forward movement, the end of which is not visible between black immensities. Let us not forget that the film lasts 129 minutes. What is left in the void of night if it isn't sound and enigmatic words starting up again and again?

Lost Highway: through this lost highway we find a path slipping away to vanishing point, we leave our cinema seat and organize the passages between multiple worlds. Are we awake? Are we in a world chosen by David Lynch and over which he has complete control and the definition of which is left up to him? Whose dream are we in from this point on? Are we not still in the dream of someone, still outsiders confronted by his mystery, the mystery of his world, the mystery of the world, but not necessarily lost? There is never any univocity, that is what this lost highway tells us; in the dream of David Lynch, if the territory is well mapped-out, no geography constrains us; we can invent the film as a story, why not? knowing as we do that what is moving, what moves us, is never clear.

The films of David Lynch economize on my dreams of which I am the prime spectator as well as the particular person conducting the experiment, the one who jumps to get hold of a fruit on a branch which is too high up, the one who does not belong to either. In this way it falls to me to ask one more question, at the end of the emergence of these figures from *Lost Highway* on my work table before they disappear under the surface as flat as the world's skin: did I succeed in getting hold of the fruit on the branch that is too high up, or did I merely want to get hold of it without risking a fall from the trapeze which had been hung there and breaking my arm? So it is that I am excluded from image and sound, never terrified nor in the place of another, forced to accept my eternal distance:

> ...perhaps that's what I feel, an outside and an inside and me in the middle, perhaps that's what I am, the thing that divides the world in two, on the one side the outside, on the other the inside, that can be as thin as foil, I'm neither one side nor the other, I'm in the middle, I'm the partition, I've two surfaces and no thickness, perhaps that's what I feel, myself vibrating, I'm the tympanum, on the one hand the mind, on the other the world, I don't belong to either...

SCOTT WILSON
NEUR*A*CINEMA

Sometimes ideas come into my mind that make me crazy.[1]

It's worst at night. It's hard to get off to sleep because I hear this throbbing sound in the background and you know what it's like when you can't get to sleep and you're tossing and turning and you get more and more agitated about it... People assume you must be hearing things, but I'm not crackers... this is not in my head. It's just as though there's something in your house and you want to switch it off and you can't. It's there all the time.[2]

A MAN WITH A DISCONNECTED HEAD

I first saw *Eraserhead* (1977) in 1978; it was the same as a dream I had, exact in every detail. I realized immediately that David Lynch was stealing my ideas; indeed he was stealing my life. I was working in a pipe factory in an industrial part of the town. My father was a boilermaker. I never saw him at the factory; all I remember is the noise of the machines, the constant hissing of the boilers, clanging pipes and the wind and the rain. The guy that used to tell me what to do worked on one of the machines, a lathe, he spent his days pulling levers. He had scars from an accident where sparks of molten metal burned his face.

Anyway, watching *Eraserhead*, the guy had my suit and white socks – we all wore white socks in those days; it was cool. I even had those pens in my top pocket when I was doing the stock take of all the different pipes. So many pipes and boilers, large and small. My father says the pipes don't grow on their own. My girlfriend was pregnant, I was just sixteen; my father was sixteen when he had me. I killed the baby. I heard this voice in my head, it said: "Of course, this world is a bleak industrial wasteland, and his baby is inhuman."[3] I wedged its tiny fingers into an electrical socket – my mother always warned me against that – and it just exploded! Of course I went up with it. The electrical socket was next to the big radiator in my room where I kept the hamster that my mother gave me in a small box to keep warm. It bit me once. It was like electricity shooting up my arm. My hair stood on end.

I'm much older now but I'm still in day care. A Dr. Fink is looking after me. He told me not to worry, psychosis was becoming much more common these days, maybe because of "the decline of the father function in

[1] David Lynch, *Lynch on Lynch*, ed Chris Rodley (London: Faber and Faber, 1997) 20.
[2] Katie Jacques qtd in James Alexander, "Have You Heard 'the Hum'?" (*BBC.co.uk*. British Broadcasting Company, 19 May 2009).
[3] Todd McGowan, *The Impossible David Lynch* (New York: Columbia University Press, 2007) 47.

Western society."[4] Dr. Fink is a buttoned-up kind of guy, like the William Holden character in *Sunset Boulevard* (Wilder, 1950). He looks all-American, very straight, but I keep thinking *Fink? Fink?* What kind of a name is that? Is he telling me that he's called Fink in order to make me think that's just his name, when actually he really is a fink? He's informing on me the whole time. Words mean what they say, right? That's why I'm still coming here even though I haven't killed anyone in years.

We like to spend time discussing the films of David Lynch. I know the secret to his films. David Lynch himself told me the secret. He called me on the phone. He said, "Henry, I'm very sure that something is happening, but he doesn't understand it all. He watches things very, very carefully, because he's trying to figure them out.... Everything is new. It might not be frightening to him, but it could be a key to something. Everything should be looked at. There could be clues in it."[5]

The secret of his films is unknowing. Since David Lynch calls me, I asked him one day what his films are all about. You know what he said? He said "I don't know, or I can't say."[6] He seems to have a real passion for ignorance, mine as well as his own. He says he's absolutely *horrified* at the idea of knowing.[7] He was especially upset at being told that Norma Desmond's house wasn't really on Sunset Boulevard. "Henry," he says, "they're happy *not* to know about it. And they *shouldn't* know about it.... Why would they talk about it? It's *horrifying!*"[8] At the same time, David Lynch does nothing but provoke me by hinting at mysteries and enigmas, offering obscure and misleading suggestions, like those ten clues to the secret of *Mulholland Drive*. He drives me crazy with all these ideas. It seems that the ideal viewer of his films is some crazy guy who will come up with all sorts of different interpretations. I think he wants to keep people puzzling forever. That's his passion. Of course un-knowing can only be the outcome of trying to know. And knowing is *horrifying*, that's an essential part of it, the horror.

I find clues everywhere... but I hear conflicting voices. There's a voice that says looking for clues means I'm "the pure subject of desire" and that my desire is "unalloyed by fantasy."[9] The voice comes from a ventriloquist's dummy that sits on the knee of an old Professor. The dummy is of an American guy in a baseball cap called Todd McGowan, and he's worked by this bearded guy called Slavoj Žižek who has this wild East European accent, straight out of central casting. They have heated debates about the meaning of Lynch's films. McGowan thinks that there are separate worlds of desire and fantasy in which the world of desire is one of "drab social reality" and the world of fantasy one of "excess and heightened presence."[10] Professor Žižek just bursts out laughing and says he is a fool and that the idea of social reality is itself the very fantasy that

4 Bruce Fink, *A Clinical Introduction to Lacanian Psychoanalysis* (Cambridge: Harvard University Press, 1997) 110-11.
5 Lynch, *Lynch*, 56.
6 Lynch, *Lynch* 72.
7 Lynch, *Lynch* 78; Lynch's italics.
8 Lynch, *Lynch* 78; Lynch's italics.
9 McGowan, *The Impossible David Lynch*, 34.
0 McGowan, *The Impossible David Lynch*, 19.

shapes desire, and that Lynch's "excess and heightened presence" is actually the Real bursting through the fantasy of social reality.[11] Or at least I think that's what he says; the trouble is his accent is so thick that I can barely understand a word. When he speaks through McGowan though, the voice is pure Midwest American. It is so weird. I wonder if McGowan is actually, by means of some elaborate contraption, working Professor Žižek himself and putting on the accent.

Dr. Fink listens to all this patiently and assures me that the reason I can't understand Professor Žižek is that as a psychotic the concepts of desire and fantasy mean nothing to me. "There is no properly human desire at all in psychosis" he says.[12] This is because I'm not repressed, which is pretty cool. I don't have desire but I do have passion. I'm passionate and I have delusions but to me they are real (I'm passionate about them). In fact for me everything is real, especially the cinema of David Lynch. Dr. Fink says that this is because I have not undergone what he calls "symbolic castration" which sounds pretty unpleasant I have to say but is necessary for people to make distinctions between ideas like desire and fantasy, fiction and reality, stuff like that. In my case the failure of the "father-function," that is to say the father as a purely symbolic idea bound up in a name and a prohibition, has made me psychotic. I became crazy – or rather I had what Dr. Fink calls my "psychotic break" when my girlfriend got pregnant. This is a classic cause, apparently, "the encounter with the Father as a pure symbolic function may [occur] when a man learns he is about to become a father."[13] But because I have no concept of this function, its absence discloses a terrible void in the world and things just fell apart. I went crazy and started having all these "delusions" particularly about David Lynch. But Dr. Fink says this is a good thing, and can help me, so we talk about David Lynch and he gets me to write essays about his films. I just started this one on *Eraserhead*.

THE HETEROGENEITY OF THE SOUND-IMAGE IN *ERASERHEAD*

Eraserhead, I say, is my most spiritual movie.[14]

Just before he began filming *Eraserhead*, David Lynch screened *Sunset Boulevard* (Wilder, 1950) for the cast and crew. This was in order, he says, to establish "a certain mood."[15] Of course, the first shot of Henry recalls the famous opening sequence of *Sunset Boulevard*, especially the image of the dead narrator, Joe Gillis (William Holden) floating in Norma Desmond's pool, shot from below. This and the final sequence in which the psychotic Desmond descends her staircase in a delusion that she's in a movie called Salome being filmed by Cecil B. de Mille provides the framework for much of Lynch's *oeuvre*, not only *Eraserhead* but *Blue Velvet* (1986), *Lost Highway* (1997), *Mulholland Drive* (2001) and *Inland Empire* (2006) where two of the main narrative strands concern an ageing Hollywood starlet hoping for a comeback and "the hallucinatory fantasies

[11] Slavoj Žižek, *The Metastases of Enjoyment* (London: Verso, 1994) 114.
[12] Fink, *Clinical Introduction*, 101.
[13] Fink, *Clinical Introduction*, 106.
[14] David Lynch, *The Air is on Fire* (Paris: Fondation Cartier pour l'Art Contemporain, 2006) 25.
[15] Lynch, *Lynch*, 71.

of a crack whore as she faces death on Hollywood and Vine."[16] At the end of *Sunset Boulevard*, Gillis comments ironically on Desmond's therapeutic state of madness: "life, which can be strangely merciful, had taken pity on Norma Desmond: the dream she had clung to so desperately had enfolded her." The dream of Hollywood, the dream produced by Hollywood, is equated with psychosis even as it is disclosed as real. Desmond, an ageing Hollywood starlet who believes she is making her comeback, played by Gloria Swanson, an ageing Hollywood starlet making her comeback, suffers from the delusion that she is in a movie when she actually is in a movie.

While the distinction between fantasy and reality is collapsed on the screen of real delusions, Lynch enfolds his audience into the dream through the use of sound that does not just enhance an image but opens up another dimension beyond the screen into the real space of the auditorium. For Michel Chion, Lynch's *superfield* of ambient sound creates a space of immersion even as it gives images their temporality through marking their duration in time.[17] Furthermore, the precision and consistency of Lynch's ensemble of sounds gives them "a kind of quasi-autonomous existence with relation to the visual field."[18]

In *Eraserhead*, sound often accompanies changes in shot so that sound thereby seems to provide the principle of editing shots or assembling them into segmented sound-images. "They are like image tensors, isolating the shots from one another even as they join them, drawing out the time of each shot in relation to its two boundaries, constituted by the two cuts confining the segment."[19] These sound-images are comprised therefore of heterogeneous elements that are linked together in chains in relations of similarity and difference. There are linked chains of images that are segmented together along with a chain of sounds that are related to each other but not necessarily the images. The chains of images and sounds follow their own logic as they are cemented together in sound-image segments. The images present the theme of psychosis while the sounds provide them with the consistency that, in the absence of language, would otherwise be missing.

The opening shots in which Henry's head floats in space above a planet (that initially looks a bit like a brain), becoming briefly superimposed over it, establish the link between the head or mind and the alien planet that it creates, constitutes and occupies. It is a commonplace to say that psychotics live on "their own planet" because they conventionally do not experience the same sense of shared reality as everyone else. At the same time, the title has not only brought into conjunction two disparate ideas, the head and the eraser, but also thereby the associated idea of the erasure of the head, the rubbing-out or loss of identity that is classically the concern of psychotics. "The psychotic's ego... is fragile" and can shatter (like the planet in *Eraserhead*) when confronting the trauma that precipitates the psychotic break.

[16] Anton Bitel, "*Inland Empire* Review" (*Film 4.com.* Channel 4, 2006).

[17] Michel Chion, *Audio-Vision: Sound on Screen*, trans. Claudia Gorbman (New York: Columbia University Press, 1994) 150.

[18] Chion, *Audio-Vision*, 150.

[19] Michel Chion, *David Lynch* (London: British Film Institute, 1995) 38.

Clearly this trauma is the onset of fatherhood something that is of course represented in the narrative, such as it is, but more powerfully conveyed in the horrifying images of childbirth and its hideous progeny. The first series of images, the planet-head-eraser assemblage that seems to be linked together according to "metaphorical" relations of similarity – the planet is a head that with its distinctive haircut looks like an eraser – gives rise to a second series to which it is metonymically related. The idea of an alien planet naturally suggests aliens, an idea immediately conjured-up by the strange spirit-form that floats out of Henry's mouth. Henry gives up the ghost, but in the shape of an in-human "cord" that seems to conjoin a spermatozoa with the umbilical cord that its successful fertiliza-tion produces in the germination of a baby. Not only are spermatozoa a kind of alien substance that is part and not part of a body, since Roswell in the 1950s generic aliens have taken the oval-headed smooth-bodied shape that suggests both a sperm and a foetus. It is also, of course, the shape of Henry and Mary X's "baby" that is comprised of just a head and a torso wrapped in bandages.

The metaphorical assemblage planet-head-eraser is therefore subordi-nated to the logic of metonymy concerning the trauma of childbirth that articulates the chain. The head fails to function as a paternal metaphor that might arrest the chain. Detached from the body, it becomes just one object among others. The severed head in *Eraserhead* functions a little like the enucleated eye in Georges Bataille's *Story of the Eye* in relation to the egg and the testicle, on the one hand, and the tears, yolk, sperm and urine on the other, all of which are placed into an erotic circuit of meton-ymy. "Using metonymical interchange" writes Barthes, "Bataille drains a metaphor" and abolishes it.[20] Consequently, "the world becomes *blurred*; properties are no longer separate... and the whole of *Story of the Eye* signifies in the manner of a vibration that always gives the same sound."[21]

In the absence of a paternal metaphor, the organizing principle of *Eraserhead* is sound, the continuum of which is given consistency through the resonance of the *pipe*. This is also, perhaps, derived from *Sunset Boulevard* where the pipe organ played by Max (Eric von Stroheim) domi-nates Norma Desmond's gothic salon. When it is not being played by von Stroheim, Gillis describes the eerie ambient noise of the wind "wheezing" through the pipes. "It sure was a cozy set up. That bundle of nerves [Norma] and Max and a dead monkey upstairs and the wind wheezing through that organ once in a while." The dead monkey, Norma's surro-gate child that is buried in a baby coffin in an elaborate ritual, when it is first seen wrapped in a blanket resembles the baby in *Eraserhead*. More importantly, it has the same role in the structure of the narrative, its death heralding the death of Gillis who replaces it in Norma's affections. This is recognized unconsciously by Gillis when he dreams of an "organ grinder, [the] organ all draped in black and a chimp dancing for pennies. When I opened my eyes the music was still there. Where was I?" It is the sound of the organ that articulates dream and reality for Gillis, existing in both

[20] Roland Barthes, "The Metaphor of the Eye," *Story of the Eye*. By Georges Bataille (Harmonds-worth: Penguin, 1982) 126.
[21] Barthes, "The Metaphor of the Eye," 125.

states, and waking him to discover that Norma's house, the expression of those "wild hallucinations of hers," now constitutes his sole reality. Indeed, from the hiss and throb of steam pipes and boilers to the melodious tones of Fats Waller's pipe organ, the pipe is in *Eraserhead* the primary industrial object that resonates throughout the soundtrack. Furthermore, the paternal function as it is evoked in both its failure and its insistence in the movie is bound up with pipes.

While Mr. X, the only father (apart, perhaps, from Henry himself) represented in the film, has no name (no name-of-the-father), he has a function: he is a plumber. In the dinner-party scene (the first to be filmed) in which Henry is introduced to Mary's family, her father sets off on a speech to Henry exclaiming "I've put every damn pipe in this neighbourhood" that everyone including the dog tries to silence. That the family has failed to become structured by the Oedipus complex is evident in the two subsequent scenes. Mrs X's interrogation of Henry concerning his relations with Mary culminates in her rapacious kissing-sucking of his neck like a vampire, suggesting the voraciousness of maternal demand unchecked by the law of the father. Meanwhile, the failure of this law is clearly demonstrated by Mr. X when he passes on to Henry the role of carving the meat (usually undertaken in any case by his wife). The carving of the meat is of course the symbolic family ritual that establishes the father as heir to the primal murder that instigated the law according to Freud in *Totem and Taboo*, the text that for Lacan underscores the centrality of symbolic castration. Passed on to Henry ("Do you carve these like regular chickens?"), the action of the knife produces a nightmarish scene of blood gushing through the legs of the chicken, waggling in the air as if in a disastrous birth or miscarriage. At the end of the scene, the father's fixed grin indicates that he has sunk into a catatonic state suggesting psychosis.

"We are born in sound," they say, and Lynch's *superfield* of ambient machine-pipe yet watery noise (steam, rushing water, whirlpools, storms) is neither diegetic nor non-diegetic. It constitutes the whole milieu which is both the social reality of the film and Henry's psychic reality, the sound increasing and abating in intensity depending on the relative perplexity if not emotional turmoil of the central character. And indeed of the audience in so far as they identify with his predicament or are drawn into his world. We are enveloped by an amniotic, womb-like world that nurtures diseased mutants. The ambient sound of *Eraserhead* is like a (psychic) body within a body and at significant moments the sound alternates between low frequency bass notes and high intensity hissing, the latter especially at moments of anxiety associated with the spermcords or the proximity of the woman with puffed-out hamster cheeks who lives in the radiator. At their most intense, the sound of steam/hissing is joined by an incredibly high organ note for example when Henry is cutting open the baby's bandages or when he is moving to touch the Lady in the Radiator.

The hamster-like Lady in the Radiator appears to be the maternal object of Henry's childhood eroticism. She is first perceived in a rare moment of reverie when he is lying on the bed listening to the maternal sounds of his wife feeding their baby. He seems to undergo some state of infantile regression as he begins to hallucinate and perceive the little stage and the tiny Lady upon it between the radiator pipes. We hear Fats

Waller's pipe organ again, though it is not clear whether the music is playing on the gramophone or in Henry's head. Nevertheless, throughout his encounters with the Lady, the pipe organ music provides the point of stability necessary to sustain the eroticism of the relation as opposed to the pure engulfment which finally occurs when he touches her. She dances to the music, it regulates her movements, and she is thereby able to squash the spermcords. As such, Fats Waller's music, as music as opposed to ambient noise, has a relative symbolic dimension. Fats Waller's organ is Henry's only connection to an external signifying system, suggested by the gramophone, some relatively exterior shots of factories and railway tracks along with scenes of domestic "normality." Crucially it is able, up to a point, to assemble a brief scene of delusory fantasy and therefore romance between Henry and the Lady in the Radiator.

Music, as a "cut" in noise, involves the repression of the ambient noise that would engulf everything in its indifferent intensity. Ironically, this is initiated when Fats Waller's music seems to suggest to Henry the solution of killing the baby with the scissors. It plays as he lies on his bed picking at the blanket as the baby laughs at him in the corner. The baby is clearly now Henry's alter ego, his double, something that is confirmed when he imagines that the beautiful woman next door sees him with the baby's head, his own having already been erased through being turned into erasers. Locked within the intensity of the imaginary register, any weak symbolic power associated with Fats Waller gives way to the intense rush of ambient noise as Henry cuts open the baby's bandages, repeating his attempt at carving the chickens, with an even more spectacular result in the production of bodily excess.

The death of the baby is intercut with an electrical overload as sparks fly out of the plug socket and his light flickers on and off. The sparks sound in conjunction with the intense, sustained high organ note as Henry's head is intercut with the baby's. The screen fills with white light and there is a final surge of electricity before it shorts out. The screen goes dark. Henry's head is again intercut with the baby's, emphasizing their equivalence, and then the planet. The planet explodes and Henry's head is surrounded by an aura of white light and dust particles (the famous publicity shot for the film) as if from the exploding planet or from his own head. The camera disappears into the hole in the planet and the screen goes black. The man in the planet loses control of his levers, sparks flying into his burnt and scalded face and the sound-image fuses in blinding white light and noise as he embraces the Lady in a "dream of incestuous fusion"[22] that is the ultimate transgression of paternal law, or would be if paternal law existed for Henry. He goes not to hell then but, we assume, to heaven where, according to the Lady in the Radiator, everything is fine.

Of course Henry actually kills himself by sticking fingers into the electrical socket. You are always warned not to do that as a child. Hence the horripilation and the aura of dust that encircles his head like a halo, as if his were the severed head of John the Baptist being held aloft by Salome (played by Norma Desmond), as she leans to kiss his "dead cold lips." The decapitated head is one of the most sublime and sacred of all symbols of

22 Michel Chion, *David Lynch* (London: British Film Institute, 1995) 46.

the experience of self-erasure at the instance of death, the eternal in-stance of "a being suspended in the beyond of oneself, at the limit of nothingness."[23] It is electricity that provides the aura, the halo, because electricity in David Lynch corresponds to excess. In Lynch's system it seems to relate to the measureless expenditures of energy that violate "the integrity of individual beings [and] is thus closer to evil than to good."[24] Electricity is evil in the sense that it is beyond-good-and-bad; this is because it is linked to the inexplicable. Lynch says: "Yeah... scientists don't understand it. They say 'It's moving electrons.' But there's a certain point where they say, we don't know why that happens."[25] The inexpli-cable secret of David Lynch's movies is animated and illuminated by the electricity of the severed head suspended "in the void of unknowable night" that is the basis of "communication" for Bataille.[26] Perhaps that is why it is re-shot at the conclusion of the movie as the blinding touch of the Lady in the Radiator. "'Communication' is love, and love taints those whom it unites."[27]

Dr. Fink puts my essay down. It needs some work, he says, but con-gratulates me on my reading of the film in terms of my own condition. He says that I have succeeded in constructing a "delusional metaphor;" he seems pretty satisfied with himself. Certainly, *Eraserhead* sets the pattern for many of the subsequent films, particularly *Lost Highway*. But from my perspective, Dr. Fink intones sagely, all of Lynch's *oeuvre* is a psycho-genic fugue that structures my relation to both the movies and the narrative of my own psychic reality. David Lynch holds everything in place for me and in this way his cinema has a therapeutic role. It unfolds a real-ity in which I can make my own sense of things where there would otherwise be just a terrifying void.

A SCHIZOPHRENIC WOMAN

For some time now Gilda just lay on Dr. Roque's couch curled up in a foe-tal position like Marilyn Monroe or Diane Selwyn in *Mulholland Drive* or a figure out of Francis Bacon. The truth be known, she's beginning to smell, and in this airless vacuum of a surgery, it is not pleasant. Added to which there is this insistent hum in the room; a kind of throbbing, pulse-like low-frequency drone. It makes me feel queasy and ill; it's torture. I have searched every inch of this sparse austere room, even all the electrical plug sockets, but cannot find the source; there seems to be no source. Dr. Roque denies that there is any such noise; he says it is all in my head, but I know it is real. Gilda is unaware of it. She just lies there, still. I'm not sure if she's asleep, catatonic or dead. The last word she said was "Dumassio!" Then she shut her eyes and lay down. That was some time ago.

Nobody knows if Gilda is her real name, she came to see Dr. Roque suffering from transient global amnesia. She said she'd been in a car acci-dent, but there were no injuries and Dr. Roque said there was no evidence of brain damage either. Indeed, it was the appearance of a healthy brain

23 Georges Bataille, *On Nietzsche*, trans. Bruce Boone (New York: Paragon House, 1992) 19.
24 Bataille, *On Nietzsche*, 17.
25 Lynch, *Lynch*, 73.
26 Georges Bataille, *The Bataille Reader* (Oxford: Blackwell, 1997) 45.
27 Bataille, *On Nietzsche*, 18.

after her PET scan that convinced Dr. Roque that Gilda was schizo-phrenic. He said jokingly that neuropathologists often remark that "it is easy to recognize the brains of schizophrenic patients because they are the ones which look normal."[28] He also told her not to worry because schizophrenia is "a surprisingly common illness with a life-time risk of ap-proximately 1 in 100 people."[29] I think he was quoting someone.

Shortly after she was diagnosed Gilda came in to day care claiming that Laura Dern had been calling her on the phone. "She says I am 'play-ing a broken or dismantled person, with these other people leaking out of [my] brain.'" She said I am "a mental touchstone" like "Catherine Deneuve's portrait of psychosis in Roman Polanski's *Repulsion*."[30] She was convinced that Dern was jealous of her and was threatening to kill her with a screwdriver. They gave her dopamine which reduced her symp-toms which mostly concerned auditory hallucinations – voices on the phone, records, tapes – and her delusions that famous Hollywood film directors and beautiful young starlets were trying to seduce her and rival actresses kill her. The drugs haven't affected her depression and inertia, however. Indeed these have increased since the delusions were taken away and she was subjected to endless tests and examination. She loved her delusions since they made her life exciting and she believed she was loved by beautiful people. According to Dr. Roque, Gilda is suffering from a kind of schizophrenia known as erotomania. She claims that a starlet named Betty was trying to kill her out of jealousy for the love of a glam-orous young Hollywood director. She knew this because Betty would break into her apartment and rearrange her ashtrays in a significant way. When she found a blue key on her coffee table she recognized it as a sign that Betty was coming to kill her. Betty was found dead with a single bul-let wound to the head. It is assumed that Gilda was the murderer, but she does not recall anything.

Dr. Roque is an innovative psychologist with a very large body, a tiny head and a passion for the movies. While he thinks that there is a genetic predisposition to schizophrenia he also thinks that the increase in the condition, from the second half of the twentieth century, is in part an ef-fect of new forms of audio-visual stimuli that affect the brain. Dr. Roque has, in this view, been especially influenced by both cognitive neurosci-ence and Deleuzian film theory. Dr. Roque has noted a recent irony in art and science concerning cinema and neurology. In an interview with *Ca-hiers du Cinéma* in 1986, "The Brain Is the Screen," Gilles Deleuze rejected the idea that "psychoanalysis or linguistics have much to offer cinema. But molecular biology, the biology of the brain – that's a different story. Thought is molecular."[31] A few years later, noted neuroscientist Antonio Damasio claimed that the cinema is the best way of conceiving how mental images are generated and edited by neural patterns.[32] "The

[28] C.D. Frith, *The Cognitive Neuropsychology of Schizophrenia* (Hove: Lawrence Erlbaum, 1993) 15.

[29] Frith, *The Cognitive Neuropsychology of Schizophrenia*, 4.

[30] Dennis Lim, "David Lynch Returns: Expect Moody Conditions, with Surreal Gusts," *New York Times*, 1 October, 2006.

[31] Gilles Deleuze, *Two Regimes of Madness: Texts and Interviews 1975-1995*, trans. Ames Hodges and Mike Taormina (New York: Semiotexte, 2006) 283.

[32] Antonio Damasio, *The Feeling of What Happens: Body, Emotion and the Making of Conscious-ness* (London: Vintage, 2000) 9-11.

neurobiology of consciousness faces two problems: the problem of how the movie-in-the-brain is generated, and the problem of how the brain also generates the sense that there is an owner and observer for that movie."[33] As the new neuroscience generally acknowledges (Damasio, Joseph LeDoux, V.S. Ramachandran and Francisco Varela), the internal world of the brain is not a sealed-off hard-wired automatism; the external world is integral to the structure of neuro-processes of self-modification. Circuits in language, art and music create and modify circuits in the brain.

Dr. Roque is fascinated by Gilda's case because he thinks that somehow she has been seriously affected by David Lynch's films, particularly *Mulholland Drive* (2000), in the way they seem to have informed the content of her symptoms. But he wants to find out if there is something more structural going on, whether Lynch has inadvertently managed to reorganize some of her brain's circuits. I have been charged with keeping her under observation and write a report. I have been observing her for some time now, but she remains in the same position and says nothing. However, this is my report:

NEURaCINEMA: THE FILMY ESSENCE OF CONSCIOUSNESS

I love dream logic; I just like the way dreams go. But I have hardly ever gotten ideas from dreams. I get more ideas from music.[34]

Following the movie-in-the-brain thesis of neurological psychology advocated by Dr. Roque, after Damasio, the characterization of the patient's pathological structure is complicated by the clear evidence that the movie-in-the-brain-of-Gilda is *Mulholland Drive*. This is further complicated by the fact that the movie-in-the-brain of *Mulholland Drive* is *Sunset Boulevard* (Wilder, 1950). Inside *Sunset Boulevard*, moreover, are (at least) three different movies: *Queen Kelly* (1929), "Dark Windows" and "Salome." These films within the film within the film within Gilda's brain not only provide the templates for a number of significant events and features (suicide, writing, murder, retroactive narration, putrefaction, delusion and the dissolution of inside/outside, illusion/reality distinctions), they also correspond to the various levels constitutive of subjectivity: proto-self; core self/core consciousness; autobiographical self/extended consciousness. This is not primarily because of the subject of schizophrenia that is amplified in the intersecting and overlapping narratives, but because of the structuring role of the constituent parts of cinematic form: sound, moving images, music, writing, speech and so on, all of which take on different roles and emphases.

It is well-known in cognitive neuroscience that the self is an illusion in the sense of a core of identity and agency, a homunculus sitting in a command and control centre, somewhere in the brain. Rather, according to Damasio, consciousness or self-perception is an effect of layers of film or movies-in-the-brain that are projected "in the brain's multiplex screens."[35] While it is important to note that the metaphorical movie "has

[33] Damasio, *The Feeling of What Happens*, 11.
[34] David Lynch, *Catching the Big Fish: Meditation, Consciousness, and Creativity* (New York: Penguin, 2007) 63.
[35] Damasio, *The Feeling of What Happens*, 21.

as many sensory tracks as our nervous system has sensory portals," his use of the term "image" to describe them is no accident, consciousness is a matter of "stepping into the light."[36] Damasio's account amounts to a photology that unfolds various layers of film.

At one level, a "proto-self" is produced as the effect of neural systems that film both the organism's encounters with its external reality and the modifications produced in the physical structure of the organism by that encounter. There is an (obscure) event and a filmed narrative comprised of movement-images that play over time, albeit in microseconds; but all this goes on at a level that is non-conscious, "the proto-self has no powers of perception;" there is no self-reflection, no awareness of self, just multiple films playing on multiple screens "that span varied orders of the nervous system" from the brain stem to the cerebral cortex that are connected by neural pathways.[37]

It is on the basis of these films that more neural patterns are produced that film a "second-order nonverbal narrative" of mental images that enable both a working memory and consequently an awareness of "self" that is brought into consciousness in and as a film. At the same time, the watcher of the brain's movies is brought into self-perception as an effect of being filmed. But there is no subject of this film, nor any object being filmed, other than another film. Self-consciousness is the film of a film, or of multiple films, the representation of representations made by neural patterns of the state of the organism.

A further, third order of representations is necessary for the extended form of consciousness characteristic of human beings. For this to happen the movies of core consciousness need to be permanently stored as "dispositional memories" that can be brought out and re-played or even re-made whenever necessary and in light of new experiences, that is, new films made at the level of core consciousness, stored, re-made and so on in a potentially infinite reflexivity that directly acts on and modifies the non-conscious state of the organism. It is the video store or DVD hard drive, upon which "experience of the past and an anticipated future" can be based, that provides the material of "autobiographical memory" and an "autobiographical self."

When interrogated about her subjective collapse, sometimes known as a "psychotic break," Gilda would simply repeat "*ay no banda*," there is no band. This of course refers to the most celebrated scene in *Mulholland Drive*, where Betty and Rita visit Club Silencio and watch various performers mime to pre-recorded tapes, particularly Rebekah del Rio's mime to her own recording of a Spanish translation of Roy Orbison's song "Crying." Both Betty and Rita cry throughout this performance, which culminates in the singer collapsing, perhaps dying, while her amplified voice continues reverberating throughout the auditorium. During the scene Betty apparently also suffers a decisive collapse resulting in her transformation into Diane Selwyn, perhaps realizing that she is already dead, or maybe "waking up" from her dream, depending on the way one reads the narrative. In any case, the scene is generally taken to be the turning point in the lives of the two main female characters and indeed of the movie as

---

[36] Damasio, *The Feeling of What Happens*, 3.
[37] Damasio, *The Feeling of What Happens*, 154.

a whole. But it is not just the collapse of Rebekah del Rio that provides the figure or metaphor for the collapse of "Betty," her dream, or of the detective-romance narrative of the first section of the film. Rather, the scene as a whole consists of a series of synthetic elements that are disclosed as heterogeneous: sound and image, music and language, song and sense. They are the constitutive elements whose co-ordination orchestrates subjectivity and the different levels of consciousness and memory that it depends upon.

The Club Silencio sequence accentuates the fact that sound and image are distinct and that their synthesis is an illusion. At various points, but most spectacularly with the collapse of Rebekah del Rio, the disjunction between sound and image is traumatically disclosed along with the essential silence of the image. This refers a viewer back to the origins of the cinema in silent movies, a cinema, played most often in theatres, that was not silent so much as devoid of speech. The movie-in-the-brain is likewise first and foremost a "silent" movie or a kind of "miming." What Damasio calls core consciousness, that underlies and is essential to the "extended consciousness" of the "autobiographical self," is "a simple narrative without words."[38] Damasio gives the example of "Jean-Louis Barrault miming the story of the watch theft in *Les Enfants du Paradis*."[39] Of course comparing core consciousness to wordless or "silent" cinema is not to suggest that the latter is more "primitive." Both Damasio and Deleuze concur, however, that the cinema of core consciousness is the classic Hollywood cinema of action images that appeal directly to primary emotions (sexual desire, happiness, fear, anger, surprise, disgust). These are the emotions that neuroscience regards as preset by nature but can be culturally stimulated and manipulated by movies. "Alfred Hitchcock built a brilliant career on this simple biological arrangement, and Hollywood has never stopped banking on it."[40] For Deleuze, notwithstanding his admiration for Hitchcock, this is "bad cinema [which] always works with the ready-made circuits of the lower brain: a representation of mere violence and sexuality..."[41] What Deleuze calls "Real cinema," by contrast, "breaks through to a different violence, a different sexuality, which is molecular and not localizable."[42] As the example of Hitchcock suggests, it is possible to produce brilliant cinema on the basis of an appeal to emotions, and so does Lynch, but in a different way.

Relative to most Hollywood movies, Lynch produces a predominantly "silent" or wordless cinema. Martha P. Nochimson notes that "the foregrounding of tonal/emotional depictions of unspoken narrative events is primary to an understanding of Lynch's work."[43] Lynch's collaborator in sound, Angelo Badalamenti, confirms in an interview on the DVD release of *Mulholland Drive* that Lynch uses so much music and sound design in his movies because "there's so much space without dialogue;" indeed

---

[38]   Damasio, *The Feeling of What Happens*, 168.
[39]   Damasio, *The Feeling of What Happens*, 185.
[40]   Damasio, *The Feeling of What Happens*, 59.
[41]   Deleuze, *Two Regimes of Madness*, 284.
[42]   Deleuze, *Two Regimes of Madness*, 284.
[43]   Martha P. Nochimson, "All I Need Is the Girl: The Life and Death of Creativity in David Lynch's *Mulholland Drive*," *The Cinema of David Lynch: American Dreams, Nightmare Visions* (London: Wallflower Press, 2004) 170.

Lynch begins with music, Badalamenti comments that "in most cases he's brought in music or had me [working] on music before he's even shot the first frame." While there are occasional narrative tensions and shocks in Lynch's movies that appeal to primary emotions, his soundtracks, particularly the use of Badalamenti's "firewood" (low abstract sounds, dissonant chords and so on) to generate "background emotions" such as "well-being or malaise, calm or tension,"[44] support an audience's apprehension of scenes, objects and environments below the threshold of sense. We feel anxious and uneasy, but more often than not, in the absence of the relevant background information, we are not sure why. Lynch exploits the pre-verbal level of core consciousness in order to disorient and puzzle rather than to excite and entertain. In *Mulholland Drive* this disorientation is for once justified in the narrative through Rita's amnesia. As Damasio writes, "the predicament of transient global amnesia underscores the significant limitations of core consciousness: without a provenance for the current placement of objects and a motive for the current actions, the present is nothing but a puzzle."[45] Solving the puzzle demands recourse not just to a working memory but to the dispositional memory characteristic of extended consciousness, the experience of full subjectivity characteristic of the "autobiographical self." In Lynch, however, this dispositional memory is comprised of movie images, music and movie dialogue.

The Club Silencio scene in *Mulholland Drive* conveys the formal and formative power of music and language strangely yet precisely through emphasizing their "otherness." Music and language are both exterior particulate systems, forms and forces, which leave an "imprint" on the mind.[46] They are "other," yet they write us. That the human mind and emotion are "already-written" by syntactic structures and acoustic signals outside itself is conveyed in the assertion that everything is "on tape." The performers simply mime pre-existing dialogue, music and song. This of course goes on throughout the movie, especially the first section, when Betty and Rita rehearse Betty's audition (that itself provides one possible pattern for the narrative of the whole movie), the miming at Adam Kesher's auditions, indeed, as Chris Rodley notes, the characters seem to be "people 'miming' their entire lives."[47] But in this, the movie is itself "miming" *Sunset Boulevard* and the processes of screen-writing and rehearsal that goes on between Betty Schafer and Joe Gillis, and between Gillis and Desmond that provide the scripts for their "real" on screen romances. Music and language provide the means, the vehicle and the content of delusion as well as its disclosure.

While he rejects the idea that consciousness is predicated upon language, Damasio has constant recourse to notions of "translating" and "converting" from one system of neural patterns to another, to the mental images of core consciousness that are re-represented in extended consciousness, and back again, in horizontal and vertical topographies traversing the space-time of the brain's deep expanse of grey corridors,

44 Damasio, *The Feeling of What Happens*, 51.
45 Nochimson, "All I Need Is the Girl," 203.
46 Aniruddh D. Patel, *Music, Language and the Brain* (Oxford: Oxford University Press, 2008) 9.
47 Lynch, *Air*, 293.

editing suites and auditoria. In the terms of Jacques Derrida, Damasio's filmy brain is clearly a text, a weave of traces, differences of force and signification, "a text nowhere present, consisting of archives which are *always already* transcriptions."[48]

It is the function of self-consciousness, which for Damasio appears by means of cinematic images, to supplement the instinct for survival of "the inner sanctum of life regulation" to which it is connected and that is perpetually threatened by death, is indeed continually dying. Cinematic images are ghosts, spirits that both anticipate the death and memorialize the life of those objects whose light they refract. Ironically, the visceral, cellular and microcellular play of forces (its "life-and-death" struggle), which it is the function of consciousness to protect and watch over, is foreclosed from consciousness. The spirits know nothing of the body but shadows. Indeed, one might even say that through being represented, re-represented and re-re-represented in moving images the life of the organism is continually being mortified even as it is being re-animated in patterns and moving images unfolding in a different time, at different speeds and in another space. "Representation is death," writes Derrida, "which may be immediately transformed into the following proposition: death is (only) representation."[49] Death only has meaning for a subject, a subject that is an effect of multiple "originary repetitions," "a system of relations between strata."[50] Similarly, Damasio's system of filmy consciousness necessarily extends, as the very condition of his metaphor's efficacy, to further levels of stratification, audio-visual machines that envelop, modify and mortify organisms, integrating them into wider machinic systems and assemblages.

As a way into *Inland Empire* (2006) and, perhaps, his *oeuvre* generally, David Lynch offers a quotation from *Aitareya Upanishad*: "We are like the spider. We weave our life and then move along in it. We are like the dreamer who dreams and then lives in the dream. This is true for the entire universe."[51] "Consciousness is all we have," he adds,[52] implying that his is supremely a cinema of consciousness though one that is filled with (rabbit) holes, dark corridors, portals, lost highways and multiple screens and movie theatres. As for example when Nikki (Laura Dern), in *Inland Empire*, walks out of a secret corridor into a movie theatre where she sees the "Lost Girl" watch Nikki on a TV screen in a hotel room, somewhere else at another time, as someone else, maybe. Consciousness is multiple but ghostly, schizophrenic, spiritual and continuous with the universe.

For Damasio, schizophrenia, in so far as it is defined by "thought insertion and auditory hallucinations" is a disorder of extended consciousness that leaves core consciousness unaffected. The transient, pulse-like experience of moment-to-moment consciousness remains but "the mental representation of the autobiographical self," clearly dependent on language, can become "anomalous," disturbed, disconnected or "so

48 Jaques Derrida, *Writing and Difference* (London: Routledge, 1981) 211.
49 Derrida, *Writing and Difference*, 227.
50 Derrida, *Writing and Difference*, 227.
51 Lynch, *Catching the Big Fish*, 139.
52 David Lynch, qtd in Michael Guillan, "*Inland Empire*: The San Rafael Film Center Q&A with David Lynch," *Twitch* (24 Jan. 2007): < http://twitchfilm.net/archives/008819.html >.

impoverished that the mind does not know where this self comes from or where it is headed…"[53] As a disorder of extended conscious that leaves core consciousness intact, schizophrenia is like the agnosias. The term *agnosia*… "denotes an inability to conjure up from memory the sort of knowledge that is pertinent to a given object as the object is being perceived. The percept is stripped of its meaning"[54] and becomes an object of mystery or anguish. Agnosias like amusia (where music is perceived as noise) are useful for cognitive neuroscience in ascertaining the contingent (evolutionary) nature of perceptual apparatuses. At the limit, the loss of certain phenomenal "qualities" may imply the emergence of new forms, and indeed new forms of knowledge.[55] In Lynch, the "autobiographical self" of his characters is always precarious, always liable to become disconnected, doubled or trebled in different contexts, becoming someone else dependent on the narrative or on the specific dimension of space/time in the parallel universes generated by the brain and its multiplex cinema. Like the agnosias, schizophrenia is evidence of a differential of forces and intensity in the circuits of the brain, of tensions and contradictions, one might also say repressions.

Lynch's cinema requires a neura*cinematic analysis since, like the brain, it consists of an assemblage of filmy surfaces without origin or end, interior and yet exterior to which moves the integral alterity denoted by *"a"* that dis-integrates them, provides them with a point, that is to say with meaning precisely through the immanence of meaning's flight, its dissolution in non-knowledge, the mortification and death of the organism that can only be imagined, yet around which the screens pulsate. Neura*cinematic analysis would seek to trace the auto-emergence of a neura*cinema interior and exterior to the brain that takes as its condition the sovereignty of the *a*cinematic symptom that the negativity of cinematic form renders both singular and common.

My recommendation, therefore, is that Gilda's symptoms should not be "cured" since they arise in response to the discontents of the state of affairs conditioned by our culture and indeed nature. Yet cultural forms – language, of course, but also music and images, cinema, the latter perhaps in more profound ways since it directly engages core consciousness, have the "power to change the nature of ourselves"[56] and thus new forms of thought and modes of experience.

I imagine Dr. Roque, if he read my report, would say it needs work. But he is already dead even as he watches himself in silence flickering on the screen. Indeed we are all dead, already film. I am just a dream that Gilda is having concerning a severed head that can speak; the dream of a putrefying corpse that is finally remembering to die. But there is still this humming noise that is apparently inaudible and about which I know nothing except that I hear it. Again I check all the plug sockets. But this is not the daemonic hiss of electricity; this is an ultra-low frequency drone.

[53] Damasio, *The Feeling of What Happens*, 215-17.
[54] Damasio, *The Feeling of What Happens*, 161-62.
[55] See Thomas Metzinger, *Being No One: The Self Model of Subjectivity* (Cambridge, MA: MIT Press, 2004).
[56] Patel, *Music, Language and the Brain*, 412.

Is this also the function of "Lynch's entire work," "an endeavour to bring the spectator 'to the point of hearing inaudible noises'"[57]? Such noises are condensed, as always for psychoanalysis, on the voice of the Other that for Žižek is inaudible because it is located in the site of "the fundamental fantasy,"[58] the comic horror of the Mother's unspeakable enjoyment. But I hear voices telling me that the noise is not a human sound, and that Mommy's dead. David Lynch says it is a "sound-vibration-thought" that opens on to an "ocean of pure consciousness" that constitutes "what is known by modern science as the Unified Field."[59] Transcendental meditation provides access to this field, offering for Lynch an experience of "bliss – pure bliss."[60]

For me, however, it is agony. Other voices say that this murmuring is the sound of the erasure of all images, all meaning and value; it is the destruction of everything human, indeed of all life. Constantly in the background, increasingly audible to new systems of perception,[61] it is the dissonant echo of the eruption of the universe and its accelerating disintegration, the desertification and disappearance of all matter. All of thought, these other voices say, must resonate in this pipe organon of extinction in which enlightenment seeks its truth in complete and utter erasure.[62]

They convince me that the sound is not all in my head; I'm not crackers.

---

[57] Slavoj Žižek, *The Art of the Ridiculous Sublime: On David Lynch's* Lost Highway (Seattle: University of Washington Press, 2000) 44.
[58] Lynch, *Art*, 44.
[59] Lynch, *Catching the Big Fish*, 4, 47.
[60] Lynch, *Catching the Big Fish*, 4.
[61] Mark Whittle, "Primal Scream: Sounds of the Big Bang" (Richmond: University of Virginia Department of Astronomy, 2007).
[62] Ray Brassier, *Nihil Unbound: Enlightenment and Extinction* (London: Palgrave, 2007).

ALANNA THAIN
RABBIT EARS: LOCOMOTION IN LYNCH'S *INLAND EMPRIRE*

Few characters in David Lynch's work are as blandly disquieting as the anthropomorphized sit-com dwelling stars of *Rabbits*. Begun as a web-based series on DavidLynch.com and featuring the voices of Scott Coffey, Laura Harring and Naomi Watts as Jack, Jane and Suzie Rabbit, their non-sequitur one liners sparking tinned laughter and applause make mysterious incursions into *Inland Empire*. Like a sit-com set within an Edward Hopper painting, the Rabbits' scenes capture not a figurative representation, but instead embody the lived effects of an audio-visual age. They are not simply *on* television, though we see them on the Lost Girl's TV, and understand that their strict and static frontality is playing to an equally mediated and absently "live" studio audience. They embody the interface itself, "rabbit ears" a shorthand for a TV antenna, sensitive receptors of invisible signals that make worlds appear. The Rabbits are living mediums, their curious embodiment rendering incommensurable and yet intimate the relation between linguistic and plastic expression. David Rodowick has proposed the figural as the best concept for addressing the effects of our contemporary audio-visual era, where linguistic and plastic expression are rendered heautonomous in uncanny fashion.[1] He sums up a heautonomous relation as such: "image and sound are distinct and incommensurable yet complementary,"[2] as in Magritte's famous painting "This is not a pipe." Magritte's example produces what I term a *vibration-image*, where a heautonomous proximity initiates a relation of felt and generative exchange. With the Rabbits, the embodied and visible interface as characters produces the same effect. This is not a *representation* of medium, but rather a heautonomous relation made visible. The mouthless and static performance of the rabbit bodies renders sound-image relations in these scenes entirely conventional, yet strange via the miss of a visual sync.[3] This disjunctive synthesis for Rodowick illustrates the way in which "offscreen space disappears in the [Deleuzian] time-image": "In this manner, the screen becomes a self-contained frame. Rather than the reversing fields that characterize the deictic features of classical editing, there is an incommensurable relation between the space of the screen and the space of the auditorium."[4] Relation is no longer given to the spectator,

---

[1] David Rodowick, *Reading the Figural, or, Philosophy After the New Media* (Durham: Duke University Press, 2003).

[2] David Rodowick, *Gilles Deleuze's Time Machine* (Durham: Duke University Press, 1997) 145.

[3] This is made explicit in the *Rabbits* series, where one high angle, long shot framing persists for the entire series. The only cutaway is in episode 7, when the phone rings and we get a close-up of the phone. This overly illustrative convention betrays an anxiety about the match, one which remains free-floating during the rest of the series and contributes to its affective charge.

[4] Rodowick, *Gilles Deleuze's Time Machine*, 145

who must create it, entering into the becoming of relation via this participation in cinema's ability to generate new bodies.

Like the constant estrangement of words and speech in Lynch, Rodowick gives as one definition of the figural "speaking and seeing at the same time."[5] This same "disjunctive synthesis," produced by the lived bodies of the rabbits is a vibration-image that distorts the clear outlines of figurative representation. The vibration-image disturbs the visible from within. At the end of *Inland Empire*, Nikki Grace (Laura Dern) enters backwards into the Rabbits set, effectuating the happy ending of the family narrative, but also generating the differential remainder of her own vibration image, living a doubled time of live/recorded, encountering an othered self again by moving backwards through the film to her first scene. The figural engages with Gilles Deleuze's concept of the time-image via time as becoming, expressed through false or aberrant movement marking where the possible is converted to potential through a "shock to thought." Reading *Inland Empire* through the figural, I explore aberrant movement in Lynch's film, paying special attention to time machines, outbreaks of dance and the aberrant movement of the interface itself.

DO YOU WANT TO SEE?

The first instance of self-aware temporal and spatial displacement in *Inland Empire*, a film riddled with wormholes, occurs when Susan Blue (Dern), wary and disoriented after her first encounter with a posse of jilted young women, responds to their claim that "in the future, you'll be dreaming, in a kind of sleep; when you open your eyes, someone familiar will be there" by covering her eyes like a child. Pulling her hands away, she seems shocked to find herself on a wintry Polish street, accompanied by two women. Susan embodies the cinematic cut (the black frame) of temporal and spatial displacement, but the transition is surprising and not smooth. She has a bumpy return as well, and displacement is redoubled when she, again seated against the wall, watches as the camera tracks away from her and over to the window, now opening onto the same snowy street below, as if the camera had gone to look on her behalf. These are two modes of negotiating the relation between human body and cinematic body: Susan makes the cut herself through a relation between hands and eyes, a direct action on her body, and then she allows the camera to take responsibility for her own displacement, to move on her behalf. Two tools of cinematic transition--the edit and the camera movement--are deployed, and they result in the first instance of *reaction* to seeing herself in the film, as if the goal of such encounters was to discover that otherness of the self, what Deleuze describes as "auto-affection." When Susan comes back from her displacements, a sequence in which she lives as if in the interior of a movie, where irrational cuts are not accepted examples of a cinematic shorthand but are lived, as for early spectators, in their shocking and disruptive immediacy, the final section of the sequence entails her seeing herself from above and below, in a shot/reverse-shot/shot sequence. This moment is not the familiar face-to-

---

[5] Rodowick, *Reading the Figural*, 68.

face frontality of the mirror-image; instead, a seated Dern looks up in a distorted close up at the impassive Susan gazing down from above, dropping a plumb line of temporal distortion through the centre of their eyeline match. While Nikki's psychogenic fugue into the world of Susan Blue can be thought of as an actress' immersion in character, this doesn't account for how this fugue is presented less as the play of multiple subjectivities and more as the stuttering of a certain mode of cinematic expression. In other words, the tools deployed to render Dern's incommensurable and yet difficult to distinguish with certainty personas are all tools of cinema itself. In this chaotic state, Susan/ Nikki receives a message from the Lost Girl, via the interface of the record player from the film's opening. "Do you want to see?" she asks, and gives Nikki/ Susan instructions to build what will essentially be a time machine: wear the watch, burn a hole in a piece of silk, fold it over and look through.

What does it mean to "see" here? Susan experiments with travelling without moving: hands over the eyes as a sampling of the real, staying seated while the camera moves for her to look out the window. With the time machine, the interface becomes the encounter in itself. When Susan looks, what she sees through the hole is, of course, more silk. Her eye is in the interior of the fold. As she looks, the watch races backwards at an accelerated rate; time is literally rendered "out of joint" here. A hole is burned in the silk that functions like an optical device to frame space, while duration (the burning cigarette as an alternative to metrical clock time) literally burns a passage through rationalized time; however, this frame doesn't hold as a window onto the world. Instead, the silk is folded over so that what is framed and highlighted is the texture of the silk itself, a doubling of perception that screens passage. The texture of the screen itself is made visible, as a cinematic time machine that doesn't look out onto a represented world as through a window, nor reflects a world as in a mirror, but instead shows us a secret coherence and connectivity of texture. What Susan seeks to see in those instants is what cannot be represented directly, but which comes to us through the figure of the interface – the figural quality of audiovisual media.

Rodowick argues that while the figural, like the Deleuzian virtual, can't be directly represented, and is thus opposed to figurative representation, "it can be apprehended in that the force of transgression acts on space, expressing itself in disordered forms and hallucinatory images."[6] This is why I suggest the vibration-image as a means of describing this apprehension, not what is represented in the image but its false or aberrant movement itself. To assess the anamorphic effects of this aberrant movement, I draw on the concept of figural analysis to discuss the interface and bodily genesis in *Inland Empire*, arguing that Lynch's film activates the production of new bodies via qualitative transformations.

Rodowick argues that figural analysis has a particular relation to the interface, in that digital technologies have rendered newly visible the interfaces that we use for habitual actions of communication and reception.[7] A renewed visibility, I argue, has also accrued to older models of the interface and their material and immaterial ticks; consider the re-

[6] Rodowick, *Gilles Deleuze's Time Machine*, 13.
[7] Rodowick, *Reading the Figural*, 217.

peated use of the scratching of a record needle that opens *Inland Empire* and which is ubiquitous in digital music, or the train whistle consistently vibrating the soundtrack, the train another outmoded interface of automatic movement. The link between the psychogenic fugue and medium forms present in many of Lynch's productions takes a new turn in *Inland Empire* where movements between mediums create a state of "loco-motion" in which habits and limits of the body become deranged. Media architectures here incorporate not only studios, theatres and sets, as well as mediums like monitor, screen and projector, but also call attention to radio waves, beams of light and electricity as modulators of bodily integrity; as such, architectures of the audio-visual body themselves become indistinctly engulfed by an "experimental night." Explorations of these extended architectures abound: the sit-com setting of a living room where rabbit ears are displaced from TV set to the bodies, the cinema studio bleeding into the home, the space of the theatre, the streets of Holly-wood, the Polish town of Lodz (sometimes known as "Holly-Lodz"), the "Inland empire" in California as home to many in the film industry. What does it mean to inhabit zones both temporal (the remake, repetition, Lynch's predilection for incorporating anachronistic elements of dress, popular music) and spatial (the camera pulling back in Dern's death scene to make the street into a set, movies watched on TV, theatre lobbies) of transitions as a means of altering the affective potentials of the body? A figural analysis is required for understanding Lynchian semiosis, where "rabbit ears" deform the opposition between the plastic materiality of signs and their signifying content, highlighting instead the incommensurable relation of the figural.

NOW IT'S DARK

In distinguishing the movement-image and the time-image, Deleuze writes that in the latter, "it is no longer time which derives from movement, from its norms and its corrected aberrations; it is movement as *false movement*, as aberrant movement which now depends on time."[8] What moves is no longer based on the linkages of achieved actions, but on the intensive aberrant movement of affect. The question shifts from "what will there be to see in the next image" to "what is there to see in this image," where the image is not explained by relation, but rather incommensurable images, lacking a common ratio of comparison, signal the potential for new assemblages and connections.[9] Here, "incommensurability denotes a new relation, and not an absence."[10] Lacking a standard by which to verify the accuracy of one image against another, one moves "beyond the true and the false" to experience "becoming as power of the false."[11] *Inland Empire* abounds in incommensurable images that resist simple reassignment, even after the fact of viewing, to a logical chronology or a sorting of the roles and masks, especially in relation to Dern's multiple incarnations. As the final credits, populated by multiple figures of uncertain memory not only of *Inland Empire*, but *Mulholland Drive, Industrial*

[8] Gilles Deleuze, *Cinema 2: The Time Image*. Trans. Hugh Tomlinson and Robert Galeta (Minneapolis: University of Minnesota Press, 1989) 271.
[9] Deleuze, *Cinema 2*, 272
[10] Deleuze, *Cinema 2*, 279
[11] Deleuze, *Cinema 2*, 275

Symphony #1, *Blue Velvet* and other Lynch productions and resisting a distinction between spectacle and acknowledgements, cheerfully suggest, "the masks do not hide anything except other masks."[12] The image evokes the indiscernible relation between the actual and the virtual, what I have termed here vibration-images. Lynch employs simple techniques to exploit this: composite images, not the smoothed verisimilitude of digital effects but the bleeding edges of colliding worlds, but also in the humble effect of a shift in lighting, the qualitative change from lit to darkened rendered as the false movement of becoming in sensational ways. A darkened room and a lit room are not the same space. The repeated use of flashlights, spotlights, projector beams render space and time shot through with potential fault lines; a beam of light does not illuminate but may well create a zone for another time to make its way into our own, to fold space-time in the aberrant movement of becoming.

Susan's death scene, with the subsequent revelation of the film set and the seeming return of a stabilized Nikki is remarked upon in almost every review of *Inland Empire*. When the camera pulls back to reveal the set, complete with film camera, extras and director Kingsley Stewart (Jeremy Irons) calling cut, this revelatory moment seems to organize at least some of the confounding questions plaguing the film thus far. For one thing, Dern's character is clearly and repeatedly identified as Nikki, and her performance is called attention to and praised. But revelation fails to halt the cascade of identities. As Nikki arises from the corpse of Sue, a swell of dramatic and foreboding non-diegetic musical suggests that the drama is not over. Nikki sleepwalks off set; the danger is momentarily suspended when Stewart stops her to offer congratulations and the threatening music stops, but as she turns away it rebegins with greater urgency. Stewart watches her walk out of the sound stage into the night in slow motion, slowing down signalling a threshold experience. Framed in a doorway, Nikki casts a gaze over the outside of the studio and then looks suddenly directly into the camera. We cut to an extreme close-up (but not an exact eyeline match) of the Lost Girl in her hotel room, weeping and waiting, where she is watching Nikki on TV. When we cut back to Nikki in the doorway, the setting has changed; the sound stage is no longer connected to an exterior, but reabsorbed into a continuous interior. Via this internal montage she walks off not into the night outside, but passes behind a column into a long curtained hallway, ending up in an old-fashioned movie theatre. In what follows she sees herself, the space around her and previous segments of the film, with the framing alternating between including and excluding the setting--we are not centered in her point of view, but oscillate between potential perspectives. This alternation between multiple versions of the same scene, the undecidability of when and where this is happening, exemplifies the play with point of view

12   Gilles Deleuze, *Difference and Repetition*. Trans. Paul Patton (New York: Columbia University Press, 1994) 17. We might think of the lumberjack (one of the only men in this scene) enthusiastically sawing away. Such a figure calls to mind the Lumberton of *Blue Velvet*, the mills of *Twin Peaks*, Michael Anderson sawing onstage in *Industrial Symphony #1*, but also the figure of the Sandman, the same kind of vibration-image as the "rabbit ears," as a popular expression for sleeping is "sawing logs." Lynch's predilection for recasting actors lends coherence to a Lynchian world, but also provokes an uncertainty of recognition on the part of audiences. See Thain (2004) in relation to Patricia Arquette in *Lost Highway*.

that circulates around Dern's centre of gravity throughout the film. Her point of view is less a single centre than a hollow point around which forces circulate, like the eye of a storm. In describing the "powers of the false," and in particular their propensity to undo a clear distinction between the camera's objective perception of a world and a character's subjective point of view, putting these poles into vibratory exchange, Deleuze writes that "there is a point of view which belongs so much to the thing that the thing is constantly being transformed in a becoming identical to point of view. Metamorphosis of the true."[13] We have here a vibration-image, a terrifying "violence of the image and its vibrations," of the thing and its double via a play of point of view, the new relation of the incommensurable. This false movement of incommensurability characterizes many of Lynch's films, but in *Inland Empire* it takes on the special characteristic of "loco-motion," the aberrant movement of becoming. In this darkened theatre, via a metamorphosis of the true, Lynch explores the potential of cinema's experimental night to make new relations sensible. Nikki sees a woman (Dern) testifying that "after my son died, I went into a bad time, when I was watching everything go around me while I was standing in the middle, watching it, like in a dark theatre before they bring the lights up." Given the family reunion of mother and son at the end of the film, this scene has sometimes been read as a revelatory kernel of psychosis, the absent child that needs to be restored for all to be well. But what Nikki is witnessing is precisely performance, not simply content, and she doesn't choose to follow the psychiatrist figure up the stairs, but instead to make her way eventually to the set of Rabbits. Through the end of the film, Nikki remains engaged in watching herself.

"An experimental night," Jean Louis Schefer's phrase in *L'homme ordinaire du cinéma* that describe cinema's ability to rearrange the world, bookends that work with two nocturnal visions. He opens with a description of an "experimental night" that cinema produces:

> A machine whirls, representing simultaneous actions to the immobility of our bodies; it produces monsters, even though it all seems delicious rather than terrible. In fact, however awful it is, it's always undeniably pleasurable. But perhaps it's the unknown, uncertain and always changing linkage of that pleasure, this nocturnal kinship of the cinema, that asks a question of both memory and signification; the latter, in the memory of film, remains attached to the experience of this experimental night where something stirs, comes alive and speaks in front of us.[14]

Schefer ends his book with a scenario in which we emerge from the cinema not as if awakening from a darkened dream into the light of reality, but instead into an experimental night, a re-enchantment of the world in the productive mystery of its potential. This world is characterized by an aberrant temporality that suspends action in a hesitation between the actual and the virtual, that reinvests perception with a haze of the as-yet-

---

13 Deleuze, *Cinema 2*, 146.
14 Jean Louis Schefer, *The Enigmatic Body*, trans. and ed. Paul Smith (Cambridge: Cambridge University Press, 1995) 111. Paul Smith has translated certain passages from *L'Homme Ordinaire du Cinéma* in an essay "Cinema" in the collection *The Enigmatic Body*. Where Smith's translations are available, I have used them; all other translations from *L'Homme* are my own.

unrealized as the lingering effects of the cinematic experience, rendered by Schefer in the strange tense constructions of his description. Time folds in on itself, making space for the sensational apparition of the virtual as a threshold experience, the feeling of one thing becoming other. This is the feeling, in Lynchian terms, of "something happening" without being able yet to see the contours of what will have happened. As he describes this "experimental night," Schefer claims that he seeks to make a threshold experience tangible, in order to argue that cinema doesn't represent a world as allow us to feel transition or becoming in itself. The visible itself is rendered new as an *act of thought* and not an *object of thought*. The final lesson of cinema, for Schefer, is that "amidst all the solids of the world, of all its images, a new matter/ subject (*matière*) becomes perceptible (*sensible*)":[15]

> The act of a thought and no longer its object (this is not a process assimilable or reducible to the figuration that we are spectating/ seeing)...it is a world which trembles, dissolves, reorganizes *because it was looked at*, in sum because the definition of the world was affected by a movement.[16]

This is a movement of in-coherence, the false movement of the time-image. As Schefer describes this, the visible is "affected and irredeemably infected by the primary incoherence of thought."[17] Anamorphosis of the image, or the world, is thus the sign of thought.

Inland Empire has been read as a scathing condemnation of Hollywood's dream factory, its oneiric quality constantly shading into the nightmarish. Dern's mocking cry "I'm a whore" has been taken as a self-referential description of the auteur himself, as well as a cry of liberation from the constraints of Hollywood production effectuated by a prosumer camera, self-regulated distribution, a stream of consciousness approach to scriptwriting and a non-Taylorist shooting schedule. Reasonable enough, but the film does something else that echoes Schefer's claim that cinema makes thought visible, or rather renders the visible as thought, a threshold of perception. Taking up Schefer, Gilles Deleuze claims that this experimental night "affects the visible with a fundamental disturbance, and the world with a suspension, which contradicts all natural perception."[18] For Deleuze, an experimental night promotes abnormal movements:

> what we mean by normality is the existence of centres: centres of the revolution of movement itself, of equilibrium of forces, of gravity of moving bodies, and of observation for a viewer able to recognize or perceive the moving body, and to assign movement. A movement that avoids centring, in whatever way, is as such abnormal, aberrant.[19]

---

[15] *L'Homme Ordinaire du Cinema* (Paris: Gallimard, 1980) 193. "Au milieu de tous les solides du monde, de toutes ses images, une matière nouvelle devient sensible."

[16] *L'Homme*, 193-94. "L'acte d'une pensée et non d'abord son objet (ce n'est pas un process assimilable à de la figuration auquel nous assistons)...c'est un monde qui tremble, se dissout, se reorganize parce qu'il a été regardé, en somme parce que la definition du monde est affecté d'un mouvement."

[17] *L'Homme*, 193-94.

[18] Deleuze, *Cinema 2*, 201.

[19] Deleuze, *Cinema 2*, 36.

In the final sequence before the credits of *Inland Empire*, Laura Dern, standing spotlit in the Rabbits set, gazing out into an empty theatre, gently weeps in a composed close-up while the image of a ballerina dancing in slow motion makes a slow cross fade into the image. The blue light of transformation is reflected in a camera lens, and we see a montage ending with Visitor 1 and Nikki from the beginning of the film, as Nikki turns to see herself on the sofa opposite. As we cut from one Nikki to the other, via an eyeline match, the line "something is happening" repeats on the soundtrack. In these images, we see aberrant movements of decentering, maintenance of uncertain relation here suspended in a state of grace.

Both Schefer and Deleuze argue that cinema does not simply represent bodies, but participates in a genesis of new bodily forms. The switch from celluloid to digital in *Inland Empire* raises questions of the cinematic body itself, and concerns over its immanent demise. In Nikki's notorious death scene, in which the camera pulls away to reveal that she is in fact simply on a set, with actors and a crew, this singular movement of self-reflexive revelation is itself doubled in another little-remarked upon move--the digital camera pulls back to show the celluloid camera. Is Nikki's death a McGuffin for another death, that of celluloid itself? Lynch himself has proclaimed that he will never work with celluloid again, citing the practicalities of faster, cheaper and more flexible shooting, and the degraded image of digital shooting on a prosumer camera where "when you have a poor image, there's lots more room to dream."[20]

However, Lynch also remains faithful to a "cinematic" experience. His notorious statement that "It's such a sadness that you think you've seen a film on your fucking telephone, get real" suggests an uneven adoption of digital technologies, even while he also claims that "the video iPod is here; we've just got to get real and go with the flow."[21] Lynch's soundtrack rumbles and distorts in an immersive "soundbath" that demands something other than earbuds, and the digital footage itself was transferred to film. In *Inland Empire*, we see the cinematic apparatus rearticulated; cinema becomes newly visible as an act, not an object, of thought. The problem of recognition pervades *Inland Empire* and becomes the motor of the film. Rather than marking the transition to a new, discrete form of media, *Inland Empire* explores the deformations of errant media, the reanimation of potential. Transformations make media newly visible; in a Bergsonian reversal of perception, they regain a luminosity that deforms the strict outlines of their contours.

Lynch is an intermedial filmmaker. Peter Boenisch characterizes intermediality as a "disruptive intangibility" interfering with the communication of meaning, and this definition nicely encapsulates the failure of simply pulling back the curtain in Lynch's films to expose the medium at work.[22] A substantial tension develops throughout *Inland Empire* around the failure to distinguish between the live and the recorded, activated by living memory as the lost time of the past. Nikki's first evident breakdown is occasioned by "stories," as Devon's agent describes this, at once dismiss-

[20] See Lynch's interview in *Variety* as well as in his book *Catching the Big Fish* (139-56).
[21] David Lynch, *Catching the Big Fish* (New York: Tarcher/ Penguin, 2006) 156.
[22] Peter Boenisch, "Aesthetic Art to Aisthetic Act: Theatre, Media, Intermedial Performance," *Intermediality in Theatre and Performance*, ed. Freda Chapple and Chiel Kattenbelt (Amsterdam: Rodopi, 2006) 115.

ing their importance and illustrating the power of the "false." Intermediality in Lynch's work involves transitions between forms of media and implicates the body in these transitional zones. Intermediality resensitizes us to the body's place within what Rodowick, drawing on Deleuze and Guattari, terms a "machinic phylum." *Inland Empire* explores the deformations of errant media, even posing in a way a question that further complicates what David Rodowick describes as "two stage media" – the fact that so much media made for one setting is increasingly consumed in another[23]. The importance of passage and the deforming effects of living the interface--the rabbit ears and anamorphosis of Dern's point of view-- ask what it might mean to feel our place within such an assemblage.

SOMETHING IS HAPPENING

The opening of *Inland Empire* activates an intermedial zone of encounter as an experience of the figural. The projector's beam furrows an inky darkness, while the harsh thrum of its mechanical movement inaugurates the double sitedness of the viewing experience. The projector beam both creates an immersive world, highlighting the textured emptiness it passes through, and draws an immaterial line between two points (projector/screen, interface/projected world). Failing to illuminate the darkness, the beam instead gives body to the space itself. After the titles, we see an image of a record circling on a phonograph, indistinctly emerging in black and white; a beam of light highlights the record needle. While the visual image suggests recording and repetition, the soundtrack, the tinny voice of a radio announcer, claims liveness via his words. A here and now also bound to continuity: "Axxon N, the longest running radio play in history. Tonight, continuing in the Balkan Region: a grey winter day, in an old hotel"; a double play between a discrete here and now and a stretched out present is inaugurated between the live and the recorded. The images begin to blur with superimpositions, the first of the film's many composite images; part of the record disappears under an amorphous flesh. This scene inaugurates a proximate layering of images, where a second image (of flesh) bleeds into the first like the spreading stain of warm breath on a cold window. What is relevant is the divorcing and layering of the live and recorded: between media of interface and mediums of record, a division or distraction of attention in the beam of the projector as the work that normally goes on "behind our backs," the live radio announcement and unfolding serial drama against the closed circuit record player and its repetition. This sequence asks us to think about living our inscriptions. Lynch's films do not figure cyborg bodies as visible imbrications of mechanical and organic; rather, it is in aberrant movement itself that such cyborg connections are rendered, what Deleuze will term the spiritual automaton. In this sequence, we have a Lynchian trademark: the body as receiver and as deformed by that reception, both a recording and playback mechanism for which it is ill-suited. We see this in the blurred heads of the hotel sequence that follows, but also in the continual interference of this record player as a composited interface that connects Dern's characters to the Lost Girl. Mediums of recording open channels across space and time. There is a heautonomous relation established be-

[23] Rodowick, *Reading the Figural*, 37.

tween material support and message, where the inert medium itself becomes invested with the potential to generate new meanings via the anamorphosis of bodies.

Rodowick argues that even before the advent of new media, older forms like cinema were already challenging a notion of aesthetics based on a distinction between linguistic and plastic expression. A rigid historical difference between analog and digital media becomes troubled: "there is a fault line in this history, in that cinema, phonography and video are two stage arts that require a technological interface to mediate perception such as the projector, turntable and amplification or the television monitor."[24] This complicates our sense of visuality, generating a disruption of the space of material inscription between hand and eye: "in the two stage arts" he argues, "the relation between presence and absence of subject and object (perceiver and object) in space and time is refashioned in new and disturbing ways."[25] We might add that two stage arts are uncannily distributed in time and space, between the corporeal and incorporeal. In *Inland Empire*, Lynch stretches out this oft-muted distinction between recording and playback, bringing them into vibratory proximity in the theatre scene near the end but never simply collapsing them.

Nicole Brenez has argued that the key question of the figural analysis in cinema is "the body, how do you find it?"[26] This is not a question of "recovering" a material body within immaterial media, but a continual rearticulation of the body within matter made "newly sensible" within the audiovisual archive. Figural analysis suggests that bodies are not simply represented on the screen. Likewise for Rodowick; while he critiques the ways in which digital media seem to mark a shift away from the understanding of the human body as "part of machinic phylum" into a false promise of "liberation" from the body, he thinks carefully about the body's renewed potential as a site for connection, mutation and creativity. To examine the modes of encounter and bodily genesis that figural analysis opens up I will focus on some of the ways that rabbit ears and locomotion are brought into contact with each other in the film as folds in its duration creating wormholes of experience.

Lynch frequently makes mediums explicit sites of spatio-temporal passage, while also making them resolutely not simply channels. Indeed, much of the film takes place in the nonplaces of streets, alleys, hallways and stairwells, the use of these locations intensifying after Nikki's resurrection. The generative nature of such movement between worlds is signaled by the use of scenes in which Dern's characters see "themselves" in other worlds; Nikki, for instance, sees herself at the read-through after she passes through the nightclub, or on the streets of Hollywood.

The hotel room becomes another site in the film that explores the idea of medium as zone of aberrant movement. If hallways are the stretched out spaces of delinked action, the hotel becomes a site for a meditation on seriality that, like the opening, brings together composite images and

---

24 Rodowick, *Reading the Figural*, 38.
25 Rodowick, *Reading the Figural*, 38.
26 Nicole Brenez, *De la Figure en Général et du Corps en Particulier* (Paris: De Boeck & Larcier, 1998) 13.

lighting as a means of generating the incommensurable relation of aberrant movement. Our first sight of the Lost Girl, who may or may not be the "whore" from the opening scene, occurs as she sits weeping and watching television; she seems to occupy the same hotel room, except for one crucial difference. Where there was only a lamp in the corner opposite the bed during the black and white sequence, there is now a television set. As the Lost Girl watches, the same lamp is indeterminately visible as either reflection (although there does not appear to be a lamp in the room that could be reflected as such) or double exposure with the television screen. The TV screen becomes a medium that brings together separate scenes in a non-agentic "zapping" (the channels change and scenes of Visitor One's arrival and the Rabbits play on fast forward intercut with static, but she is not working the controls) and, like the cinema screen later on, seems to occupy an ambivalent position between worlds. The double image of lamp and television does two things: it reorients the representational force of media images to the immersive qualitative transformations of light, and reimbues the materiality of the medium interface with an immaterial presence. In much of Lynch's work, lamps function as nodes of passage, calling attention to the current of electricity ambiguously animating objects and architectural spaces. Lighting in Lynch, especially the flickering light of alternating current, always marks a phase shift. In discussing the propensity of bodies to enter into new configurations and thus generate new bodies, Brian Massumi describes a phase shift from "the substantial to the potential" as the "opening through which empirical contingency – the intermingling of already constituted bodies, things and signs – expresses itself as coordinated becoming."[27] This is the condition of "collective change" where "change is emergent relation."[28] In Lynch, such phase shifts charge existing entities and open them to the process of connection and change. This is usually tremendously eerie and even terrifying in Lynch, at minimal output of effect, involving how electricity and lighting are cinematic shorthands for the reanimation of bodies, and Lynch's use of simple shifts in lighting to make something radically new felt not between scenes, but within the scene itself. Such shifts force us to ask "what is there to see in this image," usually amidst sensational effects of terror and foreboding that the actual scenes do little to justify. Instead, it is the visibility of this phase shift at work here. Lighting changes are one of Lynch's most effective techniques of internal montage. Thus, when Nikki shoots the Phantom, she does so not with bullets but with drawn out flashes of light; we witness his "death" not through the signs of organic destruction such as bloody holes, but via spotlighting and composite imagery.

A figural analysis stretches out on the interface between form and meaning: a key question that we must ask is in what ways does film participate in a genesis of bodies not yet recognizable in terms of discrete forms? In *Inland Empire*, Lynch repeatedly uses slow motion within scenes to highlight transitions as "deforming" or decentering the human body as fully part of the machinic phylum. One cannot move in slow motion; while

27 Brian Massumi, *Parables for the Virtual: Sensation, Affect, Movement* (Durham: Duke University Press, 2002) 77.
28 Massumi, *Parables for the Virtual*, 77.

slow motion reveals actions *of* the body (micromovements) invisible to everyday perception, it also reveals forces acting *on* the body. Slow motion makes relation newly visible. An early scene in the film encapsulates passage in Lynch. The male rabbit enters a darkened drawing room from French doors; a crossfade brightens the room as the rabbit disappears. The phantom and another man are having a conversation, in which the Phantom is looking for "an opening." "You understand" he says, and the shot of him goes to slow motion. Another crossfade brings the rabbit back and fades out the men, and then the entire scene goes dark. The scene conflates direct presentation of the machinic phylum's effects (slow motion) with the lived medium, where the rabbit ears are literally an exchange station between worlds.

To understand how the audiovisual architecture of *Inland Empire* generates bodies, I turn to an example in which the anamorphosis of the body in terms of the temporal possession of mediums is made apparent: the "Locomotion." Lip-synching and performance have a special relation to commentary on medium in Lynch. Elena del Rio's elegant reading of lip-synching scenes in *Mulholland Drive* and *Blue Velvet* emphasizes how they mobilize competing intensities at the cost of the coherence of character body and moral identity. These stagings of a Deleuzian "powers of the false" point to the emergence of as yet unactualized experiences, what Schefer calls the primary incoherence of thought. Characters participate in what Del Rio describes as an "affective contagion," often without knowing what has instigated such a phase shift of affective tonalities.[29] We might think of the Giant's visit to Agent Cooper during Julee Cruise's performance in *Twin Peaks*, during Madeleine's murder by Leland/Bob to the relentless click of a the end of a record.[30] "It is happening again" he intones to a bewildered Cooper who alone (perhaps with the Log Lady) can see him in the paused crowd. When the scene restarts, those close to Laura (Donna, Bobby, James) are suddenly caught despite themselves in an affective contagion of sadness. In *Inland Empire*, Lynch experiments with the collective bodies of performers to explore a seriality not seen before in his work, and an unusual displacement of performance from the stage or set to the home.[31]

The "Locomotion" sequence takes place amidst the world-jumping of the middle section of the film enabled by the time machine; Sue is back in the house after a scene in Mr. K's office. She enters a room to find the time machine still smoking. Another pass of the same room in slow motion registers a time lag, a repetition of difference, typical of how Lynch repeatedly signals change by the proximity of repetition. Suddenly, Sue is seated on the floor in the living room of Smithy's house. The room is also filled with a group of the other women, who seem to be addressing Sue and commiserating with her abandoned state. No shot includes Sue and the women together, however, and her non-verbal reactions are slightly delayed and not always appropriate to the conversation. This editing opens up gaps in the space of the room, emphasizing the temporal dis-

---

[29] Elena Del Rio, *Deleuze and the Cinemas of Performance: Powers of Affection* (Edinburgh: Edinburgh University Press, 2009) 181.

[30] *Twin Peaks* (episode 14). This scene also uses spot-lighting and slow motion to underscore possession whenever Bob is visible.

[31] Of course, Smithy's house is a set.

continuity of the scene. The women lounge around, lazily depressed and commiserating. As they speak, a train whistle (the film's refrain) blows faintly in the background, and one woman sings lowly "you've got to swing your hips now," as she and two others snap. Another whistle sparks an irrational cut; suddenly the women are choreographically distributed in the centre of the room, performing a synchronized routine to Little Eva's "Locomotion." We cut throughout to reaction shots of Sue; despite being in the same space, the flashing lights of the performance sequence don't touch her.

Given the frequent and sinister irrational cuts in the rest of the film, it is easy to forget how delightfully bizarre and unexpected the Locomotion scene is the first time we see it. Its "sleepover in jilted purgatory" feel belies its genuine strangeness, and how it sets up a relation of non-reaction and incommensurable cutting within the discrete space of Smithy's house that should remind us that that "When am I" is as urgent a question for Dern's characters as any sense of where. This image of automated movement, both in the performance to the recorded song and the choreography of the collective women, pulls against the temporal movement of the scene itself. The collection of women, the choreographed motion, and the sense that they are all cast-offs of the same man, evokes both seriality and simultaneity in the scene and in the performance. Preceded by the group's appreciation of some clearly artificial tits, making clear a certain connection between a mutability of the body even as there is a resistance and recuperation of all too familiar forms, the scene explicitly folds into *Rabbits* through the sound of the train whistle that sparks the song "Locomotion," a sound heard in all the *Rabbits'* scenes. The scene turns on the figural tension between plastic and linguistic signification--between the sound of the train whistle and the song title, the song's lyrics "Jump" are not only literalized in the hopping movement of the women, but also immediately doubled by a jump cut within the space as they vanish. As in Sue's first encounter with the women, cinematic movements (there editing and camera movement, here, the jump cut) are heautonomously related to bodily movement.

This scene is also linked to a different effect of the irrational cut, which is not just cinema's ability to join two temporally and spatially distinct sequences, but to repeatedly fold and retrace those sequences on themselves, playing with duration. Thus the "locomotion" scene is inaugurated by a moment that both calls attention to and breaks the marriage of sound and image – a different sort of irrational cut opening up a "pure opson" image. As the first woman sings just before the choreography, she finishes the line with a discrete snap of her fingers. This snap, keeping time, actually loses it, becoming a magical sonic instance that stretches the snap into an extended hissing of a match being lit, a spark that continues to burn. This audible cue only receives its visual "match" much earlier and much later in a scene with the Rabbits, when an animated match head suddenly appears in the upper right corner of the screen, again calling attention not to lived time but to the duration of the cinematic body itself. The "Locomotion" sequence serves as a shorthand for the crazy motion that will characterize the film as a whole not only because it is so out of place--although there are memorable performance sequences throughout Lynch's oeuvre, there has rarely been one so completely deframed from a performative or participatory setting--but because the affective joyousness of performance and movement here, despite drawing just a wan smile from Dern, gives us a key to the way that affective shifts in tonality are the product of the powers of the false.

One final example of the figural exists in the repeated failure of performance to cut itself off from reality, a failure that emerges from the incommensurable relation between plastic and linguistic expression, in the mysterious graffiti of "Axxon n." This is the title announced at the beginning of the film as the "longest running drama in the Baltic region," evoking the world without end of serialized drama, and is also the name of an unrealized original series announced in 2002 on David Lynch.com. It appears at crucial moments to initiate a marked though ambiguous passage between worlds, always accompanied by an arrow, which I would argue is part of the word itself; it is a word whose meaning slides into passage deliberately. An axon is part of a nerve cell that acts as the transmission lines of the nervous system. As Daniel Smith writes, the Figure "is a form that is connected directly to a sensation, and that conveys the violence of that sensation directly to the nervous system."[32] Axxon N is such a figure. Spoken aloud, the word deforms "action" – literally and figuratively, that repeated injunction that marks the distinction between film world and real world, the settling onto actor's body of character possession. Here "action," like "cut" is repeatedly a failed command in Lynch's film. Rodowick defines the figural as "a force that erodes the distinction between letter and line"; here, the arrow taking off opens the word outside of its significance to its work creating and not just referring to a world.[33]

Schefer argues that the cinema offers a being without memory: "in the cinema we are dealing with a new experience of time and memory which alone can form an experimental being." This is what he terms the "enigmatic body"; Paul Smith describes this as "the unknown centre of ourselves," emerging from the encounter between subject and object in art, and which undoes our accepted, habitual or what Schefer calls "doxical" understandings of ourselves. The interface produces one such sense of the being without memory, in opposition to arts of "gravure" that rely on the inertness of the material support. Figural analysis suggests that rather than see this lack of inscription as bodiless, we must pay attention to the new connections that are formed, the new modes of embodiment that occur. For Rodowick, the figural as a concept, by virtue of its ability to signal the formation of relation, and the temporality of becoming, raises this critical question: "how is our experience of collectivity changing...how are our collective arrangements in social time and space being restructured by the new communication architecture of digital culture?"[34] To begin to answer this question, we must return to Brenez's claim that the goal of figural analysis of a repeated return to the question "the body, how do you find it?" In other words, what new forms of the body can happen, especially when we understand the body precisely in terms of the

---

[32] Daniel Smith, "Deleuze on Bacon: Three Conceptual Trajectories in *The Logic of Sensation,*" *Francis Bacon: The Logic of Sensation* (Minneapolis: University of Minnesota Press, 2002) xiii.
[33] Rodowick, *Reading the Figural*, 1.
[34] Rodowick, *Reading the Figural*, 210.

connections it can enter into and the change it undergoes in doing so? As Rodowick notes: "new potentials of power are also new opportunities for criticism and resistance," and thinking the figural means that "visuality needs to be reconsidered."[35] What is means to see and be seen is the key question in Lynch's film and a figural analysis asks us to think of this encounter not as the meeting between two constituted subjects, but as the experience of change as emerging relation – the positivity of locomotion. The plays between actress and roles are thus a relation of the double outside of the scopic mirror. As Schefer reminds us: "it is a world which trembles, dissolves, reorganizes *because it was looked at.*"[36] This vibratory world is Lynch's *Inland Empire*.

[35] Rodowick, *Reading the Figural*, 210.
[36] Schefer, *The Enigmatic Body*, 194, my italics.

JASON T. CLEMENCE
"BABY WANTS BLUE VELVET": LYNCH & MATERNAL NEGATION

THE FEMININE AND THE MATERNAL

It has become a dicey task, in the realm of Lynchian criticism, to invoke psychoanalysis as an interpretive lens. Lynch's oeuvre is so awash in the unsubtle presence of the phallus and the fetish that a modicum of defensiveness, a pre-emptive justification for employing the language and tactics of a psychoanalytic reading, has worked its way into a variety of recent essays, as though the only way to employ such a reading is to acknowledge its inevitability. In his essay on *Eraserhead* (1977), for instance, Steven Jay Schneider, discussing the moment in which Henry Spencer is decapitated from within by his own mutated offspring, precedes his analysis by apologetically remarking: "I have made it this far without resorting to hackneyed Freudianisms, but ..."[1] David Foster Wallace points out that "despite its heaviness, the Freudian stuff tends to give Lynch's movies an enormous psychological power" and adds that what often makes such "stuff" work is that it is presented with unwavering sincerity; that "Jeffrey Beaumont's interslat voyeurism may be a sick parody of the Primal Scene, but neither he nor anybody else shows any inclination to say anything like 'Gee, this is sort of like a sick parody of the good old primal scene.'"[2]

In discussing *Blue Velvet* (1986), to continue on Wallace's example, the most thematically complex element to be dealt with is indeed the one which is encapsulated in the notorious (primal) scene in Dorothy Vallens' (Isabella Rossellini) apartment; that is, to what extent can one assume that certain psychoanalytic concepts – such as the symbolic and obscene fathers (and their regulation of desire and enjoyment), Oedipal triangulation, and the ideology of the maternal subject – inhere in the parental figures of the narrative? While Jeffrey Beaumont (Kyle MacLachlan) is unmistakably the subject proper, the one whose experiences and observations directly inform the way in which the viewer experiences the film,[3] it

---

[1] Steven Jay Schneider, "The Essential Evil in/of *Eraserhead* (or, Lynch to the Contrary)," *The Cinema of David Lynch: American Dreams, Nightmare Visions*, ed. Erica Sheen and Annette Davison (New York: Wallflower Press, 2004) 15.

[2] David Foster Wallace, "David Lynch Keeps His Head," *A Supposedly Fun Thing I'll Never Do Again* (New York: Back Bay Books, 1997) 198.

[3] Consider, for instance, the way in which Lynch forces viewer identification with Jeffrey, especially in the suspenseful scene in which a flushing toilet drowns out the car horn warning of impending danger. Or that perhaps the most disturbing effect of the film involves the revelation that Jeffrey possesses the capacity to think, desire, and act like Frank – this revelation would not be nearly so traumatic if the viewer were not fully invested in Jeffrey as a normalizing agent, a protagonist ostensibly deployed to correct the degeneracy of Lumberton rather than participate in it. It is not enough to say that Jeffrey is merely a protagonist – there are after all plenty of filmic protagonists who are offputting and vile – the success of the film hinges totally on the viewer's ability to see him or herself in his place.

is Dorothy who drives the narrative through her position as the mutable feminine subject, her alternation between the vamping hypersexualized lounge singer and the nurturing, protective mother. *Blue Velvet* tells the story of how Jeffrey, home from college to tend to his sick father, finds a severed ear in a field and enlists the local police detective's high school daughter Sandy (Laura Dern) to help him figure out where it came from. This leads him to Dorothy, who is in the midst of a crisis: a local sociopath, Frank Booth (Dennis Hopper), has kidnapped her son and husband and threatens to kill them if Dorothy does not submit to his perverse sexual advances. Dorothy begins to seduce Jeffrey and initiate him into a similar realm of fetishized sex. This arrangement lasts until Frank catches the two of them at Dorothy's apartment and reacts, to say the least, violently.

As Eric G. Wilson points out, "Even though Dorothy is the prototypical femme fatale, she is most moved by motherhood."[4] Wilson aligns this relationship of – one might like to presume – diametrically-opposed feminine behaviors with the notion of "order dissolving into chaos," suggesting that motherhood involves a redirecting of desire from a sexual object to the welfare of one's offspring. This, of course, alludes to the very maintenance of societal *order*. But, as Freud famously puts it, "the *sexual* life of adult women is a dark continent."[5] The complexity of Dorothy Vallens' character stems from the manner in which she shifts from one mode to the other – and in which the ideological order of the maternal function gives way to the chaos of feminine desire.

As the maternal subject, Dorothy only wishes for the safe return of her son (and to a lesser extent, her husband). But as the femme fatale, her desire (as in classic film noir) exists somewhere outside of the phallic symbolic order – indefinable, by definition. As Todd McGowan puts it, "both Jeffrey and Frank Booth confront her desire, and each fails, despite their efforts, to fantasize a way of making that desire meaningful."[6] Since neither man is capable of addressing Dorothy's feminine desire, it becomes necessary, instead, to focus more closely on her maternal subjectivity; to treat her motherhood as the quintessence of femaleness, as the point of entry from which they might adequately satisfy and possess her. Lynch thus invites us to regard the split between domesticated motherhood and sultry feminine sexuality as simply one more instance of *Blue Velvet*'s fascination with dramatic bifurcations that turn out to be not mutually exclusive, but wholly complementary.

Jacques Lacan famously and controversially declared that *la femme n'existe pas* – that "Woman does not exist." This claim is frequently misunderstood as pertaining to a negation of women as individual subjects, but in fact pertains to a non-existence of an *essence* of Woman; it suggests that there is no single principle by which one can universalize femininity. This distinction of men and women takes place strictly at the level of the symbolic order; masculinity, after all, can be organized under

[4] Eric G. Wilson, *The Strange World of David Lynch: Transcendental Irony from* Eraserhead *to* Mulholland Dr. (New York: The Continuum International Publishing Group, 2007) 57.
[5] Qtd in Mary Ann Doane, *Femme Fatales* (New York: Routledge, 1991) 210; my emphasis. Sigmund Freud, *The Question of Lay Analysis*, ed. James Strachey (London: Norton and Company, 1978).
[6] Todd McGowan, *The Impossible David Lynch* (New York: Columbia University Press, 2007) 99.

the banner of the phallus. Because the phallic function is in fact the symbolic function, which is in turn the arbiter of language, Lacan claims that "That means we can't talk about Woman. A woman can but be excluded by the nature of things, which is the nature of words."[7] That is to say that feminine jouissance is the locus of the failure of phallic jouissance to encompass all. Lacan writes "there is no chance for a man to have jouissance of a woman's body, otherwise stated, for him to make love, without castration, in other words, without something that says 'No' to the phallic function."[8] Because sexual enjoyment is attached to phallic signification, the masculine subject cannot sexually appropriate the feminine subject. Lacan's thesis is that phallic jouissance is recognizable – it is essentially sexual enjoyment – and that Other jouissance is not. The feminine subject is capable of both kinds, but only that which takes place in the symbolic order – that which is under the marker of the phallus and is thus overseen by masculine subjects – can be conceptualized and understood.

This is why Jeffrey and Frank exhibit sexual behavior which, although it is at times shocking or disturbing, can also be understood through the lenses of castration and fetish. Dorothy's desire, because it is defined by her femininity and is thus outside of the symbolic order, cannot be articulated. The masculine recourse to this problem in *Blue Velvet*, I will argue, is to isolate and appropriate the maternal and domestic functions of the woman (insofar as Dorothy represents the non-existence of Woman), because these functions, unlike feminine *sexuality* and desire, can be contained and exploited on behalf of masculine desire. Paradoxically, the film's method of *engaging* Dorothy's maternal subjectivity is in fact to *negate* it by deploying Frank to annihilate the bonds of domesticity which give the maternal its symbolic meaning. Psychoanalytic theory suggests that the role of the child in the Oedipal paradigm is to "be" the phallus. As Darian Leader puts it, "When the child picks up on the key place of the phallus for the mother, he or she will try to incarnate this object for her, although knowing full well that he or she is not identical with it ... the child is trying to be the object which it *thinks* the mother lacks."[9] Whereas Frank violently negates the maternal bond in an attempt to appropriate and objectify feminine sexual desire, Jeffrey attempts to be what Dorothy "needs;" to position himself as a corrective to Frank's extreme and fetishistic influence on her in the same way that the Oedipal child attempts to position himself as a substitution for the phallus in order to short-circuit the mother's desire that surpasses the maternal function. The traumatic content of the film, however, emanates from this theoretically chivalrous gesture, as Jeffrey's involvement with Dorothy consistently conflates the maternal with sexual desire.

THE (GOD-)FATHER AND RESTRICTED ENJOYMENT
In what will perhaps be viewed as a typically phallocentric gesture, before exploring the maternal function in *Blue Velvet*, I want to establish how the

[7] Jaques Lacan, *The Seminar of Jacques Lacan, Book XX: On Feminine Sexuality, the Limits of Love and Knowledge*, trans. Bruce Fink (New York: Norton, 1998) 73.

[8] Lacan, *Book XX*, 71-72.

[9] Darian Leader, *Introducing Lacan* (Cambridge: Icon Books, 1995) 102-03.

paternal function lays the groundwork for the film. As I've suggested, along with elements which lend themselves to "wild psychoanalysis," the most common viewer reaction to *Blue Velvet* is surely the observation that "good" and "evil" appear to be presented as existing in a precise 1-1 relationship. The opening scene iterates this when the almost imbecilic depiction of small-town banality gives way to the chaotic writhing of insects below the ground's surface. Many critics have noted that it is Jeffrey's father Tom's fall, ostensibly due to a stroke, that inaugurates the narrative, and it is easy to posit a psychoanalytic reading of this event. One of the core tenets of psychoanalytic thought is that the paternal figure represents the authoritative Master Signifier whose presence holds together Law and meaning. In the perpetual slippage of signification, it is the pretext of the Father's phallic potency which anchors the symbolic order and allows the illusion of a *signified* to exist. And so when the Father collapses, his fundamental impotency is exposed and the signifying chain ceases to maintain meaning, just as Tom's garden hose becomes kinked and ceases to flow smoothly. Furthermore, one might be tempted to argue, the collapse heralds a suspension of Law and the opening up of transgressive possibility; as Todd McGowan puts it, "The absence of the father within the fantasy structure allows for the introduction of desire."[10] Although the father typically stands in for prohibition, Tom Beaumont's primary function is to prop up the illusion of Lumberton as an ideal, benign locale. So long as this fantasy is maintained, McGowan argues, desire is kept suppressed and the subject has little reason to imagine the existence of anything that does not conform to the ideal.

Mr. Beaumont's activity at the time of his collapse provides our first indication that these two halves of Lumberton, the ideal and the perverse, are not distinct but infinitely interrelated, a Mobius strip in which one side is perpetually turning into, and revealing elements of, the other.[11] Although his collapse is represented as one distinct spectacle – and the burrowing into the lawn which reveals the seething "underworld" as another (the shift from one to the other suggests the camera's restless boredom with the tableau of a middle-aged patriarch laid out on the ground, a desire to move on with the story) – it is important to note the nature of Tom's yard work. He is not cutting the grass or raking leaves or mending the heavy-handedly symbolic white picket fence in front of his house. He is *watering* the lawn, thereby feeding and nourishing the very subterranean zone which the film, from the outset, associates with the world of desire that poses a threat to the phallic social order. The soon-to-be-exposed realm of perversity and fetishism is not merely an outlying

---

[10] McGowan, *The Impossible David Lynch*, 95-96. As this quotation suggests, McGowan's thesis is that the idealized representations of Lumberton embody fantasy – in that such an ideal can only exist as the object of fantasy – while the perverse representations embody desire. Further, he argues, it is ideologically expedient to keep the two separate so that the failure of the former can be attributed to the insidiousness of the latter, rather than to its own inherent shortcomings.

[11] In his book *David Lynch* (1995), Michel Chion deploys the Lacanianish figure of the Mobius Strip in order to describe the relationship between Dorothy and Sandy. While I would concur that those two characters are so related on the level of representation, and will discuss this dyad later in my paper, it is important to note that the film's opening scene makes the connection between Tom Beaumont and his obscene counterpart on the level of form as well.

aberration, but something that feeds off of and extends from the realm of idealized normalcy. Lynch emphasizes this relationship in other, more technical, ways as well. For instance, the soundtrack does not abruptly change from Bobby Vinton's rendition of "Blue Velvet" to the cacophony of insects below ground, but rather fades gradually; thus, the music which one almost instinctively associates with the opening montage of idealized small-town life continues even as the camera abandons these images for more foreboding ones.

In his *Ethics* seminar, Jacques Lacan presents us with his own account of the Primal Father mythology from Freud's *Totem and Taboo*. Lacan reiterates the "tight bond of desire and law,"[12] and notes that Freud addresses this issue in *Civilization and its Discontents* when he (Freud) claims that "whoever attempts to submit to the moral law sees the demands of his superego grow increasingly meticulous and increasingly cruel."[13] Put simply, Freud posits that if you give the superego an inch, so to speak, it will take a mile. The more we submit to moral law, the more we may worry that we have not submitted sufficiently. This, it would seem, would be the genesis of a particular sort of neurosis. Lacan's point here, however, is that the inverse, a pursuit of uninhibited jouissance through a rejection of morality, does not come up against this recursive cycle. That is to say, jouissance is not simply something to be attained through transgression which then requires a more perverse or outrageous transgression in order to be attained once more. Without transgression – transgression which is defined by its opposition to Law – Lacan claims that the subject would always be returning to "the rut of a short and well-trodden satisfaction."[14] In *Seminar II*, Lacan remarks: "If God doesn't exist, the father says, then everything is permitted. Quite evidently, a naïve notion, for we analysts know full well that if God doesn't exist, then nothing at all is permitted any longer."[15] Slavoj Žižek responds to this statement by describing how the lack of an authoritarian injunction to prohibition and obedience undercuts the possibility of jouissance, which can be approached only through the field of transgression. This paradox of enjoyment, God, and superegoic oversight is nicely summed up in these terms:

> "If God doesn't exist, then everything is prohibited" means that the more you perceive yourself as an atheist, the more your unconscious is dominated by prohibitions that sabotage your enjoyment. (One should not forget to supplement this thesis with its opposite: if God exists, then everything is permitted – is this not the most succinct definition of the religious fundamentalist's predicament? For him, God fully exists, he perceives himself as His instrument, which is why he can do whatever he wants, his acts are redeemed in advance, since they express the divine will...)[16]

[12] Jaques Lacan, *The Seminar of Jacques Lacan, Book VII: The Ethics of Psychoanalysis, 1959-1960*, trans. Dennis Porter (New York: Norton, 1992) 177.

[13] Lacan, *Book VII*, 176; Lacan's paraphrase.

[14] Lacan, *Book VII*, 177.

[15] Qtd in Slavoj Žižek, *How to Read Lacan* (New York: Norton, 2006) 91; Jacques Lacan, *The Seminar of Jacques Lacan, Book II: The Ego in Freud's Theory and in the Technique of Psychoanalysis* (New York: Norton, 1988) 128.

[16] Žižek, *How to Read Lacan*, 92.

Lacan also uses the Nietzschean aphorism "God is Dead" in a manner that we must work around with caution before applying it to Lynch's depictions of transgressive enjoyment. While Nietzsche deploys this phrase to suggest that a singular system of moral order cannot be maintained through religion, Lacan suggests that the God/father "has never been the father except in the mythology of the son."[17] This would seem to suggest that moral order is never an inherent, self-directed agency, but one which is always *posited* to exist, and based on that very existence, assumed to be justified. It is in this same sense that the God/father is invested with moral authority by the son. When we say, in the Lacanian sense, that "God is dead" we are saying that morality is only ever the self-interested insistence of an *ideology* that sovereign good exists. In other words, that moral order is a social/symbolic construct in the service of normative culture. We see this especially emphasized when Lacan, discussing the (actual, not primordial) father, says that there is a "virile identification which flows from the love for the father and from his role in the normalization of desire. But that result only occurs in a favorable form as long as everything is in order with the No/Name-of-the-Father ... with the God who doesn't exist."[18] This emphasizes the ability of both the void that in fact constitutes paternal authority, and the role of this non-existent paternal agent, to endlessly reproduce the rules and regulations of the social order under the guise of an *a priori* morality.

We can see some helpful cinematic examples of this idea, acting as explicit precursors to Lynch, at work in Hitchcock's *Psycho* (1960). The down-and-out Sam Loomis is breaking his back and deferring his own desire in order to pay off debts incurred by his dead father, which prevents him from normalizing his desire by entering into domesticity via a "respectable" relationship with Marion Crane. The real father, the literal paternal authority, in this case, *no longer exists*. With the paternal figure dead, one could suppose that everything is now permitted; but Sam's father binds him to a particular place in the symbolic and social orders, one which bars him from completing the normalizing romantic union. In other words, that the God/father is dead does little to establish autonomy and jouissance for the subject.[19]

Sam's potential breaking out of his prescribed role in the social order continues to be prohibited by the Name of the Father even in the absence of his physical presence and vitality. Marion's attempt to short-circuit this prohibition between father and son – to transgress on her lover's behalf – results, as we well know, in both her own violent death and, for Sam, a radical rupture, courtesy of Norman Bates, in the very conception of normativity that he wished to attain. Rather than achieve the apex of normative sexuality, marriage and reproduction, Sam must live with (or repress) the newfound knowledge, so lovingly described by the psychiatrist in the film's final moments, of an alien, non-normative mode of

---

[17] Lacan, *Book VII*, 177.
[18] Lacan, *Book VII*, 181.
[19] This of course parallels Norman Bates, who continues to the end to be controlled by his long-absent mother; but whereas Sam's prohibition is aligned with his father and Norman's with his mother, we are receptive to Sam representing masculine virility and Norman embodying feminine timidity.

sexuality.[20] Like Jeffrey, Sam's impulse toward *de*tection (directed at Frank and Norman, respectively) and *pro*tection (directed at Dorothy and Marion/Lila), an impulse triggered by the instability of the paternal function, brings him into confrontation with perversity, decay, and anality.

I've discussed above how the common interpretation of *Blue Velvet* involves the idea that because the Father is "dead," Jeffrey Beaumont is freed to explore the perverse underbelly of small-town America that Lumberton embodies – and indeed, this exploration is directly catalyzed (on the level of plot, at least) by the discovery of the severed ear, a discovery made as Jeffrey leaves his father's bedside – but one must note that Jeffrey's enjoyment heretofore is consistently foreclosed. A new, inverted, paternal prohibition, the obscene father embodied by Frank Booth, moves in immediately to fill the void. And while the very definition of the obscene, or anal, father, is that he encourages enjoyment and rejects prohibition, Frank's hedonism nonetheless leads to violence and chaos which must be, at least ostensibly, corrected in the film's denouement.

Like the quintessential Hitchcock film, *Blue Velvet* narratively ends on a note of restored normativity; a normativity ostensibly enacted by repression. As Robin Wood puts it in his essay discussing Lynch's film in contrast with *Shadow of a Doubt* (Hitchcock 1943), "If Frank represents – as the film seems to suggest – an unrepressed version of Jeffrey, then what is there left to do but repress?."[21] Because Frank's extreme perversity left Jeffrey with no taboo to be transgressed – because jouissance was, for him, always right out in the open and never veiled – Jeffrey could not properly enjoy in spite of his transgressions. The "dead" God/father has the effect of simply removing prohibition which, paradoxically, *restricts* rather than enables enjoyment. The restoration of patriarchal order, at the end of the film, ironically, opens up a new avenue for Jeffrey to enjoy through his apparently unproblematic heterosexual coupling with Sandy – the daughter, not coincidentally, of the *de facto* agent of masculine authority, the small-town police chief. Yet, still, this pursuit of enjoyment is more likely to result in the "rut" of enjoyment since, as Lacan attributes to Freud, "there is nothing in common between the satisfaction a jouissance affords in its original state and that which it gives in the indirect or even sublimated forms that civilization obliges it to assume."[22] In other words, while civilization will allow a degree of regulated pleasure and enjoyment to seep through, it does not approach the ecstatic nature of jouissance. Likewise, we could conjecture that, had Marion lived to marry Sam in *Psycho*, both of them would have found the socially-sanctioned domesticity of marriage to pale in comparison to the transgressive enjoyment they took from their hotel room trysts. In *Blue Velvet*, Jeffrey's inevitable relationship with Sandy Williams would appear to be essentially his (inadequate) consolation prize for his lost access to the sublime/grotesque feminine Thing embodied by Dorothy, an access which is lost when repression is reengaged. However, we will encounter the possibility that by refusing to fully repress his own transgressions,

[20] For these various insights concerning *Psycho*, I am indebted to Lee Edelman, whose fall 2008 Hitchcock class at Tufts University, for which I served as a teaching assistant, was instrumental in my thinking about this and other Hitchcock films.
[21] Robin Wood, *Hitchcock's Films Revisited* (New York: Columbia University Press, 2002) 48.
[22] Lacan, *Book VII*, 199- 200.

Jeffrey ensures, rather than sabotages, the success of normalized, domesticated desire.

Blue Velvet does not present, then, as Wood suggests, a vindication of the urge to repress. Rather, somewhat paradoxically, it celebrates the restoration of unthreatened maternal and ideological subjectivity – located in Dorothy as the social order's preferred version of feminine subjectivity, and presented as concurrent with the normalization and domestication of *masculine* desire through Jeffrey – as a result of an unfettered indulgence in the Oedipal impulse, the realization that maternal and sexual desires are in fact inseparable. In short, the film, along with Freud, embraces the very *opposite* of repression.

THE MASK OF FETISH AND DRIVE

Martha Nochimson argues that in encountering and emulating Frank's brutality, Jeffrey's narrative arc serves to "demystify the Freudian narrative ... it reveals the problem of cultural definitions of masculinity – the maiming of a father and husband (Don Vallens) by a shadow father figure (Frank Booth) who is too willfully divorced from, not too much possessed by, subconscious feminine forces."[23] Frank's imposition of his own body upon Dorothy is heavily thematized through a parent/child dyad; in his initial appearance, he commands Dorothy to call him "daddy" and bring him his bourbon (this part of the scene suggests an eerie inversion of the domestic trope of a husband returning home from work and being served a cocktail by his stay-at-home wife) while referring to himself as "baby" (as in "baby wants to fuck" and "baby wants blue velvet"). That is to say, Frank appropriates and sexualizes the roles of the two males that he has abducted and that would complete the domestic and Oedipal circuit for Dorothy. His own slippage between these two roles is essentially the first impression that the viewer, occupying Jeffrey's vantage point in the closet,[24] has of Frank:

> Dorothy: Hello baby.
> Frank: Shut up! It's "Daddy," you shithead.

However, it is only shortly after this correction that Frank takes on the persona of "baby." His project is clearly not one of base sexual gratification, but of control[25] – of wresting control of the Oedipal paradigm by removing two of its key players and then filling in for both of them. The

---

[23] Martha P. Nochimson, *The Passion of David Lynch* (Austin: University of Texas Press, 1997) 102.

[24] My own comparative reading of *Blue Velvet* and *Psycho* notwithstanding, there are several other distinct stylistic gestures, especially in this scene, which recall Hitchcock's film. The mise en scene of Jeffrey's "interslat voyeurism," as Wallace calls it, is nearly identical to that of Norman Bates' spying on Marion, and the two scenes are imbued with a similarly prurient motivation. The music that plays as Dorothy discovers Jeffrey in the closet is also uncannily reminiscent of Bernard Herrmann's score for *Psycho*. That each film is widely considered the magnum opus of its respective director is rather fitting.

[25] This characterization of control trumping sexual gratification in a violent encounter, of course, recalls the common politically correct aphorism that rape is about power and violence, not sex. If *Blue Velvet* conveys any message about sex, it is that this aphorism is essentially redundant; that sex *is* already about violence and control *before* issues of consent even enter the equation (for this insight I am, again, indebted to Lee Edelman, who made a similar point in his fall 2008 Hitchcock seminar [see n19] concerning the film *Frenzy*).

apex of this system of control lies in his ability to dictate which role he is performing at any given time, and to harshly correct Dorothy when she misunderstands whether he desires to embody the persona of man or child at any given time.

Upon Frank's shift to the role of child, initiated by his use of the iconic gas mask to inhale an unspecified substance, Dorothy's calling him "baby" does not provoke the same response. Instead, he stares rapturously between Dorothy's legs, unmistakably reenacting the traumatic moment to which Freud attributes the genesis of the fetish: the realization that the mother lacks a penis. The tableau of the "closet scene," then, serves to demonstrate Frank's mutable desire. But this mutability does not fully parallel Dorothy's. Rather, it is a performance, a series of gestures toward his arrested development, his inability to fully inhabit the subjecthood of the helpless infant *or* the authoritative paternal figure. Whereas Dorothy's mutability shifts between the (symbolizable) maternal figure and the (unsymbolizable, ensnared in the Real) figure of feminine desire, both sides of Frank's duality – two sides of the same coin of perverse desire – can be located in a psychoanalytic model.[26]

The mysterious mask which fuels his performance aligns Frank with what Lee Edelman, in his book *No Future*, has termed the *sinthom*osexual: the figure whose inherent queerness is understood as a threat to reproductive futurity and the maintenance of the symbolic order; a figure "beyond the correlative logic of the symptom and its cure," who is defined "no longer as subject of desire, but rather as subject of the drive. For the subject of desire now comes to be seen as a symptomatic misprision, within the language of the law, of the subject's sinthomatic access to the force of a jouissance played out in the pulsions of the drive"[27] Earlier in *No Future*, Edelman points out the uncanny similarity between the facial apparatuses worn by two characters in the cinema of Jonathan Demme: the cannibalism-prevention muzzle – easily as iconic, if not more so, as Frank's gas mask – worn by Hannibal Lecter (Anthony Hopkins) in *The Silence of the Lambs* (1991) and the deathbed oxygen mask worn by AIDS patient Andrew Beckett (Tom Hanks) in *Philadelphia* (1993). While Edelman's comparison of these two representations is meant to suggest that the latter film is something of a *mea culpa* for perceived homophobia in the former, it is also instructive to view these masks as conduits of death drive, as signifiers of their respective wearers' displacement from the organizing principles of civil society, as institutional scarlet letters identifying insidious non-normativity. For Hannibal, the mask signals his past aberrant behavior and his utter disregard for the consequences of that behaviors' repetition. For Beckett, it signals the consequences of engaging in sexual acts that are not sanctioned by the parameters of heteronormativity. And for Frank, we see the maintenance of perversity and brutality filtered through a performance of infantile innocence. This confluence is exemplified later in the film when Frank takes Jeffrey "for a ride." After inhaling the gas, he again begins to touch Dorothy's body

---

[26] In other words, whereas only a portion of Dorothy's subjectivity is thus locatable, we can fully make sense of Frank. Or, as Todd McGowan puts it, "Even if Frank horrifies us as spectators, he nonetheless provides a horror that makes sense" (103).

[27] Lee Edelman, *No Future: Queer Theory and the Death Drive* (Durham: Duke University Press, 2004) 113.

with the same childish excitement he exhibited as he gazed between her legs. But once more, the role of the child is quickly abandoned for the role of the violent patriarch when Jeffrey attempts to intervene and is severely beaten.

Frank's status as a *sinthom*osexual is particularly complex and extreme. He has abducted Dorothy's child and husband, thus separating her from the fruit of her own reproductivity as well as the only man who could (within the boundaries of domestic and paternal law) contribute to her future reproductivity; what more can the *sinthom*osexual (who so often exudes queerness and negation of futurity *representationally* rather than through actions performed at the narrative level) do than actually, remorselessly, abduct a child and violate the child's mother? But Frank does so, it is clear, for the purpose of inserting *himself* into this very paradigm, not merely in accordance with the drive to undermine futurity and childhood. Unlike Dorothy, then, Frank's desire is clear: he is profoundly invested in a cyclical perpetuation of, and participation in, the Oedipal Crisis. That continued perpetuation is contingent on annihilating the bonds of maternal subjecthood in order to leave a gap that he himself can fill. This, in turn, requires Frank to force Dorothy to orient herself strictly within the maternal sphere and thus abandon the opaque feminine sphere. But the violence, and threat of same, that Frank consistently represents, is not merely a pragmatically thuggish means of attaining what he wants; as McGowan puts it, it is a plainly homosocial form of violence, "an attempt to arouse Dorothy's desire – to motivate her to desire something rather than nothing."[28] As I've argued, such a project necessarily takes the form of maternal negation.

Jeffrey's interference, as many critics have noted, triangulates this Oedipal structure, naturally positioning Jeffrey in the role of the child. The problem is that this forecloses Frank's ability to assume that role at will and relegates him fully to that of the father. This is the essence of Frank's pathology: an unwillingness to fully assume the mantle of the paternal, and a lack of compunction to destroy the "child" who has usurped his position. As Nochimson points out, Frank is compelled by the feminine only insofar as it is the *object* of his fetish. The constitution of his drive toward that object is emphatically masculine, whether he is embodying the fully-developed phallic father or the child in the throes of latency.

ETIQUETTE AND THE ABJECT BODY

Dorothy and Frank's embodiment of the maternal and paternal roles with respect to Jeffrey – as well as to each other – takes on myriad forms. Frank becomes something of a mentor to Jeffrey, a stern and dedicated instructor of social graces. When he asks Jeffrey what kind of beer he likes, and Jeffrey replies "Heineken," Frank's oft-quoted outburst – "Heineken! Fuck that shit! Pabst Blue Ribbon!" – is positioned less as a declaration of beer preference than a forceful induction into the proper behavior and accoutrements of the perverse world over which Frank presides.[29] Just as we could suppose that his biological father, Tom

---

[28] McGowan, *The Impossible David Lynch*, 103.

[29] It is significant that Pabst is stereotypically associated with blue-collar masculinity. The implication, then, is that Heineken, by contrast, is to be associated with an effete *non-*

Beaumont, imparted the rules of etiquette within the fantasmatic realm of Lumberton,[30] Frank (at least when he is engaged in the paternal rather than infantile mode) is more than willing to dispense instruction and punishment with an air of fatherly authority. The scene in which Frank and his gang force Dorothy and Jeffrey to go with them to Ben's (Dean Stockwell) house is exemplary, to the point of absurdist parody, of this trope. After pouring and distributing glasses of beer to the assembled inhabitants of Lumberton's underbelly, Frank insists that Ben toast "Here's to your fuck" – an irreverent toast, essentially meaningless beyond its ostentatious vulgarity. Frank then offers a toast in response, one which is comparatively civil: "You are so fucking suave. We love Ben ... Here's to Ben!" Noticing that Jeffrey has not joined in the toast, Frank rushes to him and hits him in the face:

> Frank: "Here's to Ben!"
> Jeffrey: Here's to Ben.
> Frank: Be polite!
> Jeffrey: Here's to Ben.

The point to be made here, simply, is that Frank is generally assumed to be to the perverse underside of Lumberton what Tom Beaumont is to its idealized counterpart: the phallic father, the Master Signifier who anchors and legitimizes the meaning of all that passes through the signifying chain. It is through Frank's influence, in particular his declaration of "You're like me!" that Jeffrey comes to recognize the underside not as a strange and mysterious place, but as a place which can in fact support articulable meaning. Though Jeffrey's anguish over hitting Dorothy himself is apparent – demonstrating that he is caught in a dialectic between the two worlds, that the two worlds overlap, rather than he has simply been corrupted by one over the other – the pleasure that he finds himself taking in hitting Dorothy is not, like Dorothy's pleasure in *being* hit, an opaque or unsymbolizable thing. It is now supported by the substitutive Master Signifer that Frank represents. This is a critical starting point for any psychoanalytic reading of the film.

Nonetheless, I would argue that it is not Frank, but Dorothy, who not only stabilizes the obscene underside, but is also capable of moving from it to the idealized side. Whereas Frank requires his Well-Dressed Man costume to elude the gaze of fantasmatic Lumberton, Dorothy needs only to put forth her maternal side in order to fit in there. This is why the moment

---

masculinity. As Kenneth Kaleta puts it, "Frank's gang is the antithesis of Jeffrey's imported-beer-drinking circle at college" (123). However, Frank's alcohol preference also extends to bourbon; a drink that, depending on brand as well as social context, can connote stereotypical "redneck" rowdiness and mayhem *or* dignified gentility – mint juleps at the Kentucky Derby, for instance.

[30] Jeffrey's interactions with Sandy's family are particularly indicative of his command of civilized gestures. While one could suggest that his desire to date Sandy and extract information from Detective Williams provides an ulterior motivation to be excessively polite and humble, his excellent manners nonetheless position him as the sort of young man who would compel elders to comment that he must have had a good upbringing, good parents, and so forth. One might expect that this is essentially the norm in the idealized version of Lumberton. David Foster Wallace goes so far as to suggest that the typical Lynch character must be "stolid to the point of retardation" (199) so as to be believable in their inability to notice the overt Freudian symbolism of what's going on in the plot.

in which she appears naked in front of Sandy's house is so alarming and so effectively defuses the relatively minor threat posed by Sandy's angry ex-boyfriend Mike and his gang of football buddies, who have come to beat up Jeffrey for "stealing" Sandy.[31] Significantly, when Dorothy first appears – disoriented, beaten-up, and nude – Mike sneers "Who is that, huh? Is that your mother?" As Nochimson points out, "[Mike's] outlaw impersonation collapses when evidence of Frank's brutality surfaces in the scene."[32]

Dorothy's appearance here is a pointed inversion of the one other way in which she appears in the public space of Lumberton: her singing performances at the Slow Club. In both instances she is on a stage of some sort (at Sandy's, the front porch) and demands the attention of spectators. At the club, she is dubbed "The Blue Lady," a reference to the glamorous dress she wears. Here, her clothing – or lack of it – is similarly the focal point, as the only thing she "wears" are the bruises resulting from Frank's savagery. In other words, Dorothy appears to be incapable of setting foot in the non-private idealized sphere of civilization without being configured as a spectacle. Jeffrey, by this point, is astute and learned enough concerning the two versions of Lumberton to recognize that collapse; as he rushes to Dorothy's aid, he blithely forgives Mike, who stammers a confused and ashamed apology.

While the common reaction to this scene involves the observation that Mike's juvenile attempt to play the outlaw serves to underscore the division of the idealized and perverse version of Lumberton, one must keep in mind that it is Dorothy's predicament, not Mike's impotent adolescent rage, around which Lynch has structured the mise en scene. Mike's question – "Is that your mother?" – is clearly meant as a garden variety insult. The implication that one's mother possesses sexual desire and a capacity for promiscuity is, after all, essentially *the* one-liner insult between men. But it is not merely the suggestion of sexuality which inheres in Dorothy's nakedness. She is not merely nude but utterly abject – she stumbles around looking monstrous. Simply, her presence in front of Sandy's house is painfully, resiliently wrong. Mike may be more astute than we give him credit for: our spectatorial gaze upon Dorothy's body does indeed seem to recall Frank's gaze in the "primal" scene, a moment in which Dorothy's subjectivity is emphatically maternal. That is to say, we are now seeing what Frank saw, what was previously blocked by the blue velvet bathrobe. We, like Frank, are initiated into the realm of the fetish by our apprehension of that maternal body.

At the same time, Dorothy would seem at this moment to be engaged in the mode of feminine desire, rather than maternal domesticity. Whereas in the scene in which Frank stares lasciviously between her legs, Dorothy

---

[31] It is perhaps too obvious to note the correlation between Mike's gang and Frank's. While Mike and his friends do pose something of a physical threat, they operate explicitly within the boundaries of fantasmatic, idealized Lumberton, fueled by socially acceptable levels of drunken teenage bravado and entitlement. After the previous night's encounter at Ben's, their accosting of Jeffrey is almost laughable by comparison (one does wonder, though, if the bottles in their hands are of Pabst Blue Ribbon or Heineken). The realization that they are being chased by Mike and his friends rather than by Frank is occasion for relief for both Sandy and Jeffrey – the latter of whom goes from considering using his father's gun to complacently getting out of the car to receive whatever sort of beating Mike has in mind.

[32] Nochimson, *The Passion of David Lynch*, 117.

is lucid and fully aware of what is happening and her prescribed role within it, here she displays the disoriented ravings of the hysteric and, simultaneously and perhaps inadvertently, the role of the Other Woman, the femme fatale who disrupts the burgeoning (wholesome, non-fetishistic) relationship between Jeffrey and Sandy: "Jeffrey, Jeffrey, Jeffrey, hold me, hold me, oh God! My secret lover." When Sandy's mother informs them that she has called the police, she shrieks "Don't get the police! Stop him! I love you, love me! He put his disease in me."

Although she comes to ask for help in recovering her husband, and in recovering her own disrupted domesticity, Dorothy proves almost immediately to be a threat to the idealized young love that is designed to reproduce the fantasmatic Lumberton and keep the underside at bay. Sandy's own mother, in this scene, remains oddly calm. Her only reaction to Dorothy is to remark that she will find a coat to cover her. Essentially, despite all that Dorothy's presence represents concerning Jeffrey's foray into darkness and evil and his sexual betrayal of Sandy, Mrs. Williams can think of little else other than the proprietary measure of concealing her nakedness. This gesture is the gesture of the fantasmatic world in general. Concealment of abjection allows one to operate under the guise that that abjection does not exist.

For Jeffrey's part, it is this strange interaction in Sandy's house that leads to the film's climax, as though the threat that is posed to his own masculine ascension to sanctioned domesticity is the last straw; now that he has attained a romantic relationship with Sandy, he can hardly have his obscene shadow-father inundating him with reminders of his slumming in the world of rough, fetishistic sex. This threat to his own stability in the symbolic order is the one and only thing that leads him to finally kill Frank, an action performed while he is concealed once more within Dorothy's closet. The locale that initiated the Oedipal crisis, then, is also the point from which it is resolved, with a well-placed bullet in the obscene father's head. Significantly, Frank takes a hit of his mysterious inhalant moments before Jeffrey kills him, indulging in the aimlessness of the drive to the very end. Frank's death, complete with an animalistic squeal, is immediately followed by Sandy and her father arriving on the scene. Sandy emits a breathy "Oh Jeffrey!," while Detective Williams – finally performing his job actively rather than leveling vaguely paternalistic threats at a meddling Jeffrey – assumes the A-stance and wildly brandishes his small caliber police-issue about the apartment before declaring: "It's all over." The ideal version of patriarchy, it would seem, is thus restored.

RESTORATION AND REPRESSION

Blue Velvet's denouement closely "recalls its prologue." We return to the color-saturated shots of manicured lawns and picket fences. But like the prologue's transition from the imagery of placid small-town life and the crooning of Bobby Vinton to the corrupt and writhing chaos of the subterranean, the restoration of the social order is not an abrupt switch but a gradual overlapping. The soundtrack switches to the light, airy song that has come to be associated with Jeffrey and Sandy's pure teenage love, but we remain fixed in Dorothy's apartment, watching as the agents of normalcy – police, EMTs, etc. – deal with the consequences of Jeffrey's interference, of his going where no nice Lumberton boy should go. The actual switch back to a fully fantasmatic Lumberton is accomplished via a fade to black and a zoom out from the abyss of Jeffrey's ear as he reclines on a lawn chair.[33] Sandy calls Jeffrey to lunch and, on his way in, Jeffrey speaks briefly with his father (100% recovered from his stroke, apparently; he assures Jeffrey he is feeling much better) and Detective Williams, who are chatting out on the lawn, the site of the former's initial fall from paternal power. A pointed shot assures us that Tom Beaumont is indeed capable of standing erect upon the domain of home and hearth. Sandy, in the kitchen with her aunt, marveling at the presence of a robin in the window, assures us that her desire will remain domesticated and contained; that she will not, some years down the line, be a Dorothy Vallens – and conversely, that Jeffrey will not be forced to re-engage the little bit of Frank Booth that he has internalized.

This interpretation of the ending could almost be taken as sincere if not for a variety of incongruencies. Sandy lightly remarks to Jeffrey that it's "a strange world," indicating a refusal to fully repress their experiences in the other side of Lumberton; surely she did not intend to suggest that the restored, aggressively banal fantasm of Lumberton is what is "strange." Sandy's aunt admires the beauty of the robin, but upon noticing the insect in its beak she bristles and remarks "I don't see how they could do that ... I could never eat a bug."[34] Lynch then fixes the camera on the bird for us to be certain that the lovely animal does indeed hold a bug in its mouth, essentially cementing the conflation of civilized, repressive beauty and the aggressive counterparts of drive, hunger, and instinct. Yet again, the two sides cannot be adequately separated.

The point, then, is that Jeffrey can*not* fully repress. He is indeed a version of Frank Booth at this point; but not a repressed one. This final scene does not validate repression but demonstrate its impossibility. There will always be disturbing material to re-engage the trauma that Frank has inflicted, even if it is as seemingly-innocuous as a feeding bird. As if to preempt the realization that Lumberton's fantasmatic restoration cannot fully overcome its own symbiotic relation to the seamy underside, we leave Jeffrey and Sandy for the even more abstracted version of symbolic idealization, a reprise of the images which opened the film: flowers in bloom, firemen mechanistically grinning and waving, white picket fences and blue sky.

But rather than concluding with the assurance of a vindicated social order, the final shot returns us to the maternal/feminine crux of the film, as a young boy walks up to a woman on a park bench. It takes us a moment to realize the woman is Dorothy; the last time we saw her she was

---

[33] This transition is somewhat on the nose, as it not only recalls the ear of Don Vallens which, by being looked *into*, initiated Jeffrey into the problems of the film, but also suggests that we are moving away from Jeffrey's head at the same time as we depart from the perverse world of desire; in other words, that that world was all a dream, a fantasy produced by a denizen of a different fantasy.

[34] Wallace claims that the aunt, immediately after speaking this line, "proceeds to put a bug in her mouth" (206). While she does take a bite of something at this juncture (she and Sandy were, after all, preparing lunch), there is nothing to indicate that what she eats is a bug or anything else in particular. Clearly, Lynch is underscoring a bit of mild hypocrisy on the aunt's part, in that she decries one living thing's means of survival and then indulges in her own – but the claim that what she eats is also a bug is, in my view, a bit of a reach.

beaten up, naked, hysterical. In instances before that she varied between sexy glamour and exhausted frumpiness. Here, she is presented as unproblematically maternal, as her appearance is purged of these complicating signifiers of feminine desire and frustration. With her son returned to her, Dorothy is able to perform the role of motherhood within the boundaries of the symbolic order, in a space which is domesticated and contained, articulable and understandable.

But we must note that this performance – and it is indeed a performance – of ideologically-proper motherhood is *not* a "return" for us as spectators. The "fall" at the beginning of the film exclusively involved the paternal authority. For us viewers, Dorothy's condition has always-already been defined by the complex split between feminine desire and maternal domesticity. The film positions this split not as something which occurs because of a traumatic instance but as the *a priori* state of Woman. Just as the ideal and obscene halves of Lumberton are intertwined and interdependent, Dorothy's two sides cannot simply be toggled from one to the other, as Lynch refuses to allow Dorothy's unsymbolizable desire to give way to a fully reformed maternal subjectivity. Instead, the look on Dorothy's face as she hugs her son turns from rapture at having recovered what she wished for throughout the film to a look of longing and dissatisfaction. This change in facial expression coincides with a shift in the soundtrack from the sappy music that has marked Jeffrey and Sandy's coupling – thus underscoring the parallel between Dorothy's ideological containment and that of the young lovers – to a final strain of Dorothy singing "and I still can see through blue velvet through my tears."

If we take this line to refer to the tears of joy that she is shedding over being reunited with her son, then we must imagine that Dorothy's final wistful gaze is directed at what she has lost in the process of recovering her maternal subjecthood: the enjoyment that inhered in opaquely desiring and in having two men attempt to penetrate that desire, an enjoyment which was metonymized by the literal presence of swatches of blue velvet. Despite being back in the position of idealized motherhood, Dorothy continues to desire and continues to exude a lack of fulfillment.

In *Blue Velvet*, Lynch attempts to bring together the two parts of Woman which the social order is deeply invested in keeping separated: the maternal figure and the object of desire. The true traumatic content of the film emanates not from Frank's outlandish violence or even from Jeffrey's mimicking of that violence,[35] but from the unabashed sexualization of a woman who is also configured to embody motherhood. Yet despite the disgust that such representations tend to instill in subjects of the social order, Freud insists that "whoever is to be really free and happy in love must have overcome his deference for women and come to terms with the idea of incest with mother."[36] Thus, when read psychoanalytically, *Blue Velvet* ends on an ominous note. If Jeffrey is, as I've argued,

---

[35] The trope of the idealistic protagonist seduced into antisocial behavior (only to reform in the end), after all, has been put to thorough use in mainstream cinema. It's difficult to imagine that such a narrative arc, in and of itself, could be traumatic.

[36] Sigmund Freud, *Sexuality and the Psychology of Love* (New York: Simon & Schuster/Touchstone, 1997) 55. Freud also includes the sister in this statement but I have omitted that portion of the quotation since the eroticization of sibling relationships is outside the purview of this article.

able to buck the urge to repress his involvement with Dorothy and Frank, then the success of his relationship with Sandy is, according to Freud, ensured. Dorothy, meanwhile, is left in the lurch, so to speak, as she continues to be suspended between tempestuous feminine desire and aggressively normalized maternal subjectivity. Although she ends up essentially unsatisfied, Dorothy (along with Frank) has ultimately served as a means to the recapitulation of a purportedly heteronormative coupling. The film's most subversive gesture is to blot that coupling with incestuous desire.

JOSHUA D. GONSALVES
"I'M A WHORE": "ON THE OTHER SIDE" OF *INLAND EMPIRE*

"He's a whore. I'll do anything for money."
["He's a Whore"[1]]

"I sing this poem to you...
On the other side I see..."
["Polish Poem"[2]]

A woman cries after sex or sex-work in a hotel room. She is shot in ex-treme close-up, looking at the TV and crying, longing, looking to the screen for a reconciliation of her heart-rending experience of sexuality. It is not the same woman who acknowledged that "whores fuck" seconds before, and who is obscurely seen performing a sex act, but she also seems to be what most women are in this film: a whore. *"Find the female who isn't a prostitute"* might be a party game to play while watching *Inland Empire*. Try it and see. In a later scene Laura Dern proclaims "I'm a whore," reveling in the access to self-recognition she has been seeking throughout the film, her face breaking apart in DV as she escapes centu-ries of hypocritical, patriarchal domination, masculinist double standards and (self-)incarcerated feminine desire.

"Yes, we want whores, whole territories dedicated to whoring, but we want our wives, mothers and daughters to be pure" – to be pure whores exchanged on the marriage market to generate capital of all kinds, as Marx, Engels, Lévi-Strauss, Pierre Bourdieu and Gayle Rubin argue.[3] This film is, after all, as the voice over the opening shot of a needle scratching a vinyl groove stresses, about the "longest running radioplay in history" (Cf. the cliché of prostitution being the world's oldest profession), an allu-sion to the story of sexual difference and the scenarios, strategies and institutions that have emerged to process the traumatic *jouissance* or gender bender consistently misrecognized as sexuality.

Inland Impire (*II* hereafter)[4] is about something? I must be mistaken. When Lynch's *Lost Highway* was released, voices were heard protesting

---

[1] Cheap Trick, *Cheap Trick* (1977).
[2] Soundtrack to *Inland Empire.*
[3] See Karl Marx and Friedrich Engels, *The Communist Manifesto* (New York: Penguin, 1992) 21-3; Claude Lévi-Strauss, *The Elementary Structures of Kinship* (Boston: Beacon Press, 1969), as complicated or de-semiologized by Pierre Bourdieu, *Masculine Domination* (Stanford: Stanford University Press, 2001), 42-53; and Gayle Rubin's feminist re-reading of Marx, Engels and Lévi-Strauss: "The Traffic in Women," *Toward an Anthropology of Women*, ed. Rayna Reiter (New York: Monthly Review Press, 1975) 157-210.
[4] See John Dee, the Renaissance imperial fantasist, in reference to an "Islandish Impire" in *General and Rare Memorials pertayning to the Perfecte Arte of Navigation* (1577), qtd in Bruce

that it wasn't about anything, that you couldn't limit the film's haunting, surreal and absurd imagery by giving it a meaning. Just let it be, go with the flow of images and unclench your interpretative consciousness, a style of non-reading Žižek defines as the "New Age Lynch,"[5] a style that is exemplified by the Transcendentally Meditating auteur. Watch Lynch's hands flutter up and down, "beautiful as the hands of an alcoholic in delirium tremens,"[6] as he fails to explain his films and you realize that the New Critics were correct. The author is not the master of his text, especially an improvised, cut and paste, or paratactic text like *II*. Lynch, like Tarantino, seems to have no idea what he is talking about when he talks about his films, yet this lack of knowledge[7] makes them geniuses in the sense of idiot savants. "We have already grown beyond whatever we have words for. In all talking there lies a grain of contempt,"[8] and so they talk of other things than what their films are about. *"Anything but sexual trauma please! We're from Hollywood! We sell sex in the movies, on TV and at the corner of Hollywood and Vine,"* a red light area of LA where star whore Dern endlessly wanders in *II*.

Todd McGowan's articles on *Lost Highway* and *Mulholland Drive* provide a virtuoso reading of what these films are about – the impossibility of the sexual relation – and Richard Peña is dead-on when he notes that *II* is about sex trafficking.[9] If McGowan exemplifies a Lacanian style of reading that engages the social abstractly, the not altogether ridiculous sublime of the brutal, statistical facticities of global sex traffic intimate why many insist that Lynch's films are not about anything. They prefer to simply consume (and not enjoy or *enjouir de...*) a stream of consciousness or apparently disconnected images as if they were watching TV, channel-surfing, or strolling around the commodity fetish fairs our globalized urban centers have become, a domestication of *jouissance* that McGowan and Kordela target in a psychoanalytic viewfinder.[10] This domesticated mood of mind is typified by those film fans who will see anything if they can gain cultural capital by these films being from or about oppressed nations,

McLeod, *The Geography of Empire in English Literature: 1580-1745* (Cambridge: Cambridge University Press, 1999) 41.

5   Slavoj Žižek, *The Art of the Ridiculous Sublime: David Lynch's* Lost Highway (Seattle: University of Washington Press, 2000).

6   Isidore Ducasse (Lautréamont), *Les Chants de Maldoror* in *Oeuvres Complètes* (Paris: Garnier-Flammerion, 1969) 203.

7   "But even angels do not know, for all real knowledge is *obscure.*" Antonin Artaud, "Position of the Flesh," *L'Ombelic des Limbes* (Paris: Gallimard, 1958) 190.

8   Friedrich Nietzsche, *Twilight of the Idols* in *The Twilight of the Idols and The Anti-Christ*, ed. Michael Tanner, trans. R.J. Hollingdale (New York: Penguin, 1990) 94.

9   Or "about the smuggling of women from Eastern Europe"; Richard Peña, paraphrased in Helene Blatter, "'Inland Empire': Just Don't Expect to See the 91," *The Press-Enterprise* (2006-09-02) http://www.thecityofabsurdity.com/inlandempire/intInlandEmpire04.html; Todd McGowan, "Finding Ourselves on a *Lost Highway*: David Lynch's Lesson in Fantasy," *Cinema Journal* 39.2 (2000): 51-73, and "Lost on *Mulholland Drive*: Navigating David Lynch's Panegyric to Hollywood," *Cinema Journal* 43.2 (2004): 67-89. In regard to the impossibility of the sexual relation, see Jacques Lacan, *Le Seminaire de Jacques Lacan, Livre XX: Encore*, ed. J.A. Miller (Paris: Seuil, 1975): "On y parle de foutre – verbe, en anglais to fuck – et on y dit que ça ne va pas" (We are talking about fucking – verb, in English *to fuck* – and we are saying that it does not work; 33) and Joan Copjec, *Read My Desire: Lacan against the Historicists* (Boston: MIT Press, 1990) 201-236.

10 See Todd McGowan, *The End of Dissatisfaction: Jacques Lacan and the Emerging Society of Enjoyment* (Albany: SUNY Press, 2004); and A. Kiarina Kordela, *Surplus: Spinoza, Lacan* (Albany: SUNY Press, 2007).

peoples or sub-groups, and not think about them in any non-clichéd (read: non-politicized) sense except in regard to whether they liked them or not. Liking, or even loving, may be many things, but they are not the "frenetic 'enjoyment'" of "*jouissance*."[11] Instead, we have non-enjoyment, domesticated *jouissance* (pleasure, liking, perhaps loving), the commodification of the visual drive, or tele-vision.

While respecting the Žižekian psychoanalytical model I also plan to situate *II* in the socio-historical real of sex trafficking that functions as the great American repressed in the displaced form of stripclubs, which litter the nation and surface in Lynch's films in the lurid form of nightclub singers (Isabella Rossellini in *Blue Velvet*, living echo of the Hollywood blacklisting of Ingrid for having her first child out of wedlock), burlesque shows in *II*, Laura Palmer in *Twin Peaks* and *Fire Walk with Me*. The obscene yet stubbornly unseen proliferation of these clubs in Puritan America suggests that there is one degraded thing Democrats and Republicans agree on. Yet these infantile empires are based on the international exploitation of women, Eastern European women especially, given the central function of Poland in the film, which, in being shot, like many parsimonious Hollywood productions, in Eastern Europe reenacts this exploitation on a global level of unseeing.

Stanley Kubrick was right. *Eyes Wide Shut* (USA, 1999) is the ur-mantra of the American consumer of women as the mammary fetishism scene at the Long Island mansion attests. This unseeing at home and abroad strives to un-enjoy the absence of the prohibitive superego – breasts, mommy and me, and no *non du père* – domesticated fantasies of the ultimate fantasy of power, the obscenely enjoying paternal pervert, Frank Black (*Blue Velvet*) or Dick Laurent (*Mulholland Drive*). I will end by querying what this consensus represses, the sociohistorical truth of sex traffic: race – that is to say, in today's global economy, some races are trafficked and some eat up the traffic, as if to obscure, in America at least, the as yet unprocessed transatlantic presence of the black race, by which I mean the consequences of evading a post-Civil War reconstruction of American race relations: racism, displaced non-enjoyment of the African-American qua dominated other, hate crimes and the post-racial problematic code-named Michael Jackson.

Since *II* is fragmented in time and space, taking place in LA and in Poland, shuttling between acting and actuality, false memories and real fantasies, bunny sitcoms and films within films, I will eschew the pretense of a step-by-step discussion and focus on specific scenes, or on themes, traumas and structures that recur across this paratactical hodgepodge of images. The basic narrative organizing this reading will be based on where I began: a whore is watching TV and crying. Why? For what money shot? For whose benefit? Who is trafficked, prostituted and killed so that this payoff can occur? What, then, is this basic narrative?

AT THE ORIGIN OF THE WORLD
Let us begin at the absolute beginning. A spotlight is searching for something to see as if doubling for me, the viewer, wanting to see. The words

---

[11] Jean Laplanche, *Life & Death in Psychoanalysis*, trans. Jeffrey Mehlman (Baltimore: The Johns Hopkins University Press, 1976) 105.

INLAND EMPIRE emerge in black and white, as if announcing what this film will be about. The last shot is, we recall, a black or biracial woman lip-synching or minstrelizing "Sinnerman" by Nina Simone. I use the verb "minstrelize" in reference to an African-American miming his or her culture for the benefit of white culture's perpetuation of racism, since Simone, a proponent of black culture and the Civil Rights Movement, finally left America in disgust over its irredeemably un-reconstructed society and ended her days in opposition to race-mixing as a reinscription of antebellum slavery. But we are getting ahead of ourselves.

We see a close-up of an old gramophone playing "Axxon N...the longest running radioplay in history" as an audience claps: "tonight continuing in the Baltic region, a grey winter day in an old hotel." This tale is told by no one and signifies the idiotic *jouissance* of the male side of sexual difference that prevents the masculine subject from knowing the other, or the feminine side of the equation, a prevention effaced by the sheer, insensate enjoyment of sexual intercourse, or the fantasm of male *jouissance*, insofar as it serves as an unknowing of feminine desire.[12] The needle tracing the record's groove can now be seen as an image of copulation. In love this non-knowledge of the woman's desire may be possible, but not in an empire of whores where the "I," the male ego, *moi* or *Ich*, rules supreme: *II*.

The darkness gives way to a darkly lit corridor, faces obscured as if a crime is taking place, or as if the actors in this TV reality show (Cf. *COPS*, *Cheaters*, etc.) didn't want their identities divulged. This is everyman and everywoman, an anonymous Adam and Eve, the primordial mommy and daddy acting out a primal Oedipal scene for me. We are at the origin of the world of sexuated suffering, the sufferings of being sexed as a subject.

Seconds before this primal scene we see the dirt-streaked window of the soundstage house into which Justin Theroux will chase a voyeuristic interrupter of his and Dern's rehearsal of "On High in Blue Tomorrows," the film within *II*. We also see an eye peeking through this dirty window, yet it doesn't seem to be Dern, who will eventually turn out to be the voyeur Theroux chased until s/he "disappeared where it's real hard to disappear": behind a fake wall. Who, then, is watching? Her jealous husband, who subsequently sees her and Theroux betray him in distended DV images of the sex act? The child as voyeur vis-à-vis a primordial fantasy

---

[12] "Phallic *jouissance* is the obstacle through which man fails (*n'arrive pas*), so to speak, to enjoy the body of the woman, precisely because that which he enjoys is the *jouissance* of the organ" (*organe* refers to both the male and female genitals; see *Littré*) – that is, the idiocy of male orgasm as a non-enjoyment of the woman's body or as the misrecognition of feminine desire: "his entire realization of the sexual relation results in the fantasm"; Cf. Lacan's answer to the question "What is [...] phallic enjoyment" (*jouissance*)?: "nothing if not this, which the importance of masturbation in our practice underlines sufficiently, the *jouissance* of the idiot"; see Lacan, *Encore*, 13, 80, 75. Unless, that is, this sublime failure is supplemented by love: "We love only in response to the failure of the sexual relationship. As Lacan put it, 'What makes up for the sexual relationship is, quite precisely, love.' Lacan, *Seminar XX*, 45" (McGowan, "Lost on *Mulholland Drive*," 79n16). Yet for Lacan "That which supplements ("*supplée* [in the Derridean sense of supplements as well as substitutes for, or in relation to] "*au rapport sexual*") the sexual relation is precisely love" (Lacan, *Encore* 44). Fink's translation minimizes both Lacan's supplementation of Derrida as well as the risk that love can replace *jouissance* instead of merely making up for it, thereby plunging the relationship back into whoring, an adulterous *terrasse* where the other seems to offer what is lacking in love: *jouissance*.

of sexuality he or she will be unable to integrate into subjectivity, a sub-jectifiction whose dominance is based on his or her inability to process this phantasmic mystery? Who is there looking, incapable of escaping? "Polish Poem" intimates that this seeing will be forever ungratifiable:

> I sing this poem to you...
> On the other side I see.
> Shall you wait, glowing?
> It's far away, far away from me,
> I can see that
> [...]
> But no one comes
> No one comes
> Where are you?

We will return to the question of who is on the other side, watching, waiting, seeing what s/he desires, what will forever remain "far away, far away from me" suspended in the song's refrain: "Something is happening." S/he, unlike the whore watching TV, has no chance of redemption from the dead-end of heterosexuality: "No one comes."

And yet the john says that they are "at our room now" as if they were a married couple returning to the only hotel they could afford after a night on the town. Like a stereotypical couple one of them is confused as to who has the key and he helps dissipate her confusion by letting her know he has it. Yet this conjugal possibility is pushed aside when they enter the room and he commands her to disrobe, cruelly asking if "you know what whores do?". "Yes," she replies, "They fuck." We are far away from love. We are at the oldest place, or the origin of history, the place where every-thing begins with whoring, symbolic, economic and sexual exchange, or marriage without the promise, illusion or possibility of love.

Undecipherable images suggest a sex act as the woman repeats "I'm afraid." We immediately hear the immeasurable beauty of "Polish Poem." We then see the prostitute post-coitus, sitting on the edge of the bed seemingly mourning the *ratage* that is the sexual relation in the same room. The camera cuts away from her to the lamp in the corner, returning to a different woman with a thicker body shot in color, yet due to the obscured face it is impossible to be certain if it is not the same whore, nor can we be sure if what appeared to be a cheap trick might have been a (loving?) married couple acting out a cold and cruel role-playing game do-mesticated by a safe word. No matter. She (Karolina Gruszka) is suffering, crying and watching a television, which is now where the lamp was. TV eclipses simulated natural light, a hyper-simulation she stares at as if it will save her from her tearful knowledge of the impossibility of the sexual relation. The screen is initially white noise or visual static, giving way to a speeded-up image of the infamous web-only Lynch sit-com "The Rabbits," an image that is superseded by fastforwarded images of Grace Zabriskie confusedly approaching Laura Dern's door in what will be the beginning of the story of Nikki Grace, a star down on her luck and in need of box of-fice gold. Zabriskie's approach to the door is superimposed on the image of the lamp in the corner, now in color and even more simulacral as a result. Static returns as the lamp continues to burn. Both images ineluctably give way to those damned rabbits.

The whore sees the Rabbit family of mommy-daddy-me. The son frozen in place, fixated on the sofa by unacted Oedipal desires as Ma Rabbit irons like a good wife and Father returns from visiting his mistress or *meretrīx*. If it is not adultery, then some unutterable secret is eating at the family in this sit-com from hell. Father enters to applause as if this Oedipal sit-com were the "longest running radioplay in history" on the model of *Anti-Oedipus*'s critique of the West's imperial extension of its problems to the rest of humanity. Father sits down. He and the son blankly stare into the space where the familial TV should be. Only mother doesn't watch. Instead, she speaks: "I'm going to find out one day. When will you tell him?".

Father and son turn to look at each other as if about to exit the domesticated enjoyment communicated by the television, but instead of anyone telling anyone anything one of them says "Who could have known?", a non sequitur that evades the question. The audience shares this desire for evasion at any price, since the silence is broken when the mother's supplemental non sequitur – "What time is it?" – provokes a cacophony of canned laughter that nervously covers up what no one wants to broach. Father rises to say "I have a secret" and pauses as if about to utter it. The mother's additional non-statement – "There have been no calls today" – cuts, however, this possibility short by producing even more canned laughter. The rabbits then hear footsteps outside the door, another possibility of revelation that Ma Rabbit's nervous laughter interrupts as if she were complicit in the cover-up. She then contradicts herself by re-desiring revelation: "I do not think it will be much longer now" (a line that can only produce real laughter given we are only five minutes into this interminably traumatic film). Pa refuses to gratify her ambivalent wish for revelation and leaves the room to investigate the noises outside, expressing a similarly ambivalent desire to reveal the secret he wants to unsee by continuing to watch TV.

He enters an ornate room where a Polish Man (Krzysztof Majchrzak) is hardly holding his cool as he screams – demonic in distorted DV – to a calm, sitting Pole (Jan Hench) that "I look for an opening," which could mean a hole to sexually penetrate, or an opening beyond sex, a place where whoring is revealed as no more than a blocked escape hatch from Oedipal blockage. Pa Rabbit seems to think both thoughts for he turns away from this luxurious chamber, yet remains on the verge of returning to his rabbit hole. He is caught, like the son, in a double bind, wanting to find an opening through whoring while also wanting to avoid returning to the mother and her demand that he reveal the dirty little secret that they ambivalently collude to conceal as the sit-com plays on. No way out of Oedipus for the son as long as this revelation is unforthcoming, as long as whoring, a key instance of the adulterous desire pervading this film, isn't revealed as a false escape from Oedipus.

To traverse this phantasm would be to undo Oedipal blockage, but we are not there yet. It remains "far away from me," an ego as claustrophobically closed in upon itself as the wombal room within which the rabbits remain to repeat the blockage to the canned laughter of the audience that is us or a globalized U.S.A. It is literally canned because we also cannot escape. What would offer, one wonders, an escape from this American sitcom of the same? David Lynch is, let us not forget, a TV auteur (*Twin Peaks*), a relentlessly folksy personage (although he says he doesn't watch television) continually low-brow(s)ing his deification as the *ne plus ultra* of American auteurism. Note too, that *the* transatlantic American auteur, Stanley Kubrick, alludes to Seinfeld's apartment number (5A) via Tom and Nicole's apartment number (5A) in *Eyes Wide Shut*, a film that also over-exposed the adulterous Other Side of conjugal Oedipalization. Film, these auteurs tell us, is *depassé*. We seek transcendence through the screen. It was television that killed the dominance of the Hollywood studio system in the late fifties and early sixties and Oedipalized us all in the comfort of our own homes, a space where "The Wound Is Healed Only by the Spear That Smote You."[13] The television is, then, the model for all the screens that haunt our lives, the screened memory where Oedipus is born, still-born, half-borne, and yet unbearably real. The whore cries, overwhelmed by her entrapment in an idiot box promising a revelation that will never occur in real time.

"DAMN, THIS SOUNDS LIKE DIALOGUE FROM OUR SCRIPT!"

Father Rabbit is caught on the threshold as the screen fades to black, fading in to a sun-dappled tree shot from below on Nikki Grace's palatial Hollywood estate. Grace approaches the house, Grace Zabriskie, double for the other Grace, or the Grace who will annunciate the trauma Nikki is to undergo when she gets the part in a movie based on a German film, *47*, based, in turn, on a "Polish Gypsy folk tale," and cursed by the brutal murder of the male and female leads. Yet Dern is not the protagonist of this film. She is being seen by the character whose desire is at issue, the watching whore, the gaze that is ourselves as we seek redemption from the TV screen (in both senses of "from"). Dern's character, as we will see, does not exist. She is trapped in an inland empire, looking in, lost, wandering as errantly as the scopic drive she figures. She is to be exploited by the watching whore to achieve resolution even though Dern will not be able to resolve the Oedipal conflict that haunts the film.

Grace Zabriskie enunciates to LD (Laura Dern as a mirror image for DL or David Lynch) the crisis of sexuation that the film will fail to resolve for man or woman, DL or LD, I and I. She tells a tale of the different fates that await boys and girls lost in the labyrinth organized by Oedipal sexuality. First, she asks if the film is "about marriage" or about the adultery that hangs over marriage, as if marriage were a childish fantasy that can only resolve sexual trauma by failing to enforce the passage to adulthood, a failure that takes the adulterating form of adultery. Nikki prevaricates, although having read the script she knows it is about the adulteration of a marriage: "Ah, perhaps in some ways but...."

Her evasion is preempted by Zabriskie. "Your husband. He's involved?," to which Dern – playing the epitome of West Coast *faux* gentility, her hair a cascade of coiffured blonde alienation, a falsity belied by her occasional and then perpetual fall into a white trash Southern accent – politely replies "No." This "No" is another evasion, since the script

13 Slavoj Žižek, *Tarrying with the Negative: Kant, Hegel and the Critique of Ideology* (Duke: Duke University Press, 1993) 165-99.

will lead her to betray her husband in the arms of Theroux despite explicit warnings by her husband and Theroux's coterie that he is not to seduce Nikki. Zabriskie blows away the evasion by telling the story of sexuation: "A little boy went out to play. When he opened his door he saw the world. As he passed through the doorway he caused a reflection. Evil was born. Evil was born and followed the boy." "I'm sorry, what is that?" Dern asks, desiring, however, not to know. "An old tale," the other replies, emphasizing that the script Dern is hoping to act out is a primordial story:

> And the variation [not "a," but "the," as if no other option were available]. A little girl went out to play, lost in the marketplace, as if half born. Then not through the marketplace – you see that don't you? – but through the alley behind the marketplace. This is the way to the palace. But it isn't something you remember. Forgetfulness. It happens to us all. And me, why, I'm the worst one. Oh, where was I?

The impossibility of sexual difference plays out differently for each side as they fall away from the waywardness of infantile sexual play. The "little boy" sees the world, but due to the mirror stage cannot grasp it or himself. Instead the "I" can only seize a reflection representing his ego's desire for wholeness, a desire that invests the other, mother or any erect adult (the child, as we all know, after seeing himself standing tall in the mirror and recognizing this illusion as himself, ingloriously falls) as this whole.[14] He will endlessly search for an other to make him whole. His dissatisfaction with mother, wife and lover will impel him to pursue (or not pursue; i.e., repress – same difference) every image of sexual resolution in the endless procession of whores that is his fallen world. "Evil" is another name for this bordello, and it is born, not the boy. The man is stillborn, never emerging out of this blocked Oedipal situation (comedy). Insert canned laughter. To say "'I am'" is really to say "'I am haunted'":[15] "Evil was born and followed the boy." Since "follow" in French is *suivre*, a homonym for "to be" – "*Je suis*" = "*Je suis*"/"I am" = "I follow" – this "Evil" is my non-coincidence with myself, a constant haunting of myself as I besmear any appearance of wholeness (mother/wife/lover) with the possibility of another (whore): "Am I evil? yes I am./ Am I evil, I am man./ Am I evil? yes, I fucking am!."[16]

If the curse of male desire is to desire another, the curse of femininity is to be placed in this impossible position of the prostitute as the resolution to an Oedipal *cul de sac*, even though the figure of the whore perpetuates this Oedipalization in the hall of mirrors that is male sexuality. She falls out of the multiple positionality of childlike play into the marketplace, into her status as exchangeable object, both valued at market price

---

14 See Lacan, "The Mirror Stage as Formative of the Function of the I," *Écrits*, trans. Alan Sheridan (New York: W.W. Norton & Co., 1977) 1-7; as elaborated by Mikkel Borch-Jacobsen, *Lacan: The Absolute Master* (Stanford: Stanford University Press, 1991).

15 Jacques Derrida, *Specters of Marx*, trans. Peggy Kamuf (New York: Routledge, 1994) 133.

16 Metallica, "Am I Evil?" *Kill 'Em All* (1988 re-issue; a cover of a *Diamond Head* song on *Lightning to the Nations*, 1980). Heavy metal is, as *Lost Highway* and *Wild at Heart* record, a symptom of the male desire for obscene enjoyment: *Kill 'Em All*! Cf. the solution proffered by "Am I Evil" to the *échec* of the *ego sum*: "My face is long forgot, my face not my own./ Sweet and timely whore, take me home."

and interchangeable with any other woman. If she – this anonymous everywoman, her face unseen in a dimly lit corridor recalling the corridors where the sexuated sufferers of *L'Anneé dernière à Marienbad* (Alain Resnais, France, 1961) wander without end[17] – is lost in the primordial *souk*, there is at least a way out through the alleyway "behind the marketplace," or the alley Laura Dern occupies after buying groceries for Theroux, since there is, as she repeats during her transgressive sex-session with Theroux, always parking there. If the male is unborn through sexuation, afloat in the amniotic fluid of the Oedipal womb-prison, the female is at least half-born. The possibility of birth beckons, in other words, from the backdoor of the Axxon N stripclub – a gender-bending backdoor she finds behind the marketplace where she is doing his shopping like a good Stepford wife. Yet when she enters this in-between space after committing adultery with her co-star in a scene where each is unsure if they are themselves or the adulterous characters they are playing, the film slips into the truly delirious, higgledy-piggledy temporality that will be its destiny on the model of *L'Anneé dernière* and other modernist monuments. The resolution the crying whore finds in this modernist narrative via Dern will be exposed, as a result, as the evasion that it monumentalizes.

Infantile amnesia or "Forgetfulness" lets us forget the canned crisis of sexuality into which we are un- or half-born. It also leads Nikki, who, having read the story in which her character, Sue Blue, ends up dying on Hollywood boulevard, ought to know, to forget the brutal murder in her script. Yet the modality of this murderous *frisson* – death by screwdriver delivered by Theroux's wife (Julia Ormand) in revenge for Dern's act of adultery – should not let us forget that the ur-repressed of this film is not our occasional fall into murder, but the brutality of insensate copulation and its consequences.

Murder is one possibility among others. Screwing is the real problem, as in the scene where Theroux's wife, looking like a down-and-out Hollywood whore, shows the cop the screwdriver in her side, as if indicating the gnawing consciousness of marriage's underside – adultery – that will lead her to resolve the unresolvable by murdering a whore. "Is...is there a murder in your film?" Zabriskie asks, her voice quavering and quickening like a bird in a place where "there is always music in the air," a space of revelation in *Twin Peaks* reminiscent of her neighborly home "tucked back in the small woods," the same Inland Empire (a designation for the Northwestern territory surrounding Spokane, Washington) where the deadly wooded areas around Twin Peaks, Washington, lurk. This dark space is akin to that place where Theroux knows an Italian restaurant perfect for seducing other men's wives. "I bet you know a cute little Italian restaurant, tucked away" Dern says as she is about to give in to temptation. "I do" he says, parodying the marriage vow he loves to violate. "Is there a murder in your film?" Grace asks herself, caught, like the

---

[17] "Once again, I advance, once again along these corridors, traversing these salons, these galleries, in this edifice from another century, this immense, luxurious, baroque, lugubrious hotel, where interminable corridors lead to yet other corridors, silent, deserted, burdened with a cold and sombre décor of wood, stucco, molded marble panels, dark mirrors, darkly tinted paintings, columns...": *Il*; see Alain Robbe-Grillet, *L'Année Dernière à Marienbad* (Paris: Editions de Minuit, 1961) 22-23.

male, in the mirror stage feminine sexuality seems to escape. "Uh no, it's not part of the story." She lie! "No, I think you are wrong about that," Zabriskie parries: "No. Brutal fucking murder!." Nikki Grace cannot handle this language, this unconscious structured like a language that she must repress: "Uh, I don't like this kind of talk, the things you've been saying. I think you should go now." Yet no one can handle the occluded thing of *jouissance*, not even Zabriskie:

> Yes. Me, I can't seem to remember if it's today, two days from now, or yesterday. I suppose if it was 9:45, I'd think it was after midnight. For instance, if today was tomorrow, you wouldn't even remember that you owed on an unpaid bill. Actions do have consequences.

This incapacity to bear Oedipus and its consequences produces a flight into an aesthetic temporality, where today and tomorrow, past and present, LA and Łódź shuffle back and forth without respite. Some would like to merely enjoy this artwork, to live on postmodern (read: modernist) surfaces. Others might want to know what we are forgetting, since Nikki enters this atemporal world in earnest only after becoming adulterous and on her way to jubilantly recognizing herself as whore, a recognition that will not, however, allow her to escape a world where all the men are named John and all the women are denominated Magdalena. Zabriskie indicates the spot on the sofa where Nikki will be tomorrow when she gets the call that she got the role. Nikki's gaze follows the indicative finger as we skip forward in time to her getting the part. Her slippage into adultery begins.

From here on in until the lines that serve as a title for this section the action is relatively straightforward for a Lynch film. Dern and Theroux meet the director, Kingsley (Jeremy Irons), and his assistant, Freddy (Harry Dean Stanton), who embodies the being-in-debt of being sexuated. Stanton is constantly borrowing money to appease his aggressive landlord or superego, a debt others pay for him as they try to forget, like Dern, the "unpaid bill" owed to the irresolvable double bind of sexuality. Paying this superego is, however, not equivalent to confronting the impossibility of the sexual relation. Rather, it is a compensatory payment to keep it forgotten so as to maintain the fabricated cohesion of the ego. So too, to go with the flow of the modernist atemporal narrative is to want to forget traumatic fables of sexuation. The two actors appear on a talk show where their upcoming adultery is bantered about and soon find themselves on a soundstage rehearsing "On High in Blue Tomorrows" before Kingsley and Freddy. The rehearsal is interrupted by the footsteps the Rabbits heard, but when Theroux swaggers off to find the source of the sound he returns to report that the interloper "disappeared where it's real hard to disappear": behind the door of a soundstage facade. Theroux returns to have the director tell him and Dern that there is a curse on this film, a curse of murder (his and hers) that everyone pretends to treat lightly.

Filming continues. The plot involves Dern and Theroux having an affair, an affair that is soon acted out as Theroux, a notorious predator, Devon Berk, where ladies, leading or otherwise, are concerned, ignores all warnings and seduces Nikki. So too, Sue and Billy (Devon) hook up in "On

High in Blue Tomorrows," a moment in which Sue, voicing Nikki's fears that her husband (Peter J. Lucas) will find out and kill them both, falls out of role and feels the invasion of the camera into her adulterated sexuality. We then see Nikki and Devon copulating in a blue-lit room, interspersing their sexplay with lines from their roles as Sue and Billy. After they both orgasm, Nikki tells Devon to "Look at me." The camera cuts away. We find ourselves approaching the door of the bedroom where they are making love from the corridor. It is the point of view of her husband. We see his gaze peeking around the corner, witnessing his wife's betrayal.

Dern wants recognition from Theroux – "member I told you? About that thing, this thing that happened?" – and tells him "a story that happened yesterday, but I know it's tomorrow." To which Theroux logically responds "That doesn't make sense." An undeterred Dern continues: "It was that scene that we did yesterday. When I'm getting groceries for you with your car and it was in that alley. And I parked the car, there's always parking there. So there I am." At this point Theroux interjects, "What? Sue, damn," forgetting that she is Nikki and that they are not on camera.

Dern: It's a scene we did yesterday. You weren't in it. That one when I'm in the alley. I'm going to get groceries for you with your car. And I park there, cuz there's always parking. You know the one. And I see this writing on metal and I start remembering something. I'm remembering. I'm remembering and – Uh...Oh – this whole thing starts flooding in, this whole memory. I start to remember. I don't know what it is. It's me, Devon. It's me, Nikki
Theroux: That doesn't make any sense. What is this, Sue?
Dern: It's me, Devon. It's me, Nikki. Look at me, you fucker. Please, please, please hold me, look at me, please

When Nikki says "please," voicing a plea for recognition from a female suffering the non-recognition of a male idiot or "fucker," Devon starts to laugh, refusing to recognize her female desire, canning it in laughter, refusing this whole memory, this whole thing that starts flooding in. Fade to black. Fade in to the husband's point of view, retreating down a passageway reminiscent of the corridor in *Lost Highway* through which Bill Pullman passed to kill his apparently adulterous, or perhaps only sexually dissatisfied, wife. No murder here. Not yet.

LITTLE GIRL LOST

The next scene shows Dern shooting the scene behind the grocery store. She sees "writing on metal" – AXXoN N – stops, and enters a door, eventually coming into focus as the interloper at the rehearsal. "Somebody's over there" says the debt-ridden Stanton, as if embodying the father figure about to exceed superegoic repression of "This memory" that Dern has entered. Dern retreats behind the stageset door, except now it is a pink room in a house existing in a no-place behind false walls: the non-space of the screen. She is a character come to life in nothingness, yet for whose benefit? Theroux is on the Other Side. He is looking for her. She is screaming his name, but he cannot hear. And she too is on the Other Side, making a movie with him in spite of being lost to the world. We see the dirty window we saw at the beginning. On the other side is a suburban front yard. Dern soon finds the room she screwed Theroux in, her husband inviting her to bed, and a room of painted women. From here on in the film gets screwy and the only constant is whoring: in Poland, Hollywood or nowhere, a world of pimps, beatings and sex worker "Locomotion." "Who are you?" Dern asks the prostitutes. She will recognize that they are she, yet at what price? Dern and two working girls find themselves in an Old World cityscape. "This is the street," one says. "Do you want to see?" asks the other. The gramophone is seen again as is the crying whore as Dern is instructed to burn a hole through silk in order to see, from above, the street of ill repute.

Dern now inhabits the stageset home. She is a housewife who burns holes in silk looking for an opening. She sees the demonic Polish man from the beginning beating a sex worker and a mustached Polish man leaving his wife as she insists that she is barren and that he will never have the other woman. He waits on the street for the other and tells a passer-by it is 9:45. We see that he is seen on a TV screen by the spectating whore. Dern is then back in the room with the working girls. "I'm pregnant" she tells her husband and calls the Rabbits asking for "Billy?." Insert vicious canned laughter. She asks two prostitutes for recognition: "Look at me and tell me if you've known me before" We see the crying whore in the screen she is watching, wishing to "cast out this wicked dream." She does so by killing or having the other woman killed in an effort to be done with "Evil" or the male adulteration of marriage. To go on with a synopsis would be pointless, yet it is clear whose desire is involved. The crying whore is imagining a variety of scenarios that will allow her to attain resolution. A modernist cinematic temporality emerges here as the key to Oedipus, a key announced by Zabriskie's "Where was I?," as if this atemporal aesthetic were the solution to the sexuation of little boys and girls "lost in the marketplace."

On the one hand, the spectating whore betrays her impotent husband, telling him via Dern – a stand-in for the vicarious figure of the Hollywood star – that she is pregnant; i.e., that she has cheated on him. He beats her in response. On the other hand, she is betrayed by her adulterous husband, she is a woman, who, like Doris Side (Ormond), the wife of Billy Side (Theroux), kills the betrayer from the "Other Side" (Dern), or has her husband killed as Naomi Watts wants to have (or has had) her lover, Laura Harring, killed as punishment both for Laura's whoring herself out to Hollywood and for betraying lesbian love in *Mulholland Drive*. Yet who she really wants killed is the Phantom/Krimp (Krzysztof Majchrzak), the suburban Dern's neighbor, who Dern is impelled to confront by a second visitor (Mary Steenburgen), but cannot, despite finding a screwdriver ready-to-hand, kill. The Phantom is the prototypical obscene father of enjoyment, the pimp of all the whores, the father who enjoys them all, beats them senseless and kills them dead. He must, as far as the crying whore is concerned, be destroyed.

At one point we see the multiple husband character, Peter J. Lucas, looking for the Phantom, looking to kill him so the lachrymose prostitute can achieve closure. Later we see him in a room of old Polish men, one of whom informs him that the crying sex worker has sent for him so he can be given a gun with which to kill the Phantom. Yet she disappears once he takes on this mission, as if to telegraph that feminine subjectivity is eclipsed by the phallic assertion of the male side, or, sexually speaking, that the phantasmic *jouissance* of a one-sided male orgasm (bang bang!) annihilates the possibility of female recognition either by the male or by herself. Instead, we see Dern wandering labyrinthine corridors of consciousness, looking for the Phantom, gun in hand. He appears. She shoots him repeatedly, yet he seems bulletproof, until we see the horrifying image of her screaming (twice), and all seems (finally!) to be well. The prostitutes are freed from the pink room and run exuberantly through the corridors. So too, the crying whore escapes interminable mourning and, after winding through the byways Dern conquered for her, finds, in a scene reminiscent of Isabella Rossellini's reunion with her child at the close of *Blue Velvet*, her husband, illegitimate son and forgiveness for her infidelity – that is, for her transgression of the proper Hollywood ideology of marriage negatively embodied by Ingrid Bergman.

Dern enables her to achieve this resolution by entering the womb of mourning and giving her half-birth via a momentary kiss. The kiss affirms a lesbian way out of the impossibility of the male-female sexual relation (a way shown to be similarly impossible in *Mulholland Drive*), yet at the price of Dern's disappearance. The kiss is apotropaic, warding off the threat to the heterosexual *ratage*[18] posed by lesbianism even as it enables the heterosexual resolution to exorcise the murdered father (Rossellini's dead husband) troubling *Blue Velvet*, a resolution that also magically undoes the violence Hollywood imposes on actresses like the one played by Watts in *Mulholland Drive* or the ones eternally memorialized by Rita Hayworth (Harring calls herself Rita) and by Bergman in *Blue Velvet*. Where, however, does Dern disappear to? Zabriskie returns as the film proper ends, gesturing with her eyes to that no-place where Dern was when she gleefully got the part in the whore's resolutive TV show at the beginning of the film, except now she turns to see herself alone, looking like a beatific Hollywood star, custom-made to be used, abused, and murdered like a whore. Why? To solve the heterosexual impasse for the benefit of another: the whore, the viewer, you (I) or I (me). All through this resolution we hear "Polish Poem," sounding even more beautiful after all the trauma, apotropaically warding off the "Other Side" where we all remain. "It's only a movie, Ingrid" (Alfred J. Hitchcock).

THE OTHER SIDE OF THE "OTHER SIDE"
What is eclipsed by this resolution? Dern. She remains on the Other Side, longing for an impossible solution she can never possess, as is heard when she calls the Rabbit room (Room 47, the cruelest curse of all) looking for Billy, or an adulterous supplement to the dead-end of heterosexual romance. Later she will be unable to enter the room. She wants to confront the Oedipal double bind where marriage is irresolutive and the counter-solution to marriage – whoring – only increases the impossibility of resolving the sexual mis-relation. To enter Room 47 would be to die as socially constructed "Man" and "Woman," DL or LD, I & I, as is witnessed

---

[18] "This screw-up (*ratage*) is the only form of realization for this relation," – that is, "the male way of screwing up (*rater*) the sexual relation," "if, as I posit, suppose or pose it (*comme je le pose*), there is no sexual relation"; see Lacan, *Encore*, 54.

by the curse that the original protagonists of the film *47* were killed during shooting. In being incapable of crossing this threshold, she remains on the Other Side, looking in through the dirty window. It is there that we see her in the final image of the film proper, questioning the eagerness of our gaze – yes, you, the non-existent hungry eye – querying why we treat actresses like whores in the interests of closure.

The film is over. Blackness lasts for a long time. We then see the one-legged woman mentioned in Laura Dern's confession, a murderer in that story, but now a gazing face, radiant with wonder, telling us how "sweet" the familiar O so Lynchian red-curtained room is. The bedeviling beat of "Sinnerman" kicks in. We see Laura Harring blow a kiss to her double, Dern, utopically resurrecting the impossibility of lesbian love in this no-place outside the diegetic interminablity of the film proper, an interminability signifying the dead-end of Oedipal blockage. "Where am I?" Dern mockingly cried in-between saying "I'm a whore" and "I'm a freak" earlier in the film. Is the modernist displacement of space, time and subjectivity – "Oh, where was I?...I can't seem to remember if it's today, two days from now, or yesterday" – mocked as an aestheticized escape from being a whorish line of flight from Oedipus for the adulterous john, a freakish female sublimation of Oedipal shame, or an adulterating (adult-rated) sex worker? Is being an adult no more than being legally able to consume pornography, prostitutes, strippers and the alcohol that fuels these global industries, or is this adulterated adulthood simply a labyrinthine evasion of the Oedipal state of being half-born, unborn or over-determined by a Rabbit hole, a Room 47 which we cannot enter, yet which continues to work our woes (and not allow us to work through them)? Either acting out an Oedipal freak or its prostituted double. No way out, hence the need for a utopic coda.

"Sinnerman" is a traditional song calling on the sinner to repent, to confess as Dern did for the blank gaze of her interlocutor – that is, for us in the service of our desire to be free from trauma. Yet here "Sinnerman" celebrates freedom from repression. The whores have been liberated from sex slavery. They revel and shimmy with total abandon. Well, not total abandon, for they are pushed into the background by a group of bare-footed black or biracial dancers, who groove with stereotypical abandon as the lead girl lip-synchs Simone's throaty growl. A male lumberjack saws endlessly at a log, while Herring holds the hand of another lumber-jacked or stereotypically masculine male. Lynch holds to the possibility that heterosexual resolution is possible (he married Emily Stofle, one of the actresses playing a whore in *II*, as if compensating for his failure to marry his former girlfriend, Isabella Rossellini) even as the non-confrontation with this impossibility is reiterated by the "patient log-man" forever sawing at a phallus he cannot cut through.[19] By making the black or biracial dancers barefoot in comparison to the elaborate "fuck-me" boot

---

[19] I am citing Ferdinand's reference to his coercion into suppressing his sexuality (or "log") through masculinized rites of labor (cutting and carrying wood), courtship and romance to win the hand of Miranda, a system of rites organized by the patriarch Prospero to extirpate *jouissance*. See William Shakespeare, *The Tempest*, ed. Stephen Orgel (New York: Oxford University Press, 1987) 3.i.66-67: "and for your sake/ Am I this patient log-man." If *The Tempest*, whose patriarch refuses to enjoy, ends with a marriage, in the inland empire haunted by the impossible phantom of the obscene father figure the sawing never stops. "Am I" evil?

and stripper heels of the "white" whores, Lynch falls into the most cliched evocation of racial difference possible, a whoring out of black girls to resolve the unreconstructed trauma of American racial politics.

In the background we see Dern's actual husband, Ben Harper, a biracial man born in the Inland Empire (a Southeastern territory in California consisting of the counties of Riverside and San Bernardino). Yet this Inland Empire, like its Northwestern double (Lynch refers to both in an interview, thrilling to a New Age coincidence that gave half-birth to a film he cannot understand),[20] is a space historically fraught with racial conflict, between Native Americans and whites, black soldiers and non-black laborers in the latter case, and between picket-fence dwelling suburbanites (white or not, "white" in either case) and the disruptions introduced by Latino/a immigrants as well as by African-American and Latino/a gangs in the other.[21] It is the epitome of race blindness to champion the interracial marriage of Harper and Dern, subject, like all Hollywood marriages to the threat of lesbianism, adultery, whoring and other mirror images of the "Evil" of male sexuality and its doubles, via a song sung by a woman who left America in disgust over racial subjugation and its perpetuation, in her eyes, by inter-racial alliances.[22] To use Harper and Dern to solve this problem is to whore them out. For whose benefit? For a viewer who remains on the other side, waiting, wanting, not-exi(s)ting.

In the same interview where Simone attacks racial mixing, she also pities Michael Jackson for his desire to be white. What a horror when a race traitor becomes a national, an African-American and a global hero. What is wrong with America and its Hollywood colonies? See *ll* and you will fail to see. Just as Rebekah del Rio lip-synchs "Crying" in Spanish in *Mulholland Drive*, so too, the final image of the black or biracial girl joyfully minstrelizing "Sinnerman" exemplifies the usage of the other to solve my "white" problems. "Who ain't a whore?" might be, then, my inconclusive conclusion. At least we have an inkling of why whoring is such a global metaphor. How this all relates to the post-racial problematic codenamed Obama is beyond the scope of this writing.

[20] See the "Guardian interview at the National Film Theatre with David Lynch" on the Two Disc Special Edition of *ll*.

[21] See Katherine G. Morrissey, *Mental Territories: Mapping the Inland Empire* (Ithaca: Cornell University Press, 1997) vis-à-vis the Northwest *ll*; in regard to the West Coast *ll*, see Michal Kohout, "Immigration Politics in California's Inland Empire." *Yearbook of the Association of Pacific Coast Geographers* (71) 2009 120-43; and Will Matthews, "Roots of Youth Violence: Gangs date back to Inland Empire's Citrus Days." *San Bernardino Country Sun* (2004-09-26), http://lang. sbsun.som /socal.gangs/articles/ivdbp1_main.asp (accessed October 17, 2009). This Other Side of America's Inland Empires is communicated by must-see TV shows (*The Sopranos, Desperate Housewives, Weeds*) even as the unseeing continues. In regard to the rise of hate crime in the *ll*, see David Holthouse, "California Conflict." *Intelligence Report* (Southern Poverty Law Center) http://www.splcenter.org/intel/intelreport/article.jsp?pid=956 (accessed October 19, 2009).

[22] Nina Simone, "You Al Capone, I'm Nina Simone: Interview with Alison Powell," *Interview* (January 1997) *Nina Simone Web* http://www.boscarol.com/nina/html/manual/interview/ interview.html (accessed October 17, 2009).

REBECCA ANNE BARR
THE GOTHIC IN DAVID LYNCH: PHANTASMAGORIA & ABJECTION

When you sleep, you don't control your dream. I like to dive into a dream world that I've made, a world I chose and that I have complete control over.[1]

The more darkness you can gather up, the more light you can see too.[2]

Darkness and the nocturnal freedoms of the self in dream are recurrent Lynchian tropes, part of the thematic and visual chiaroscuro of "New American Gothic" literature and film. As Michel Chion has noted, Lynch's visual work may reflect his interest in romanticism but is better described as "Gothic" in its combination of "the grotesque and the terrifying, the supernatural and familiar."[3] Lynch's films have frequently been identified as Gothic both in subject matter and aesthetics. The picket-fence idyll of a timeless American dream is menaced by violence and physical and sexual aberrancy. Not merely do Lynch's films flood white Middle America with anarchic and irrational brutality, but they portray it as "infested with psychic and social decay, and colored with the heightened hues of putrescence. Violence, rape and breakdown are the key motifs."[4] Such extremist aesthetics can be seen from *Twin Peaks* (1990-91) to *Mulholland Drive* (2001). This amenability to the Gothic can be seen in the way in which *Twin Peaks* became a paradigm for late twentieth-century postmodern culture, heralding a burgeoning in "Television Gothic."[5] Lynch's "Gothic" tendencies therefore seem clear: the dark, dramatic *mise en scene* of his cinematography; his interest in the violent and taboo forms of human behavior; the psychoanalytic structure of his narratives in which hidden and repressed desires are made horribly manifest.

Yet it is not merely Lynch's utilization of recognizable formulae that makes the Gothic crucial to an understanding of his work. Gothic is not solely a model but an artistic disposition; a set of aesthetic conceptions. Its status as a flexible and responsive mode, rather than a genre *per se*, provides a means of comprehending key concerns and cinematographic style in Lynch's corpus as a whole. Gothic's insistent rupture of system-

[1] David Lynch, *Lynch on Lynch* (London: Faber and Faber, 1977) 15.
[2] Lynch, *Lynch*, 23.
[3] Michel Chion, *Audio-Vision: Sound on Screen*, ed. and trans. Claudia Gorbman (New York: Columbia University Press, 1994) 159.
[4] David Punter, *The Literature of Terror: The Gothic Tradition*, vol.1 (London: Longman, 1980) 3.
[5] Lenora Ledwon, "'Twin Peaks' and the Television Gothic," *Literature-Film Quarterly* 21:4 (October 1993): 260.

atic knowledge by unreason, the repressed, and the abject provides a paradoxically coherent framework for Lynchian film. I will argue that the most compelling motivation for Gothic's importance in Lynch's work is its opposition to naturalist aesthetics and its refutation of realism. From *Blue Velvet* (1986) to *Mulholland Drive* and *Inland Empire* (2006), I will link Lynch's interest in Gothic tropes to his anti-realist aesthetics. Lynch's Gothic heroines crystallize his interest in the fictiveness or artificiality of cinema as a form. As an analytic tool and category the Gothic enables a reassessment of these films and their female characters in particular. Gothic's fascination with femininity and gender here illuminates Lynch's work, countering the persistent charges of misogyny made against his films. I show how Lynch's Gothic women are indicative not only of the self-conscious artificiality of his form, but are celebrated as such: these are not naturalistic "women" but celluloid phantasmagoria. Moving from the representation of Dorothy Vallens to his later heroines, I show how Lynch represents a specifically female abjection as salvaging and even redeeming damaged post-Reaganite society. The Gothic, therefore, is crucial as an ideological diagnostic as well as an identifiable schema of tropes, concerns and dispositions. As such it offers us a means of comprehending the willful perversion of quotidian meaning in Lynch's work, its stylized and stylish incomprehensibility. Gothic's repudiation of realism allows us to contextualize these films' unreason without neutralizing their affective power.

GOTHIC GENEALOGY, FROM RADCLIFFE TO *TWIN PEAKS*

As a genre, Gothic derives historically from the literature of late-eighteenth century Europe. The Gothic was a commercial "rage,"[6] a cultural reaction to the political and social upheavals of the French Revolution, industrialization and the dominance of enlightenment reason. In contrast to the Augustan reason, order and decency that had set the standard for respectable literature, the gothic novel fuelled the reading public's insatiable appetite for scurrilous and extremist literature. Popular novels, poetry and plays concerned with dark, tempestuous romance and set in exotic locations or the imagined past saturated the market. Characterized by superstition, supernatural occurrences and the externalization of psychological or subjective states, these works aimed at the production of horror, terror and extreme emotion in their readers. Gothic literature rehearsed certain key themes such as the double or doppelganger; supernatural or ghostly visitations; villainous fathers or husbands; transgressive desires and actions. Its plots often featured the persecution or terrorization of innocents, frequently at the hands of corrupt paternal power, and the victimization of female characters. Metaphorizing the bloody turmoil of revolutionary France and the political instability of England and its colonies, the Gothic served as a talking cure for the taboo of the eighteenth and nineteenth-centuries. Yet the tropes and subject matter of early Gothic are clearly recognizable in modern and postmodern manifestations and permutations, even as those originals have been transformed. The Gothic craze begun by Horace Walpole's *Castle of Otranto* in 1764 has

[6] Rictor Norton, *Gothic Readings: The First Wave, 1764-1840* (London: Leicester University Press, 2000) vii.

transformed from a disreputable genre to what is perhaps the pervasive mode of the late twentieth and early twenty-first century. The fascination of the ghostly, the unknown, the taboo, and the stimulation of extreme states of emotion or response are all marks of contemporary cinema and televisual culture. Once a derided literary and artistic mode is now a primary constituent of mainstream culture, as seen in the proliferation of series such as *True Blood*, *American Gothic*, *The X Files* and numerous feature length films. Contemporary American culture is in many ways fundamentally Gothic; dark, haunted by violence and transgression, self-reflexive, metaphorizing its discontents through popular media and the discourses of pop psychology. Modern Gothic represents otherness, in monstrous forms that require control or exclusion, and sympathy as an exception. For Jerrold Hogle modernity "thus constitutes and polices its boundaries on the basis of the exceptions, the others or monsters it excludes: workers, women, deviants, criminals... are produced as the antitheses fantasmatically and ideologically establishing modern norms of bourgeois rationality."

Gothic is not merely a formula. Resurrecting the irrationality that Enlightenment reason and empirical science had denigrated and excluded, the Gothic has its roots in the political and cultural reactions of romanticism. The Gothic is therefore inherently revisionist, oppositional in origin. It is part of a cultural dialectic, which raises the specters of uncontrollable passion in order to question and destabilize notions of the civilized, the orderly and coherent. Its representations of horror and fear act as simulacra of historical and social repression. From the outset, then, Gothic, is intimately concerned with power and the exercise of power on the individual subject. David Punter argues that Gothic writing and art revolves around the "dialectic of power and impotence."[7] Its "concern with paranoia, with barbarism, and with taboo" provides the vital animus of Gothic fiction; it is "these are the aspects of the terrifying to which Gothic continually, and hauntedly, returns."[8] Nor is the Gothic reducible to its components. Eve Kosofsky Sedgwick and David Punter, among several, have suggested, that the Gothic is a plurality of recognizable literary or formal codes. For Sedgwick Gothic provides a set of converging or associated set of themes negotiated by different verbal / non-verbal conventions. In a supplemental fashion Punter sees the radical discontinuities of Gothic literature as exposing and highlighting the fragmentation of the individual subject, opening up ruptures *as problems* rather than hermetically sealing them in an autonomous art form. But as Robert Miles has convincingly argued, the generic flexibility and thematic obsessions of Gothic works actively problematize the deployment of accurate critical tools: the focus on subjectivity threatening to dehistoricize a heterogeneous multiplicity of works. Miles' Foucauldian genealogy enables a historically embedded theory of influence, revision and intertextuality whilst allowing for the further complication of the shift from text-based Gothic to a film Gothic.

---

[7] David Punter, *The Literature of Terror: The Modern Gothic*, vol. 2 (London: Longman, 1996) 184.

[8] Punter, *The Literature of Terror: The Modern Gothic*, 184.

Lynch's *Twin Peaks* series is undoubtedly responsible for the infiltration of mainstream culture by Gothic tendencies, effectively normalizing the abnormal. Writing on the cult of *Twin Peaks* and its overwhelming and unprecedented popularity, Lenora Ledwon identifies Lynch's "new Television Gothic" as one that produces "familiar Gothic themes and devices such as incest, the grotesque, repetition, interpolated narration, haunted settings, mirrors, doubles, and supernatural occurrences."[9] The claustrophobic Palmer household is a quintessentially Gothic construct, with its overbearing, sexually abusive father and the dominated but vital young woman. Transposing the Gothic from its exotic, often Continental, old world locale, Lynch intensifies its effects by refusing the displacement found in pre-Victorian Gothic in which taboo or repressed subjects are negotiated through an apparent alterity. Andreas Blassman has called the series a "Gothic soap opera" and *Twin Peaks'* hybrid of domestic, relational drama and uncanny, malevolent archetypes re-charted the acceptable generic conventions for both TV and film. Yet whilst Hartman and Ledwon's identification of Gothic motifs is certainly utile and indeed valid, their insistence on thematic continuity obscures a fundamental aspect of the Gothic as a sophisticated *discourse*. If Gothic's energy derives from the "relentless exposure of the paucity and deception of traditional criteria of realism"[10] its discourse is one that seeks to expose conventional visual form, to expose and de-authenticate moral, social, and formal archetypes that have been naturalized as accurate representations of reality. Lynch attempts this via a sophisticated and dizzying countermanding of the components of the Hollywood machine.

Therefore, his explicit Gothic themes and motifs are inextricable from controlled cinematic artifice, his dark materials of celluloid and fantasy. For Lynch, TV and films are stage-managed dreams; a haunted territory whose revenants are disturbingly self-conscious. Indeed, David Foster Wallace describes "Lynchian" as "particular kind of irony where the very macabre and the very mundane combine in such a way as to reveal the former's perpetual containment within the latter."[11] Though it is debatable whether the macabre is "contained" by the mundane, Lynch's films certainly posit a relationship between the two. The irony that structures Lynch's films is part of a very Gothic paradox in which self-reflexivity generates humor as much as darkness: it depends upon gathering darkness to make sense of the light. Yet the morbid comedy of Gothic co-exists with its channeling of the subconscious, though "much of its content streams forth from the unconscious, but is carefully channeled by the hyperconscious."[12] Here the Gothic can be seen to approach self-parody in its tendency toward excess. Both *Twin Peaks* and *Blue Velvet* solicit the archetypes of wholesome 1950s America, creating a form of nostalgic atemporality populated by clichés exaggerated to grotesquery. Lynch excels at a form of Middle American kitsch – picket fences and manicured lawns, coffee and pie, good-girl, cheerleader chic of Sandy and Laura Palmer, the earnest decency of Jeffrey Beaumont and Agent Dale Cooper

[9] Ledwon, "'Twin Peaks' and the Television Gothic," 260.
[10] Punter, *Literature of Terror 2*, 143.
[11] David Foster Wallace, "David Lynch Keeps his Head," *A Supposedly Fun Things I Will Never Do Again* (London: Abacus, 2009) 161.
[12] Norton, *Gothic Readings*, xii.

all recognizable tropes. Yet, as in the Gothic Novel of the eighteenth-century, nostalgia is a means of negotiating generic and existential crisis. Lynch's films are not set in the present but they nonetheless conjure archaism. This nostalgia is a variation on what Susan Stewart calls "distressed genres,"[13] works that invent their own "temporal grounds" in order "to conceive of its own context as being encapsulated within the form of representation."[14] Lynch's retro-land is an eternal present whose terms are not temporal but imagistic, imaginary, and purely artificial. Its context is cinema, artificiality: a phantasmagoria corresponding to subjective desires and fears rather than a correspondent objective reality. The Gothic obsessively reworks older forms, layering interpretation and metatextual narrative into a dizzying fabrication. In this way Lynch's films are part of a Gothic discourse that presents the instability of contemporaneity through the formal appropriation and détournment of golden age Hollywood.

Viewing Gothic as a primarily self-reflexive and artificial form allows us allows us to reconsider Lynch's cinematic style and content. In her discussion of the uncanny in *Blue Velvet* Laura Mulvey notes the film's clear binary oppositions, topographical as well as psychoanalytic, commenting that "the specific formal properties of cinema"[15] play a central role in structuring connections, resonances and the plot itself. Mulvey's reading locates the cinema itself as a locus for the symbolic rendering of the unconscious. In this way, the dark, undulating material of the opening credits conjures not only sensual pleasures and linking to its use as a sexual prop within the film, but it also recalls the veil that covers both the theatrical stage and that of the cinema screen. The veil itself has a Gothic genealogy. Ann Radcliffe's *Mysteries of Udolpho* contains a "black veil" appearing to conceal a painting. Presumed by the heroine to cover a representation, a picture – a mimetic likeness – it inspires fascinated curiosity and horror. Momentarily brave, Emily lifts it to see beneath and perceiving that what concealed "was no picture,"[16] falls away in a faint. In Radcliffe's novel terror stems from the idea that if what is hidden is *not* a representation, then it must be a "real" body. Terror stems from the possibility that what lies beneath the veil of representation is the horror of the "real." Jeffrey Beaumont's love of mysteries in *Blue Velvet* and his desire to "see something that was always hidden" may seem to recall Radcliffe's dispelling of supernaturalism through empirical reason, but what Jeffrey sees is fundamentally staged, artificial. Dorothy Vallens is woman as masquerade: a consistent spectacle, a self-conscious role within the visual economy. The much-analyzed close of *Blue Velvet* is most convincing as a Gothic parody. The anti-naturalistic appearance of Sandy's dream robins at the close of the film signals the form's inherent artificiality, its status as contrivance and entertainment. It is the reinstatement of its context as aesthetic. The robins are as un-nerving a corrective to the happy ending as a dark or Gothic resolution. As Steven Dillon has noted, Lynch's directorial habits repeatedly display ideological

[13] Susan Stewart, *Crimes of Writing: Problems in the Containment of Representation* (Oxford: Oxford University Press, 1991) 66.
[14] Stewart, *Crimes of Writing*, 73.
[15] Laura Mulvey, *Fetishism and Curiosity* (London: British Film Institute, 1996) 152.
[16] Ann Radcliffe, *Udolpho* (London: J. Limbird, 1826) 197.

and stylistic affectation: "Lynchian weirdness appears theatrically, not naturalistically."[17] Again, Dillon echoes Lynch's own description of the film as a "dream world" controlled by the director. This is not a simple subconscious mode used to represent inchoate emotions, but "the staged quality of the dream."[18] The film concludes by refusing realism and reinstating fantasy. Whilst Radcliffe seeks to dispel her heroine's horror by revealing what lies behind the black veil to be no more than a wax model, Lynch opens *and* closes *Blue Velvet* with the soft ripples of the curtain. The veil remains, the robins sing.

Twin Peaks excavates the constructed nature of reality through a hyper-artificial and stylized exploration of images. Like *Blue Velvet*, *Twin Peaks* refutes the constraints of realism, transforming what is ostensibly an investigation into something approaching paranormal transcendentalism. *Twin Peaks* displays a Gothic mistrust of objective sensory data as a reliable source of knowledge about the world, as seen in Cooper's intuitive readings and Log Lady's spiritualist messages. In its privileging of subjective, often prophetic or intuitive forms of knowledge, *Twin Peaks* implies that realist cinematography is not merely inadequate but misleading. Instead, Lynch at every turn reminds the audience that his work is phantasmagoria, illusion and artifice. If one is to perceive the truth the screen must foster a radical mistrust in its audience; a dark misgiving over the images presented to them. Critical disappointment and anger at *Twin Peaks: Fire Walk With Me* was in part a response to its Gothic rewriting of *Twin Peaks* rather than a conventional prequel. The characters of *Twin Peaks* are themselves "incoherent, fissured, interrupted, multiple and self-critical,"[19] unfamiliar even to themselves. The scene at the Bang Bang Bar is an instance of Lynch substituting images for objective knowledge. The disorienting aural onslaught overpowers verbal audibility. As the music plays, Laura Palmer discusses Theresa Banks' death, her words impossible to hear under the pulsations of the music; the scene shot in blood red, the corpuscles of the screen itself seeming to throb with lurid desire. Lynch makes the film a process to be undergone rather than analyzed. This is not our dream, and we have no power to request clarification. Lynch risks our alienation in order to achieve our awareness, the striving of the viewer who attempts to piece together background noise, music, the voice beneath the image. Though understanding is refused, the harsh discordance of this scene is intensified by a radical lack of anything to hold it together other than the screen and the viewing subject. The horror here is in the breaking apart of the traditional unity of image and what Chion calls "visualized sound."[20] Here the Gothic affect is directly reliant on the fragmentation of our senses: it is our subjective look that remains as traditional screen co-ordinates de-cohere. This elevation of subjective agency seems like a version of the sublime – the reactivation of mental energy in the face of aesthetic power. Indeed Martha Nochimson's romantic description of the gaze in Lynch is couched in the self-same discourse:

[17] Steven Dillon, *The Solaris Effect: Art and Artifice in Contemporary American Film* (Austin: University of Texas Press, 2006) 88.

[18] Dillon, *The Solaris Effect*, 88.

[19] Peter Wollen, "Godard and Counter Cinema: *Vent d'Est*," *Narrative, Apparatus, Ideology: A Film Theory Reader*, ed. Philip Rosen. (New York: Colombia University Press, 1986) 122.

[20] Michel Chion, *Audio-Vision*, 101.

"Longing to see... ceases to depend on human control and moves toward involuntary transportation beyond ordinary limits into a Lynchian contact between logic and the subconscious."[21]

Yet the sublime, of any form, is not unambiguously positive: in essence it is a transaction of power that involves subjection to the screen image, and a relinquishing of agency that is in itself problematic and liable to resistance. This can be seen in the representation of Laura Palmer at the close of *Twin Peaks: Fire Walk with Me*, where the broken and abused schoolgirl is subjected to pursuit and battery by the predator now revealed as her Father. At the moment of death, Laura's companion receives exculpation by an angelic figure from the picture on Laura's wall. Laura herself is transformed into a heavenly creature: purged of material grossness she achieves a form of religious apotheosis, shining, other-dimensional. This foreshadows her iconic representation throughout the *Twin Peaks* series where her silent corpse garners the allure of a frozen Madonna. Such anti-realism oscillates between morally queasy specular pleasures and the offer of pure escapism, the spectator of Lynchian film is radically compromised and profoundly self-conscious. There is no supremely powerful point of view; whilst certain characters are given preeminence, this is often undermined and problematized by a radically non-individuated camera gaze – mobile, yet non-editorial, non-narrative, almost detached. Emma Clery has argued that the Gothic mobilized the sublime as a "solution to the defects of a commercial society" (104), its re-affirmation of the individual subject proving a bulwark against the alienating effects of capitalism. In contrast, the Lynchian Gothic sublime leaves us bewildered, impotent – aware of its status as *ex machina*. The viewing subject is left with a sense of the inadequacy of comprehension: the dramatic residue of pessimism.

FEMALE GOTHIC AND THE ABJECT

From its very origins Gothic has been associated with problems and explorations of gender and power. This raises questions as to whether Gothic is "possessed by or possessive of women...[whether there is an] intrinsic link between femininity and the Gothic imagination...because Gothic imagination is peopled by women."[22] The centrality of women in eighteenth-century Gothic literature can be seen in how its focus is often on "corruption in, or resistance to, the patriarchal structures that shaped the country's political life or its family life."[23] As is clear, Lynch's cinematic fascination with women places them at the heart of his Gothic aesthetic: as objects whose performative qualities exemplify the tension between depth and surface, nature and artificiality, and as subjects whose emotions, fears and perceptions generate the atmosphere and structure of his dreamlike films.

Lynch's experimentation with the subject-object relationship is undertaken primarily through the prism of female characters. Moers argues that

---

[21] Martha P. Nochimson, *The Passion of David Lynch: Wild at Heart in Hollywood* (Austin: University of Texas Press, 1997) 78.

[22] David Punter, "Death, Femininity and Identification: A Recourse to Ligeia," *Gothic: Critical Concepts in Literary and Cultural Studies*, ed. F. Botting and D. Townshend (London: Routlegde, 2004) 156.

[23] Donna Heiland, *Gothic and Gender: An Introduction* (Oxford: Blackwell, 2004) 5.

historically "female Gothic" views women from a woman's perspective, but more importantly gives *"visual* form to the fear of self."[24] The terror evinced by the veil in *The Mysteries of Udolpho* is paradigmatic of this type of Gothic: focused in the scopic drive, the fear produced in female Gothic is founded on the indescribable, a fear which terrifies and compels. Unlike the "Terror-Gothic" found in Lewis's *The Monk*, or contemporary horror films, "the female Gothic depends as much on longing and desire as on fear and antagonism."[25] The strangely seductive menace of his films relies on the creation of "female Gothic," one in which erotic obsession is produced in tandem with a profoundly disquieting fear. In *Blue Velvet* Dorothy Vallens' role is as sexual fetish: male desire triangulated around her person. Yet Lynch includes the polar opposite to Jeffrey's voyeuristic complicity in her sexual perversion by including Sandy's revulsion. When Dorothy appears toward the film's end, battered, naked and desperately declaring her love to Jeffrey, Sandy's disgust is clear – "I love you, but I can't watch that." The simultaneous disgust and desire that Vallens provokes in characters is mirrored in the viewer's discomfort: we are both voyeuristic *and* moralistic. The inclusion of Sandy's perspective complicates what would otherwise be a simple construction of the male gaze. Lynch therefore innovates the gender allegiances that would typically be associated with "female Gothic," enabling a profound ambivalence on the part of the audience.

The power of this ambivalence is the lure of the abject. Vallens' open, desirous, yet victimized body is the axis for Lynch's Gothic abjection. Canonically, the abject is that which we must expel from ourselves in order to *be* an individual subject. The abject is that which must be rejected and defined as other to establish a proper self, expelling the phantasmatic and imaginary contents of non-individuality found at the pre-oedipal stage. The re-appearance of the abject exposes the artificiality of the boundary between self and other; provoking the revelation that what we exclude from our self-definition is "something rejected from which one does not part, from which one does not protect oneself... Imaginary uncanninness and real threat, it beckons to us and ends up engulfing us."[26] In "Approaching Abjection," Julia Kristeva calls the abject a horror that is "as tempting as it is condemned ... a vortex of summons and repulsion."[27] The prospect of "engulfing" of the self threatens self-loss, dissolution and debasement. The abject – that which is cast off – thus proffers an ambivalent means of both defining the self, and of debasing it to the point of un-selfing. To abject is to separate, reject – to *be abject* is to be "repulsive, stuck, subject enough only to feel this subjecthood at risk."[28] Lynch's work revels in abjection – the suspension of temporal, spatial and subject-object relations – with the intention of provoking a particular engagement from his audience. In essence, Lynch attempts to engender abjection in his viewer.

[24] Ellen Moers, *Literary Women: The Great Writers* (New York, Doubleday, 1986) 106, 109.
[25] Clare Kahane, "The Gothic Mirror," *The (M)other Tongue: Essays in Feminist Psychoanalytic Interpretation* (Ithaca: Cornell University Press, 1985) 342.
[26] Julia Kristeva, *Powers of Horror: An Essay on Abjection*, trans. L.S. Roudiez (New York: Columbia University Press, 1982) 4.
[27] Kristeva, *Powers of Horror*, 1.
[28] Hal Foster, *The Return of the Real: The Avant-garde at the End of the Century* (Cambridge: Massachusetts Institute of Technology Press, 1996) 156.

If the abject is experienced as a cognitive disturbance in which the co-ordinates of reality and identity are thrown into doubt, the subject be-comes aware of a gap, or lacuna in the real. The incoherence of sense opens up anxiety as the rational epistemic system is thrown into doubt. The components of traditional narrative cinema (sound, plot, image etc) are deployed by Lynch in an antagonistic fashion The Lynchian "look" is a scopic relation in which the viewer "hangs in an essential vacillation on a fantasy."[29] Lynchian cinema is designed to abject its spectator.

However, unlike many avant-garde artists, Lynch does not repeatedly deploy "shocking" or obscene images, but he does prioritize the imagistic over the narrative. Lynch's Gothic focus on the signified above the thing itself approaches what Hal Foster calls the "artifice of abjection":[30] an aesthetic signaling the collapse of the system of representation. In all of Lynch's films we are faced with the dissolution of perceptual codes and the end of signification as a stable set of sign and signified, emptying out. Yet Lynch eschews the shock-value of obscenity: his films invoking glam-our as frequently as grotesquery. Here Kristevan abjection helps elucidate Lynch's Gothicism, and his depiction of women in particular. Martha No-chimson reads Lynch's depiction of feminized, often vatic characters (such as Log Lady and Agent Dale Cooper) as a refutation of the Carte-sian self, and a demonstration of the energies of a non-coherent subjectivity. The female Gothic's stress on the visual as locus of experien-tial horror is complicated by the way Lynch portrays his female characters as celluloid constructs, as objects of desire which invite abject responses in his audience – both male and female. Lynch's films create a viewing dynamic, which though "pleasurable in form, can be threatening in con-tent, and it is the woman as representation/image that crystallizes this paradox."[31] This paradox is supremely Gothic and mobilizes the abject as the means of its horror.

So whilst female characters most frequently produce this look, male characters are subject to its disorienting effects. In this way *Lost Highway* is a narrative of Gothic abjection that subjects the audience, via its male character, to the dizzying effects of abjection through his relationship with a Gothic female. Renee Madison, as played by Patricia Arquette, is a 1940s femme fatale whose brooding sexual attraction and emotional hau-teur elicits a dialectical emotional reaction in which the viewer and Madison "oscillate between both attraction and repulsion, worship and condemnation."[32] *Lost Highway* doubles Arquette as Gothic woman: both wife and whore, brunette and blond, each an artificial creation – a cine-matic fantasy. Madison/Wakefield is an ambivalent character, one which inspires fascination which propels the narrative toward the dissolution of erotic thanatos. Object of uncanny desire, Wakefield is a cipher whose attraction deconstructs male subjectivity in its compact of sexual avail-ability and psychic absence, whispering to Pete Dayton at the climax of lovemaking "You'll never have me." The pivotal importance of these fe-male archetypes seem to bear out Laura Mulvey's critique that in cinema

[29] Lacan, qtd in Rosen, *Narrative, Apparatus, Ideology: A Film Theory Reader* (New York: Columbia University Press, 1986) 212.
[30] Hal Foster, *The Return of the Real*, 153.
[31] Mulvey, qtd in Rosen, *Narrative, Apparatus, Ideology*, 202.
[32] Punter, *Literature of Terror*, 190.

women are commonly "the bearer of meaning, not the maker of meaning."[33] Yet Lynch's heroines are the bearers of non-meaning, icons whose allure triggers crisis in the viewer.

In true Gothic fashion, *Lost Highway* substitutes "transformation, condensation and projection for clearly defined patterns of cause and effect," prioritizing "subjective experience and the dynamics of inner life"[34] for definable causal relationship. As the Gothic aesthetic is one of violent contrasts, Lynch continually emphases the relationship between those contrasts. *Lost Highway's* multiplication and subsequent fusion of personae, its dereliction of chronology and the embrace of the uncanny are part of a systematic disruption of the normal and normative boundaries of the self. The voice from the empty street on the intercom that initiates the film's spiral into murder confuses and disorients because it is already known. Knowledge is *a priori* in the film, whilst understanding is not. Chronologically the film works backwards toward the primal horror, the founding violence, which is repressed at the beginning by the surface of bourgeois life. At root, *Lost Highway's* horror is entirely abject. The gap between power and powerlessness narrows, as the rebirth as Pete Dayton suggests that the secure demarcation between self and other, husband and murderer, is ultimately imaginary. Dayton's eruption as self and narrative from Madison's incarceration is "some spooky shit" – inexplicable and haunting. The lack of explicable continuity between the film's two sections reveals the arbitrariness of cinematic narrative as well as the vulnerability of subjectivity, the way in which our coherent construction of the world is based around our imaginative actions. The narrative expresses subjective suture, a metaphor "for the relation of a subject to a signifying chain... the impulse to coherent identity which...must maintain itself through the gaps of difference."[35] Lynch makes suture visible – showing the breaks in that chain, the stitchmarks of identity and culture so often hidden in the seamless selves of Hollywood. *Lost Highway* deauthenticates not only the idea of self, but space, sound and vision are similarly deracinated. The disembodied voice on the intercom from the empty street is the initial sign of the inadequacy of objective rational data. This moment is the dizzying "emptying out of the object...a horrifying moment of the birth of a new space which ruins habitual space."[36] Lynch uses technological dislocation to summon up the effects of the supernatural:

> Mystery Man: Call Me. Dial your number. Go ahead.
> [*Fred dials the number and the Mystery Man answers*]
> Mystery Man: [*over the phone*] I told you I was here.
> Fred Madison: [*amused*] How'd you do that?
> Mystery Man: Ask me.
> [*Fred remembers the anonymous video tapes*]
> Fred Madison: [*angrily into the phone*] How did you get inside my house?

[33] Qtd in Rosen, *Narrative, Apparatus, Ideology*, 198.
[34] Steven Jay Schneider, *Horror Film and Psychoanalysis: Freud's Worst Nightmare* (Cambridge: Cambridge University Press, 2004) 4.
[35] Lindemann, qtd in Rosen, *Narrative, Apparatus, Ideology*, 170.
[36] Parveen Adams, *The Emptiness of the Image: Psychoanalysis and Sexual Difference* (London: Routledge, 1996) 154.

Mystery Man: You invited me. It is not my custom to go where I am not wanted.
Fred Madison: [*into the phone*] Who are you?
[*Both Mystery Men laugh mechanically*]
Mystery Man: Give me back my phone.
[*Fred gives the phone back*]
Mystery Man: It's been a pleasure talking to you.

Bemusement turns to anger following the recognition of Madison's power-lessness – the gothic joke is on him. The Mystery Man's ghastly appearance recalls the ghoulish villains of Hammer Horror, his sinister de-meanor and cryptic omniscience at once compelling Madison to question him and to flee him. The Mystery Man's doubling enables him to speak from within the home, communicating with his other: "Call me. Dial your number." Madison's question, "Who are you?" is redundant and met with "mechanic" laughter. Like Freud's uncanny automata, the Mystery Man mimics vitality whilst spreading a deathly contagion. Madison's visceral disgust at the Mystery Man is an attempt to separate the self from what already infests it – psychic decay, violence and sexual jealousy. The sur-plus that the abject creates distorts the object of his desire, Renee Madison becomes the degenerate Alice Wakefield, a violent and sexually exploitative woman. Madison's complicity with the Mystery Man is his subsumption by the abject. Fleeing from the desert where Dick Laurent has been murdered, the camera films from the interior of the vehicle, the white road markings flashing up in an infinity of movement through fluid darkness. No defining landscape is visible: instead Badalamenti's music wells up mournfully over a prolonged shot and credits. Space, time and self have been undone. The close of the film ends in psychic limbo, a total "dislocation of spatial, physical, and fantasmatic coordinates."[37] This is dénouement as anti-resolution: knowledge is circular, obsessive, abject. Eschewing closure, Lynchian Gothic opens up abjection's temporal and existential abyss.

GHOSTS AND THE MACHINE: LYNCH'S GOTHIC PHANTASMAGORIA

Neighbor: A little boy went out to play. When he opened his door, he saw the world. As he passed through the doorway, he caused a reflection. Evil was born. Evil was born, and followed the boy.
Nikki: I'm sorry, what is that?
Neighbor: An old tale, and a variation. A little girl went out to play. Lost in the marketplace, as if half-born. Then, not through the marketplace – you see that, don't you? – but through the alley behind the marketplace. This is the way to the palace. But it isn't something you remember.[38]

Dialogue as aporia and imagist nightmare is another of Lynch's character-istic traits as a filmmaker. Lynch's films stage a confrontation in which both audience and protagonist are presented with systems of signification (whether musical, visual or linguistic) that seemingly refuse comprehen-sion, transparency and reciprocity. Yet these systems' obduracy, opacity

[37] Fred Botting, *Limits of Horror: Technology, Bodies, Gothic* (Manchester: Manchester University Press, 2008) 10.
[38] *Inland Empire* 2006.

and multiplicity also compel and seduce. Nikki's neighbor's narrative comes from nowhere in the conversation they are having within a setting of starched neighbourly politeness. The eruption of dark narrative is symptomatic of Lynch's production of Gothic menace and atmosphere in the saccharine technicolor of the Hollywood dream. The fairy-tale archaism of the old woman's story carries with it the freight of archetypes and symbols, acting as a foundation myth for something as vague and as concrete as "Evil." Her explanation, that it is "an old tale, *and* a variation" implies an incipient doubleness: Gothic tales are always familiar, repetitive, identifiable as such, and open to appropriation. *INLAND EMPIRE* and *Mulholland Drive* is late Lynch's Gothic diptych. Both films explore cinema as a realm of Gothic opposition to realist aesthetics – focusing on the confusion and absorption of fictiveness, artifice, symbols. By rendering Hollywood and the film industry the site of postmodern Gothic horror Lynch transposes traditional, old world Gothic onto the new. As in *Mulholland Drive*, the film demonstrates a "poetic reliance on intensity of imagery, the violence, supernaturalism, and vivid coloring of legend and folklore."[39] From this perspective, *Mulholland Drive* is a fairy tale of Hollywood: the story of the self negotiating and destroying itself through the Gothic misprism of cinema. Steven Dillon's outstanding analysis of *Mulholland Drive* as a deconstruction of the cinephilic fantasy reads the film as reflection of the director's love of the screen, its ability to permeate our conscious and subconscious life, to mould and distort through its seductive images, its immaculate imaginary. For Dillon, *Mulholland Drive* explores our ability to feel intensely about that which we know is unreal, despite or because of its unreality: the film is not only "a nightmare of love, but a nightmare of artifice."[40] Filmed in his signature palette of tehnicolour clarity, and Hollywood style, Lynch also steeps *Mulholland Drive* in the pooling darkness of his earlier films. If *Mulholland Drive* is indeed a film about artificiality, its exposure of the solitary pleasures and sadness of film is double-edged; implying at once that what we watch is fantasy and illusion, it poses the Gothic possibility that there is no alternative to this artifice.

Central to Betty and Rita's story is the Hollywood film industry, the economic, imagistic and technological apparatus that creates and sustains the artifice of beauty that Betty so desires, and whose projections structure her dream-like story. Arriving in Los Angeles, Betty represents herself as a sweet ingénue whose aspirations to stardom will be rewarded by the traditional format of Hollywood filmed narratives. Yet benign coincidence is swiftly belied by the rage, impotence and confusion of Betty as she meets and falls in love with Rita, whose dark beauty and amnesia are emblematic of the two-dimensional erotic fantasies of cinema – she is what Betty wants, not a subject. Named after the femme fatale flick *Gilda* (1946), Rita is a commercial product torn from the screen. The intensity of Betty's feelings are incommensurate with Rita as a person, but reflect the voracious, illogic of obsessive desire, of the loss of self in the abyss of idealized love. The uncanny, convoluted love affair detourns into a degrading obsession and murder is highlighted, as in *Lost Highway*, by the Gothic effects of technology. Lynch's interest in the technological un-

[39] Punter, *Literature of Terror*, 182.
[40] Dillon, *The Solaris Effect*, 91.

canny is clear from Rita's murmured "it's strange to be calling your self" as she makes the call to an answering machine, while the violent shifts between conventional Hollywood film style and hand-held camera foreground the technical contrasts of the film. Lynch's emphasis on the texture of technology, its ability to produce effects beyond the real stresses the power of artificiality – its sinister allure most powerfully rendered in the *No hay banda* section of *Mulholland Drive*. Set in a film noir theatre full of the deep hues of cabaret decadence, Betty and Rita watch a performance that is entirely artificial – whose simulated music is merely lip-sync and acting, and which proclaims its fabrication as a condition of the audience's enjoyment and absorption. Directing the audience with the gravitas of a priest or a TV host, the MC declares "*No hay banda*...it's all recorded; it is all a tape: it is an illusion." Sung in Spanish by Rebeka del Rio, "Llorando" is a version of Roy Orbison's "Crying" – "an old tale, and a variation." The intensity of del Rio's performance, which almost consumes her in a melodramatic faint, brings both women to an ecstasy of tears. Two beautiful women weeping at a simulacrum causes a profound surplus of emotion, as Lynchian Gothic approaches the sublime even as it undercuts the stability of the transcendental with the mundane. The aural artifice recalls Man Ray's "Tears," its aestheticized glass drops on a woman's face more beautiful and evocative than the real tears of human sentiment. The imagery and symbolism of the *No hay banda* section underscores the illogical but overwhelming emotions of the Gothic – its ability to inspire emotion due to its artificiality, problematizing the emotion felt by the audience aware of its formal aesthetics.

Film-critic Stephen Holden calls *Mulholland Drive* an "ever-deepening reflection on the allure of Hollywood and on the multiple role-playing and self-invention that the movie-going experience promises... What greater power is there than the power to enter and to program the dream life of the culture?"[41] The uncanny ability of the artificial to penetrate not merely into our subconscious, but to structure our desires and emotions, is a Gothic trait. Cinema is the post-modern phantasmagoria – the early nineteenth century technology used to entertain and terrify, to allow audiences to see their fears and to produce responses through visual and aural machinery. Art historian Henri Focillon described the representational power of objects as a spatial and imaginary eruption into the real. "Form prolongs and diffuses itself through our dreams, we regard it, as 'twere, as a kind of fissure through which crowds of images aspiring to birth may be introduced into some indefinite realm."[42] The "fissures" caused in the somatic imaginary of the viewers of early phantasmagoria and contemporary cinema alike can be seen as generative, creating a populace of phantoms seeking habitation in the real. Robert Miles' recent work on the link between Gothic and romantic phantasmagoria suggests a rich connection between the increased visuality of culture and the rise of the Gothic as a pervasive commercial form. Focillon's use of fissure to describe the aesthetic's ability to open up in the subconscious mind

---

[41] Stephen Holden, "Hollywood Seen as a Funhouse of Fantasy," *New York Times*, 6 Oct. 2001: 13.
[42] Henri Focillon, *The Life of Forms in Art*, trans. C.B. Hogan and G. Kubler (New Haven: Yale University Press, 1942) 3.

associates it further with the abject. One literal meaning of phantasmagoria is an assembly of ghosts: early magic lantern shows often represented death masks of animated simulacra of the dead. In this way, Lynch's creation of dream worlds structured by sight and experience directly relate him to Gothic's infancy, its fascination with the spectral and its imbrication in commercial activity.

If *Mulholland Drive* rewrites Los Angeles as the City of Nightmares, its concern with phantasmagoria is part of a desire to make the audience more conscious of the corruption of dreams. The film's dizzying plot shifts, and alternate realities jostling against one another, culminate in pessimism about the gloss of the cinema. Betty's suicide is the climax of a solitary fantasist. *INLAND EMPIRE* continues Lynch's investigation into cinematic Gothic. The choice of Laura Dern to play Nikki highlights the director's self-reflexivity, his referencing of his earlier work in what seems like an auto-cento of the Gothic sections of *Blue Velvet*, *Lost Highway* and *Wild at Heart*. In many ways *INLAND EMPIRE* is Lynch's most Gothic film since *Lost Highway*. Moving away from his trademark camera style, *INLAND EMPIRE* uses digital camera to draw attention to film's visual surface, its artificiality as a form. Instead of the technicolor hyper-reality of earlier works, Lynch's film is grainy, muted in palette and production value. Beginning with European footage resembling a snuff movie opens the film, the film replaying in its obscure menace. Initially without context, it becomes clear that the film Nikki is acting in is a re-make of an original German film, itself based on a Polish folk-tale, in which someone has died. Nikki's dreams or rememberings of a previous European existence resonate in the film's present through the figures of her sinister husband, and the ancient Neighbor who tells her "there is a murder in your film...brutal fucking murder!" Nikki's peculiar existence becomes more and more somatic, her affair being undertaken as if through a haze of dream, the repetitions and surreal transmissions of the "Rabbit Ears" sequence creating an atmosphere of almost unsustainable horror in which time and experience are repeatable, obscure and fantastical. The camera and film itself become gothic agents which actively obscure and distort the subject and her relationship to the world, even as they grant that subject centrality and meaning.

INLAND EMPIRE pushes Nikki to the limits of characterization: victimizing and abusing her through marital intimidation, through the resurgence of a buried alternate identity and the threatened supernatural curse of the original film, *47*. Her status in the film is almost impossibly refracted: "I'm a whore. Where am I? I'm afraid," and yet Dern retains the level of performative artifice – what we might call "star quality" to justify and retain the camera's gaze. It is arguably due to this noumenal quality that Lynch returned to Dern for this role, since the film travesties the delights of Hollywood still further. Broken, dying on a street that is also a screen-set, Nikki is not resuscitated or revived: as extras around her discuss their performance, her death appears "real," a token either of the power of narrative or of the fatal toll such cinematic fantasies can take.

The final frames of the film constitute an idiosyncratically Lynchian moment. In an incredible sequence, which travesties the glamour and choreographed ecstasy of a Busby Berkley special, twenty cheaply dressed and provocatively made up women dance to "The Locomotion," as Laura

Dern gazes beatifically at the camera. The spectator is literally elevated as the camera POV rises above the surreal scene, and the accompanying aural candyfloss. This is a phenomenal close to a seemingly dark and complex film in what is arguably Lynch's most abrupt and wonderful shifts in tone. The intensely stage managed feel of this final scene refuses to allow the viewer a continued absorption, or the option of clean cathar-sis. Instead we are returned to the artifice of the screen, and the fact that the Gothic heroine we have been watching for over two hours is an un-canny double – an actress, rather than a character. The Gothic horror of the film is transmuted in its final sequence, which at once intensifies our confusion and disgust and yet also proffers us a state of bliss and joy, even if that spectacle is debased. The discordance of this moment is a quintessentially Gothic celebration of the inextricability of contrasts – Dern as whore and as glossy film-star, as proper middle-class wife and adulteress – and one based on a kitsch celebration of Gothic irony. Whether this makes the fantasy-element of the resolution a problem, or allows the viewer to accommodate its status as wish-fulfillment or illusion is questionable. What it unarguably does is to highlight cinema as visual phantasmagoria – a media which produces pleasure through artifice and the content of which should not be confused with "the real" but con-fronts the viewer with his/her emotional and cognitive confusion as a prime result of the spectacle. We are not provided with any clear position for comfort or indeed of identification. Both Nikki's death, and that of Laura Palmer are staged, symbolic acts rather than realist or even plot-driven deaths. *INLAND EMPIRE's* finalé confronts us with the cheapened extras of transcendental epiphany in a fantasy world where "stars make dreams, and dreams make stars" is a statement of profound anxiety.

CONCLUSION

Lynch's shift toward feminocentric narrative is synonymous with his ex-ploration and exposure of the technology of artifice in cinema as a form. The economy of excess, repetition and abjection developed in his films since *Twin Peaks: Fire Walk with Me* is inherently Gothic in its militant anti-realism. Portraying film as the ultimate in phantasmatic projection, Lynch extrapolates the cultural and personal abjection resultant from our misrecognition of the dream-screen for the real. That two of his female characters, and one of his male, suffer forms of amnesia suggests that the supersaturation of images has destroyed the solid, coherent self of traditional cinema. His representations of phantasmatic women imply the darkest truth of all, that artifice might be the dominant means of negotiat-ing identity and abjection. Countermanding ideal images in service of cinema of ambivalence, confusion and symbolism, his films creates a phantasmagoric confusion of cinematic representations and subjective hallucinations: mental phantasms as entertainment, and vice versa – and both are capable of being sold. These cinematic fantasies fuse the two contraries of Lynchian aesthetics – the mawkishness of sentimentality and the terror of the Gothic –in the erotic phantasmagoria of liminal and vulnerable women.

LOUIS ARMAND
THE MEDIUM IS THE FETISH

1. Just as pathology implies the idea of the normal, so the "uncanny" implies a habitude, and a habituation – yet these terms are in no sense opposable. The mark of the perverse is not a descent into aberration, but the obsessive, domineering work of correction; of discipline; of normalization, and *hyper*normalization, in the service of an ideal object. The sexualized logic of taboo and transgression venerates order and derives its pleasure principally from it; but order in a ritualistic, stylized and austere form which masks its own ridiculousness. Just as, in the economy of the pornographic image, what is on view is not some obscure object of desire but precisely its conventionality, its generic rationalism, its fetishization by way of a type of "autistic cult" of signs.

But what does it mean to speak of a pornographic *image*, if by pornographic we mean an image which *merely* depicts; an image whose form is laid bare to expose a forbidden "content" and is in fact nothing more than a veil of insubstantial signs superimposed upon *the thing itself* (the pornographic *idée fixe*)? There is obviously no point in naming or attempting to catalogue *what* this thing is: it will always ultimately escape us, however banal it may be made to appear; knowing that this fascination with anatomical detail conveys nothing but a pseudo-physiology, whose eroticization is fugitively metaphysical.

If such a thing as the *pornographic image* exists, it could only be an "image" whose form, whose very technicity, lays bare the "cause of desire in which the subject disappears"[1] – annihilated, as Jean Baudrillard says, by transparency.[2] Not a transparency which allows us "to see with clarity," but which puts on view the very operations of seeing, in the conjunction of *porneïa* and *graphē*: the libidinal economy of visible signs.

This eroticization of seeing is first and foremost technological. The "object" is not some thing we perceive by means of a picture or image – as though films, photographs or "mental concepts" are mere instruments – it, the object, is rather an imaginary prosthesis. Just as we might say the *ego* is a prosthesis of the unconscious. Which is to say, of a certain "libido" whose operations take form at the level of a fantasised *real* – as a type of "videodrome."[3] Such a view calls to mind Bazin's well-known observation that "the quarrel over realism in art stems from a misunderstanding, from a confusion between the aesthetic and the psy-

---

[1] Jaques Lacan, *Écrits* (Paris: Seuil, 1966) 10.
[2] Jean Baudrillard, *The Perfect Crime*, trans. Chris Turner (London: Verso, 1996) 7.
[3] David Cronenberg, *Videodrome*, 1983.

chological"[4] – a misunderstanding exacerbated by the production of images by mechanical and "automatic means."

Photography accedes to the pornographic at that instant in which it is no longer seen as a *mere* depiction of, or even substitute for, the so-called real, but as its *expropriation* – its de-piction within the operations of the visual – a "transference of reality," as Bazin says, leading him to observe that the "photographic image is *the object itself*, the object freed from the conditions of time and space that govern it... it shares, by virtue of the very process of its becoming, the being of the model of which it is the reproduction; it *is* the model."[5] It is not for nothing that Marx had earlier defined the logic of the commodity in similar terms, or that Guy Debord will have synthesized these two views in his dialectical ontology of the *spectacle*.[6] Nor that in each case the expropriatory function (of the photographic image, of the commodity, of spectacle) will have come to be equated with that of the fetish.

David Lynch, from *Nudes and Smoke*

2. A camera. Lights and smoke. A body defined by increments. Mouth, legs, breasts, eyes blacked-out like the eyes in a crime scene photograph. A warp of the lens, a blurred movement, a smear. Exposures multiply, overlaid with shadows. A décor in weird chiaroscuro, building the oppressive density of an image.

In 1994, film auteur David Lynch produced a color photo series entitled "Nudes and Smoke," one of several projects that extend Lynch's preoccupations beyond the confines of cinema. The photographs, highly textured, explore the paradoxical obscurity and clarity of *smoke* captured on film, and its capacity to transform bodies and objects into compositions of surface and depth, both spatially and temporally. The figure of the *nude* is redistributed as a quality of the medium as such, rather than of the pictorial "object." The body is rendered as a locus of intensities, shadow and exposure, doubled in the framing and arrangement of the image's "décor," and by the infinitely complex topologies of smoke.

In short, "Nudes and Smoke" achieves nothing less than a photographic *articulation* of its supposed subject. The words "nude" and

---

[4] André Bazin, *What is Cinema*, vol. 1, trans. Hugh Gray (Berkeley: University of California Press, 1967) 12.
[5] Bazin, *What is Cinema*, 14.
[6] Guy Debord, *The Society of the Spectacle*, trans. Donald Nicholson-Smith (New York: Zone Books, 1995).

"smoke" could just as easily stand for the texture of the image *as image* – not as terms designating exterior objects, but as a poetics of light, aperture, celluloid, retina; the whole complex of technical operations by which we come to *perceive an image* and not (or not simply) a verisimilitude of objects fixed on a type of screen. Nor just to perceive, but ultimately to be visually aroused, through that curious and disquieting conjunction of apprehension and apprehensiveness: the *eye's* desire to possess and consume, and the evanescent, fleeting, yet fixed, overwhelming and threatening aspect of that desire itself made manifest before us.

The "image" for Lynch is this whole *pornographic* drama of desire played-out, as it were, in the theatre of the eye. "A dream of strange desires wrapped inside a mystery story."[7] The framework of the image becomes a stage in which the object functions primarily as a type of prop: the aim here is not depiction in any straightforward sense, but rather an *embodiment*. The pictorial object, the "model," is here the prosthesis of the explicitly photographic body. Its objecthood is expropriated (*de-picted*) to the fetish economy of the image *as image*.[8]

3. "Film," Lynch says, "is really like voyeurism. You sit there in the safety of the theatre, and seeing is such a powerful thing. And we want to see secret things, we *really* want to see them. New things. It drives you *nuts*, you know! And the more new and secret they are, the more you want to see them."[9]

The object mimes being in possession of a secret that the eye searches to see but is never able to attain. A body, genitals, a mask, a pair of shoes. Each functions not as the index of a hidden desire but as the metonym of the image itself – the image *through which*, and *by means of which*, we seek to apprehend the secret it seemingly contains the way a mirror contains a reflection.

If we choose to entertain the idea that Lynch's work, his photography and also his films, participates in this perhaps eccentric notion of *pornography*, then it is easy to see the danger implicit in the many attempts to view Lynch (in *Blue Velvet*, 1986; *Lost Highway*, 1997; *Mulholland Drive*, 2001), as more or less *illustrating* a psychoanalytical orthodoxy. Cinema, photography, are here reduced to the commonplace "pornography" of that which merely explicates or merely depicts – even if *what* is depicted ultimately remains an enigma. Indeed, despite much assertion to the contrary, there is very nearly nothing enigmatic about Lynch's work itself: it conceals no "secret message," no enveloped "content," no revelatory "schema," but is comprised almost wholly of surfaces, formal textures, *découpage*. Lynch's work is structurally lucid in the way Thomas Ruff's photo manipulations may be called structural, or De Chirico's paintings, or the novels of Robbe-Grillet. Like dreams, they *articulate* rather than "de-

---

[7] Lynch's description of *Blue Velvet* (1986) in *Lynch on Lynch*, ed. Chris Rodley (London: Faber, 2005) 138.

[8] We are in fact confronted here with a kind of revelation that the fetish *is not* a sign that masks a "lack" since, in any case, a lack is always symbolic. Rather, it masks the "absence" of a lack (the fetish is only castrative, to borrow the Freudean term, in the absence of castration). The fetish's ritualisation of desire displaces and reifies into situations the very logic of the mask, by which the image assumes what we might call a *persona*.

[9] *Lynch on Lynch*, 145.

pict;" or, *in spite* of what they "depict." Their logic is the already deconstructive logic of a *de-piction*.

Marc Atkins, from *The Teratologists*; Lynch, from *Nudes and Smoke*; Thomas Ruff, *Bond Girl*

With the exception of the 1992 *Twin Peaks: Fire Walk with Me*, this is perhaps nowhere more explicit than in Lynch's much more recent (digital) film *Inland Empire* (2006), with its fragmentary, collage-like narrative, its recursive image-hysteria and its relentless "foreignness" (in the manner of a type of *Alice through the Looking Glass*). *Inland Empire* is a type of visual prosthesis of itself and of Lynch's oeuvre as a whole (its cast alone is a pot-pourri of earlier films: Laura Dern, Justin Theroux, Laura Harring, Naomi Watts).

Shifting between the Hollywood studio setting of *Mulholland Drive* and post-communist urban-industrial Łódź (in central Poland), the texture of the second half of *Inland Empire* recalls the disquieting work of British photographer Marc Atkins, whose 1998 series *The Teratologists*, and 2001 series *Equivalents*, both echo and anticipate Lynch. Atkins's "shadowed portraits" evoke a *mode of seeing* whose objects stand for, and therefore symbolize, an absence which, at the same time, they seek to disavow.[10] A body or a room translated into the "previously unseen activity" of the camera, the dark place behind the eye, the "escaped frames from a film."[11]

These objects are the "Teratologists" that inhabit the technics of the photographic image the way the "mystery man" in *Lost Highway* inhabits the "continuity" of Lynch's cinematography – as a type of prosthetic *agent* directing the way we see. The Teratologists, Atkins says, are "creators of uncertainty and desire. Within a dark room, a place of memory, a curtain momentarily blows open. The glance of light from beyond the window exposes the previously unseen activity of the room: sculptural forms, shadowed portraits, escaped frames from a film..."

[10] Cf. Sigmund Freud, "Fetishism," *SE* XXI 152-57.
[11] Marc Atkins, *The Teratologists* (London: Panoptika, 1998).

David Lynch, from *Nudes and Smoke*; Marc Atkins, from *Equivalents*

In *Equivalents*, Atkins – working between factory locations in London and Łódź – creates interior parallel worlds, images within images, lost, obscured or reconstituted, their contours bleeding, visually over-saturated, into a "de-pictive" space or "de-pictive" time that has no other location than the image.

> The image of the flash obliterates the identity of the model. An auto-portrait of the photographer *whose face is held close to an illuminated lightbulb* (this motif repeats elsewhere) lies on the floor. (The illusion here of a staged reflexivity, that we must come to recognise that the image of the camera is no more the spectre *in* the photograph than this "double" exposure is *in* the camera: what we would call a "hypomensiac" machine.)
> ...
> A torn photograph of a woman's face nailed to a brick wall above a heavily eroded sign: "AMONIAK." One half of the face is entirely in shadow, the other half over-exposed. The shadow of the nail falls across the sign, cancelling it out: a cancelled sign, an anti-portrait...[12]

4. Myth, Roland Barthes once wrote, "is not defined by the object of its message, but by the way in which it utters this message: there are formal limits to myth, there are no 'substantial' ones."[13] It is for this reason, Barthes continues, that anything at all may be a myth. Myth is realizable not in the *things themselves*, but as a potentiality to signify; which is to say, discourse. And this potentiality is both medium-bound and generalizable, *as a formal condition*. Even if we attribute a certain *formlessness* to media per se: the necessary degree of formlessness of situations in flux, of evolutionary pathways.

[12] Louis Armand, "Equivalence Relation," *Interstice* (London: Panoptika, 2002).
[13] Roland Barthes, "Myth Today," *Mythologies*, trans. Annette Lavers (New York: Vintage, 2000) 109.

Marc Atkins, from *Equivalents*

Myth, discourse, evolve, just as media evolve. Or just as technology and neuroses evolve. It is for this reason, too, that myth stands at the horizon wherever a *future* comes into view, as an expressible idea. But the future, naked of fantasy and hypothesis, has no content, only potentialities, or rather probabilities. It is the *formalization of ideas* that conveys "content." The medium – as what Barthes calls a semiological *system* – not only constitutes the message, but inaugurates it.

"There is no point identifying the world," says Baudrillard. "We cannot even identify our own faces, since mirrors impair their symmetry. To see our own face as it is would be madness, since we would no longer have any mystery for ourselves and would, therefore, be *annihilated by transparency*. Might it not be said that man has *evolved into a form* such that his face remains invisible to him and he becomes definitively unidentifiable, not only in the mystery of his face, *but in any of his desires*?"[14]

How to see with clarity that, after all, it is the mirror that is the face of the world? And on the other side of the mirror: no things, but forms of transparency, radiating into myth. The error is in believing that anything here is *no longer*. Nothing *evolves into a form*; evolution *is* form. *Formalization* – the desire for system – is simply the restitution of a primal objecthood, the reification of myth into cliché and archetype by way of inversion (the message is the medium). The desire for identification, "to see our own face," becomes the horror of "transparency." Defending our "selves" from madness, we cling to mystery. And from mystery to necessity, "evolving" towards a definitive state of unidentifiability. Which indeed bears all the hallmarks of the pathological, not because it implies that the sole defense against a type of madness is to relinquish the idea of reality, but because it insists upon an idea of the normal.

What we are confronted with here is this invocation of a *redemptive perverse*. That in the face of "reality's" dissolution, or of some empirical limit of our knowing anything about *it*, a condition of the "normal" can nevertheless be reconstituted through the dogmatic? hysterical? assertion of its impossibility. Veiled in signs, the real becomes that unknowable *thing* that sends forth its avatars in the guise of a "system of objects." But objects which *have always already disappeared*. We live, says Baudrillard, on the basis of an *unreality*. Reality "itself" does not take place.

[14] Baudrillard, *The Perfect Crime* 7. My italics.

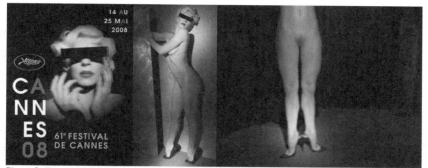

Pierre Collier and David Lynch, *Cannes 2008*; David Lynch and Christian Louboutin, from *Fetish*

5. In March 2007, Lynch commissioned well-known couturier Christian Louboutin to design some shoes for an exhibition he was curating for the Cartier Foundation. In return, Louboutin proposed a collaboration with Lynch for a second exhibition, for which he planned to create a series of extreme fetish shoes which Lynch would then photograph. The resulting installation, entitled simply *Fetish*, opened 3 October in Paris, in Pierre Passebon's *Galerie du Passage*, near the Palais Royal. The exhibition comprised five limited edition pairs of shoes and signed photographs of the shoes modelled by two nude dancers from the Crazy Horse cabaret ("Nouka" and "Baby").

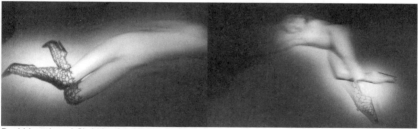

David Lynch and Christian Louboutin, from *Fetish*

While Lynch's photographs for the *Fetish* exhibition have been compared to the work of, among others, Guy Bourdin and Francis Bacon, they retain a particularly Lynchian quality, though only in part due to the familiar vocabulary of constricted space, color-saturation and lighting ("a décor populated with shadows"). If in many of Lynch's films the moving image often appears weighted down to the point of immobility, the tableaux in *Fetish* exhibit a weirdly ethereal kinetics. Kinetic not solely by virtue of the similitude of effect (the movement of the camera, the distortions of a warped, unfocused lens, the use of multiple exposure and stop-motion), but through the disjunction between the *agitated visuality* of the images and the rigid constraint imposed by the eponymous fetish as both object and idea.

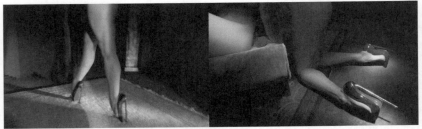

David Lynch and Christian Louboutin, from *Fetish*

Louboutin's shoes (10 inch stilettos, Siamese heels, spikes on the instep, etc.) by themselves represent a type of functional enigma – recalling Meret Oppenheim's "Ma Gouvernante" (1936) and "La Couple" (1956), in which the aesthetics of rigid constraint and bodily distortion are allegorically condensed into the sculptural transfiguration of the "shoes" themselves.

Like Oppenheim's "sculptures," the forms of bondage implied by Louboutin's shoes are no longer those of a body subjected to a sort of sadomasochistic discipline, but rather those of a *fixation*. Like Moira Shearer's red ballet shoes in The Archers's 1948 film. We witness the accession of the *thing* to the status of autonomous object – mysteriously acting on its own behalf, and not only acting but *subjecting* us to its "will." In *Red Shoes*, Shearer's character is, as it were, traversed by a type of alien ego: her shoes *dance* her. Her own actions become *intransitive*, as though some demon in the shoes had come to inhabit her against her will, exposing the horror of a mind trapped, imprisoned or in bondage, doll-like within a body, a situation or environment which *acts for it*, like a secret, irrational, external intelligence.

David Cronenberg, still from *Videodrome*; Michael Powell & Emeric Pressburger (The Archers), publicity still for *Red Shoes*

In Lynch's photographs, this logic of the fetish as both object and agent is transferred onto the images themselves. Louboutin's shoes become merely conventional signifiers of a fetish *genre*, for which the naked bodies of "Nouka" and "Baby" serve as compositional props. The images summon forth a paradox, between an excess of conventionality and excess as such, evoking a kind of *vertigo*. There is something in these images that recalls Roquentin's moment of epiphany in *La nausée*[15] – the eye's disquietude, its mortification, its uncharacteristic inertia, brought to the verge of something that contradicts and overwhelms it. Something that renders the eye *naked*.

6. "I like to remember things my own way... Not necessarily the way they happened." In *Lost Highway*, the eye that sees is constantly under threat of its gaze being returned by some externalized agency: images on a video tape, the Mystery Man's camera, the feedback loop of telephones, intercoms, interior architectures, parallel worlds, doubles, reflections, reality gaps. Inertia, entropy, static blur the division between memory and "what happens." There are ghosts in the cinematic machine: the eye becomes the prosthesis of an inverted desire to see, an automaton into which it is absorbed by way of an unrelenting enervation.

Early in the film we "see" – at the end of a long tracking shot – Fred Madison kneeling beside the naked, bloodied corpse of his wife, Renée. We "see" his silent scream. Something splitting apart. The footage is from a video tape – one of a series of three – that has mysteriously turned up on the doorstep of the Madison house. According to the script:

> On the tape is the same night-time interior of the house, accompanied by the DRONING SOUND. The camera moves eerily down the hall toward the bedroom, sliding at a high angle. The camera turns slowly into the bedroom – looking down.
>
> BLOOD is splattered over the floor, bed, walls. The camera drifts. THE DEAD BODY OF RENEE lies on the floor at the foot of the bed. She is badly mutilated. Fred is hovering over her on the tape, ON HIS KNEES, A HORRIFIED, UNBELIEVING EXPRESSION ON HIS FACE. On the tape, Fred turns away from Renee – his hands raised, dripping blood – her blood. His movements are almost mechanical, constricted, as he strains strangely upwards seemingly against his will, as if feeling some enormous pressure. He looks directly at the camera, his face a ghastly grimace, contorted, just before the taped image goes to snow.

The video image remains opaque, almost impenetrable, as though what is being presented has nothing whatsoever to do with the two figures in the frame. The camera's point of view, high up near the ceiling, creates a type of anamorphosis which seemingly distorts *what* we see at the same time as it "reveals" the geometry of *how* we see. The nakedness of the corpse becomes the "sign" of a more deadening nakedness: the mortification of the eye exposed to its own interior illusionism. The image is no longer simply that *of* a naked object, but also *of* the rigidifying fixation of the eye's "desire to see more" – from Elysium to *basso inferno*.

If the brief video footage of Fred beside Renée's corpse suggests an allegory of Madison's divided personality, it is also a kind of allegory of this division of seeing, in which the *image* stands as an immoveable blindspot that we encounter only by indirection – a topology of dislocated affect. And yet it is solely by means of this blind *that we see*. Nothing, no

[15] Jean-Paul Sartre, *La Nausée* (Paris: Gallimard, 1938).

"truth," is lost in the medium, as it were. It is not a question of verifying or not verifying that *what* we see in the video of Fred and Renée's corpse is what we *think* it is, or what Fred *thinks* it is.

David Lynch, still from *Blue Velvet*; David Lynch and Christian Louboutin, from *Fetish*

Like Isabella Rossellini/Dorothy Vallens's body in *Blue Velvet* – and the "blue velvet" that acts as its metonym – we are never close to the nakedness it seems to present to us more than at the moment our own seeing enters into the obsessive, violent iteration of the *object coupled to its negation*: Dorothy's unnaturally red mouth juxtaposed, in Jeffrey Beaumont's disturbed memory, with the distorted mask of Frank Booth's psychosis. Here we see at work the particular violence by which a radical *decoupage* evokes an equally visceral and intellectual sado-masochism; its alienation-effect *constituting* the spectator (the voyeur) as *subjection to* – we might say – *the desire of the image*.

The nakedness of the image is always an interstice – something into which the *visualization of desire* is constantly projected in a type of *pornographic* monomania. Within this economy it is the medium itself which is the "fetish" – the invisible *deus-ex-machina* whose myriad avatars traverse the surface of the eye in an unrelenting equivalence of a *de-picted* pure object, of an "object which is not an object."[16] But this "object which is not an object" continues, as Baudrillard says, to obsess "by its empty, immaterial presence" while threatening at the same time to materialize its very nothingness.[17]

This then would be the essence of the pornographic image: that in place of a "subject" there is only subjection; in place of an object there is only this prosthesis of seeing, absorbed into itself in the form, perhaps, of an impossible exchange; the libidinal economy of an eye that desires only what it cannot see.

[16] Baudrillard, *The Perfect Crime*, 6.
[17] This transcendental weirdness has its echoes, too, in Lynch's off-screen presence – by way of the David Lynch Foundation for Consciousness-Based Education and World Peace. One recent example would be the surrealism of the Taufelsberg fiasco and the subsequent efforts of Lynch's lawyers to remove footage of the event from the internet under section 512(c)(3) of the Digital Millennium Copyright Act.

ERIC G. WILSON
SICKNESS UNTO DEATH: DAVID LYNCH & SACRED IRONY

In 1966, during his second year at the Philadelphia Academy of Fine Arts, David Lynch decided to complement painting, his preferred medium up until that time, with filmmaking, a new form of expression for him. The result was a short film called "Six Men Getting Sick." This work is the first manifestation of Lynch's enduring vision of what images should do — make us sick.

Lynch projected the film onto a specially made screen. From the upper left corner jut three human heads. The head to the far left rests its jaw in its palm; like Rodin's thinker, it looks pensive, melancholy. The head immediately to the right is a fragment, lacking a top. The face is shadowy on one side and stares downward, its mouth slightly open as though in pain. The third protruding face apparently has just violently vomited; from its gaping mouth a darkish liquid has spewed and now it flows down the canvas. In the center of the screen is a fourth man; he is painted flat and in profile. On the far right is a fifth figure; he has also been painted, and he is facing straight ahead.

A siren sounds and the exhibition begins. Strange moving images explode on the screen in quick sequence — drawings of stomachs and other digestive organs, bare black lines flowing in several directions, a sixth face between the two painted ones, an x-ray shot of a ribcage, the stomachs catching fire, and the men forcefully throwing up. All of this occurs in about one minute. The loop runs continuously.

This bizarre production, like many of Lynch's later projects, defies clear interpretation. Regardless of how hard we try to understand this piece of art, we remain disarmed, shocked anew with each turn of the loop. Still, certain antimonies emerge. The exhibition reveals unforgettable interpenetrations between the disgusting — projectile vomiting — and the beautiful — stomachs blooming to flame. Likewise, the piece melds the sacred and the profane — an apocalypse of purgative fire and a display of gross sensualism. Finally, this mixture between painting and film combines total silliness, the scatological humor of puking, and complete seriousness, the tragic possibility that life, in essence, is as absurd as this piece of art.

Pitting one pole against the other, "Six Men Getting Sick" is the first instance of Lynch's interest in self-contradictory images. Each picture in the film erases itself, trying to be one thing and its opposite all at once and thus ending up being neither thing at all. But Lynch's first venture into cinema also points to another of his recurring motifs: the fullness that comes when one experiences the reverse of the negation, the robust sense that contradictory images don't cancel themselves but rather reveal how oppositions actually complement each other, how death and life, sickness and health, decay and growth, darkness and light are mutually inclusive.

Lynch's self-effacing combinations of annihilation and abundance suggest that negation need not be nihilism but a sacred path, a way to experience the sublime profusion of being. In Lynch, we encounter a weird melding of cynicism – everything is ultimately insubstantial – and hope – the void, the lack of substance, is actually being itself, the nothing vitalizing all things. Such a mixture is sickening. We get squeamish over the possibility that life is meaningless, a sordid affair only of mindless rot. But we also get another kind of illness: when we realize that this lack of clear signification is potentially liberating--a transcendence of logic into a fecund abyss where one thing is all things, and all things, one--then we get that strangely ecstatic nausea that comes with too much vertiginous motion.

This is the sickness that heals: the revolting *no*-thing of the void can also be, when the gaze slightly turns, the no-*thing* that is plenitude, a superabundance of meaning, a reservoir of infinite potential that overthrows delimiting categories, finite structures. Though this boundlessness blows our tiny minds, we are exhilarated over the world's teeming energies, its sublime being.

Lynch's images throughout his career are both annihilations of meaning and profusions of signification. They express horror of hovering in the blankness and the exuberance of encountering being itself.

Lynch's own remarks on his art substantiate these claims. He once observed that his films challenge Hollywood conventions by focusing more on idea and image than plot and character. He says, "I love the delicate abstractions that cinema can do and only poets can do with words."[1] The comparison to the poem is telling. Among other things, an effective poem is a series of disarming images expressing a complex idea. The idea is too paradoxical for simple narrative and thus requires dense images for its ambiguous expression. The image is too mysterious for simple allegory and therefore often gestures to barely graspable abstractions. In this way, poetic images, like Lynch's visual ones – here called "delicate abstractions," gossamer pictures pointing to wispy concepts – pull two directions at once: toward an irreducibly unique image resistant to clear meaning and an idea so subtle that the mind can never grasp it once and for all.

Another time, Lynch described his artistic images as mixtures of revelation and mystery, sites that disclose the infinite but also undercut clarity. In creating his pictures, he is careful to keep from knowing too much about "what things mean or how they might be interpreted." If he did have a clear purpose in mind in making his art, he would be "afraid" to let the work be spontaneous, unexpected – to "let it keep happening." Once his forms are "reduced to certain neuroses or certain things," once these pictures are "named and defined," they lose their ambiguity and their "potential" for "vast, infinite experience."[2] Such an experience would be bounded and boundless at the same time, a finite event as well

[1] David Lynch, Interview by Chris Gore, "David Lynch Interview: Is David Just a Little Weird?" *Film Threat* (Gore Group Publications, 17 January 2000) 200.
[2] Breskin, qtd in John Alexander, *The Films of David Lynch* (London: Letts, 1993) 2; Breskin, David. "*The Rolling Stone* Interview with David Lynch," *Rolling Stone* (6 September 1990): n. pag. Print.

as infinite rush. This is the potential of the "delicate abstraction," the picture that fades before the idea, the idea that dissolves into the image.

One interviewer describes a visit to a Los Angeles art museum with Lynch. She and Lynch gaze at a Pollock painting. When the interviewer confesses that she doesn't understand the work, Lynch replies that she does. He knows this because he sees her eyes "moving." As the interviewer concludes, this remark from Lynch presupposes a level of understanding below consciousness, a "subconscious" understanding.[3] Not "unconscious," this sort of apprehension *is* conscious but in a way that lies below mental representation. The eyes roving over a Pollock painting – both pattern and turbulence, too abstract for perception and too concrete for apprehension – instinctively organize splotches of seemingly random color into somewhat cogent structures. These structures, however, escape stable representation. They engage the sight but elude the mind. But this engagement is meaningful – moving and magnetic. Currents of being below the radar of consciousness are energized. They direct the eyes to focus on this drift of color, that crossing of shade and light. The mind behind the eyes is baffled yet opened to depths and possibly heights that had heretofore been hidden.

Existing in the gap between concrete and abstract, part and whole, representation and ineffability, appearance and reality, Lynch's images are necessarily ironic. They are, one the one hand, visible structures that express discernible meanings, such as the duplicitous nature of existence, whether this duplicity be growth and decay, light and darkness, clarity and ambiguity, turbulence and pattern. But they are also, on the other hand, self-effacing artifacts, both "A" and "not A" at once, one antinomy and its cancelling opposite, sites that elude logic and clarity and thus point to the possibility that all is meaningless, empty, a void – a void that might be the negation of being but that also might be the plenitude of being itself. His images, then, exist in a nauseating but giddy limbo "is" and "is not."

But what kind of irony, precisely, is this, this simultaneous declaration and erasure? The type of irony informing Lynch's images is Romantic irony, developed by Friedrich Schlegel at the turn of the nineteenth-century. For Schlegel, human existence itself is thoroughly ironic because of the gap between our representations of the world and the world as it is. All of our statements, no matter how seemingly true, are inherently false. The only way to avoid total skepticism over this situation is to be aware of it, to undercut representations the instant they are posited. This perpetual creation and destruction is actually exhilarating, leading to vital participation in the energies of the cosmos, itself a constant metamorphosis from form to formless, formless to form.

The exemplar of this kind of irony is the Socrates of Plato's dialogues. Socratic irony is, according to Schlegel, the "only involuntary and yet completely deliberate dissimulation."[4] Both "perfectly instinctive and perfectly conscious philosophy," Socrates' method grows from his raw desire

[3] Martha P. Nochimson, *The Passion of David Lynch: Wild at Heart in Hollywood* (Austin: University of Texas Press, 1997) 5.

[4] Friedrich Schlegel, *Philosophical Fragments*. Trans. Peter Firchow (Minneapolis: University of Minnesota Press, 1991) 36.

to know more and his studied performance of ignorance.[5] This opposition between the quest for truth and the feigning of stupidity "arouses a feeling of the indissoluble antagonism between the absolute and the relative, between the impossibility and the necessity of complete communication."[6] This is the tension of all gestures, all utterances: between the fullness of the cosmos's becoming and the fragments by which humans attempt to represent this abundance. To become conscious of this conflict and to enact it oneself through "continuous self-parody" is to achieve freedom from fixation on any one representation and to suffer the limitation of never knowing anything finally.[7]

Though skeptical of reaching the absolute, this irony is "transcendental."[8] In measuring the real against the ideal and the ideal against the real, irony never becomes set on one form. Destroying as it creates, standing in itself and outside of itself, irony approaches the infinitude of self-consciousness, the mind's ability to think and watch itself think. This is the terror of never being able to rest on any representation of the world, the joy of escaping any final structure.

One persistent motif in Schlegel's kind of irony, especially in its Socratic form, is this: one is never entirely sure if it's present or not. This is of course yet another irony – irony that doesn't appear as irony, lack of irony that is ironic. In this regard, think of two famous moments in Lynch's films, both of which force us to ask – is this serious or ridiculous, or somehow both?

The dinner scene in *Eraserhead* is obviously an absurdly silly pastiche of the traditional family dinner, with ludicrously awkward conversations and cooked chickens that come to life. But these disturbing shenanigans also seem to point to a deep epistemological problem – the possibility that all experiences, no matter how ostensibly authentic, are mere performances of cultural conventions, stale imitations of long-used scripts. How do we feel in the face of such a scene? Maybe we feel slightly off-balance, unsettled, dizzy, unsure what to think, if we should laugh or lament.

Or recall the scene in *Blue Velvet* where Sandy tells Jeffrey of her dream of the robins. The two young people sit in a car beside a church. As the organ plays a hymn, Sandy says that she dreamed that the world was dark because there were no robins but then one day thousands of robins flew into the darkness bearing this "Blinding Light of Love." The meaning of this vision, she concludes, is that there's "trouble to the 'til the robins come.'" Jeffrey responds to this allegory by rather sheepishly calling Sandy a "neat girl." Sandy awkwardly replies: "So are you. I mean, you're a neat guy."

This scene is obviously a parody of Hollywood teen romances, especially those of the fifties, where two innocent, squeaky-clean kids clumsily but cutely flirt. However, the scene also points to the transformative power of love, a power that eventually redeems the characters damaged by the evil Frank Booth. Again, we don't know quite what to

---

[5] Schlegel, *Philosophical Fragments*, 36.
[6] Schlegel, *Philosophical Fragments*, 36.
[7] Schlegel, *Philosophical Fragments*, 36.
[8] Schlegel, *Philosophical Fragments*, 45.

think. Should we be moved by this description of love reviving the waste-land or amused by the satire of Hollywood cheesiness?

Beholding Lynch's images, we can never be sure if we're meant to brood over the nature of being itself or if we're supposed to laugh out loud. Feeling both somber and silly at once, we are likely to commit fully to neither mood and thus find ourselves unmoored, hovering in a herme-neutical void. The emptiness is of course that – emptiness, nothing, with no meaning, no power. But it, this negation of all things, is also the re-verse of emptiness. It is fullness, potentially all meanings, all energies.

Lynch's images in this way could be called "sacred," if we remember that the word really means both holy and accursed. They invite us to con-template the grandeur of being; they force us to face the horrifying void. Ultimately, Lynch's images make us experience both holiness and accurs-edness at once and thus invite us to seek an impossible third position that somehow reconciles the two.

Can there be such a third term, a state in which horror and holiness, nothing and everything, can exist in dynamic concord? If so, what would it be like?

Around the same time that Schlegel was developing his theories of irony, Friedrich Schiller was thinking about play. In Schiller's view, play discovers a way to bring oppositions into a vital harmony in which one appreciates the virtues of both poles without suffering the limitations of either. To achieve this balance, one must embrace and reject both poles, take them seriously and laugh them off, take an ironic stance toward each. Achieving this position, one enjoys, however briefly, the elusive third term.

For Schiller, most men and women are obsessed with sensuality or ra-tionality. The man overcome by the sense drive is concerned only with "physical existence" or "sensuous nature."[9] He is set "within the bounds of time" and therefore little different from matter.[10] He is determined, pulled into the flows of ephemeral material. In contrast, if a person is bent on the form drive, he associates with a rational principle above vicissi-tude. He believes that his reasonable ego is an eternal substance untouched by the accidents of matter. He thinks he is free, beyond na-ture. Both the formal theorist and the sensual practitioner are limited, though, attaching themselves to one half of existence and ignoring the other. The sensuous man is confined to matter, and the formal man is trapped in his mind.[11]

A person escapes these binds through the play drive: the energy be-hind the contemplation, embodiment, or creation of beauty. Engaging in aesthetic activities, one finds "a happy midway point between law and exigency."[12] She draws from the powers of the sensual and formal, but is bound to neither. She realizes that the sensual, when measured against ideas, becomes "*small*," and that the reason, when related to perceptions, grows "*light*."[13] She places the formal and the sensual into a creative dia-

[9] Friedrich Schiller, *Letters on the Aesthetic Education of Man*, trans. Reginald Snell (New York: Frederick Ungar, 1965) 64-68.
[10] Schiller, *Letters on the Aesthetic Education of Man*, 64-68.
[11] Schiller, *Letters on the Aesthetic Education of Man*, 64-68.
[12] Schiller, *Letters on the Aesthetic Education of Man*, 74-77.
[13] Schiller, *Letters on the Aesthetic Education of Man*, 79-80.

logue in which one side delimits and ennobles the other. She knows that each impulse is required for beauty but that neither alone can provide aesthetic education.

This aesthetic vision, this third term within yet beyond content and form, requires an irony: the ability to take the antinomies of existence at once seriously and in jest. You turn on a Lynch film, *Wild at Heart*. You are immediately pulled in by the billowing flames filling the entire screen as the opening credits run, explosive orange colors, horrific and gorgeous at once. Ominous music accompanies the conflagration. (It is "In Abenrot," by Richard Strauss, though you probably don't know this yet.) Then, as the credits end, Glenn Miller's sumptuously upbeat "In the Mood" replaces the portentous tone, and you see the words "Cape Fear" written across a background of deep greens, crimsons, and browns. Only as the camera continues to pan do you realize that this is a high arched ceiling, and then you find that the domes cover the foyer of a grand hotel. The camera moves slowly down to the ground and there is a blond-haired woman standing behind a large column. She wears a peach-colored dress. She is young and very attractive. A young man in a two-toned coat, gray and black, kisses her and the two walk down the wide staircase leading to the outside. Then an African-American man walks toward them. He accuses the younger man of trying to seduce the girl's mother in the toilet, pulls a knife, and attacks. The music shifts to hard-driving heavy metal. (This is Slaughterhouse's song, "Powermad," but you likely don't know this.) The younger man brutally beats his opponent, eventually smashing his brains out on the marble floor. All the while, the girl shrilly screams the name, "Sailor." He then stands up over his dead victim, and lights a cigarette. He points to someone at the top of the stairs, an older blonde-haired woman looking disturbed, guilty. She is seemingly the girl's mother. Glenn Miller's music resumes.

This sequence is a bewildering assault of shifting images and sounds. There is no meaning here, only the mesmerizing, disturbing flux. You take a weird kind of joy in the surreal succession, pictures just for the sake of pictures.

But then, by the end of the succession, meaning emerges. You realize that the younger man and the woman in the peach dress are lovers; you understand the woman has a mother who hates the young man named "Sailor"; you understand that Sailor is extremely violent and has been before; you guess that the mother has tried to have Sailor killed out of rage or jealousy or a combination of both. The starkly juxtaposed images cohere into significant patterns. You take your attention away from the fragmented sights and take pleasure in the emerging concepts, glad to know that there is order within the chaos.

Then, however, you quickly fall back into the fray, once more losing yourself in Lynch's subsequent images, just as unsettling as the ones you've just seen, pictures of seemingly irreconcilable extremities: violence and comedy, tragedy and satire. You don't know how or what to feel and you just go with it until once more structures rise out of the crazed currents and grants a modicum of comfort.

Such is the rhythm of viewing this Lynch film, an especially playful work, in Schiller's sense, one that forces us constantly to place into conversation seductive material currents and more stable intellectual forms.

Moving back and forth between these two poles, you realize the virtues and limitations of both and thus accept and reject them at the same time. You find yourself in a dynamic middle ground, a border land where the powers of content energize form and the powers of form vitalize content. Attached yet unattached, you can play with each pole without becoming consumed by either. You experience the joy of dynamic wholeness, the third term.

In one of the few instances in which Lynch actually discusses the relationship between his own vision of wholeness and his filmmaking, he beautifully consolidates these ideas – irony and play. In a 2005 interview, Lynch discusses his spiritual commitment. Since the early 1970s, when he was making *Eraserhead*, Lynch has been a devotee of Maharishi Mahesh Yogi and his method of Transcendental Meditation.

Based on the Hindu discipline of yoga, this form of meditation is simple. For twenty minutes a day, the practitioner sits with his eyes closed and repeats his one-syllable mantra. This mantra is designed to focus the mind on one idea and thus to inspire a feeling of unity. This feeling is supposed to breed relaxed, passive acceptance of the way things are, openness to the flow of thoughts and things, a gentle balance between attachment and detachment. Allegedly, this condition allows the body to gain a deeper state of relaxation than it gets in regular sleep. But this state also apparently increases mental awareness and focus, empowering the practitioner to experience the world more vividly.[14]

Lynch maintains that this practice has exposed him to an idea of God as a "totality" beyond any one name. He calls this divinity the "almighty merciful father, and the divine mother, the kingdom of heaven, the absolute, divine being, bliss consciousness, creative intelligence." This God is "unchanging, eternal." It "is," yet it is also "nothing." Awareness of this full void has expanded Lynch's consciousness. He believes that "there's just too much happiness and consciousness and wakefulness and understanding growing" for anyone to be "suffering so much, or caught up in some narrow little thing." Part of this expansion is his appreciation for many kinds of religious seeking. He suggests all religions at root are devoted to "mystery" and to turning their practitioners into "seeker[s]." This feeling of boundlessness, Lynch further claims, often just "happens," unexpectedly and spontaneously. One suddenly wants "to know," to "experience," to "learn about things."[15]

Lynch describes the feeling he has at times achieved while meditating. Sometimes, when the "experience" "kicks in," he undergoes "intense bliss," as if "the unbounded ocean" had poured into him. This condition is called "bubbling bliss," a sensation that has made Lynch feel as though he is a light bulb flooded with light.

Most importantly, Lynch's meditation has played a major role in his creativity. While meditating, he sometimes sinks into a "field of pure creativity," the "source" from which ideas come. His egocentric "anxieties and fears" fade away, and he dissolves into a subconscious realm that resembles a "pure open channel of ideas." Out of these experiences grow

14   Cathleen Falsani, "Lynch: 'Bliss Is Our Nature,'" *Chicago Sun Times* (16 Jan. 2005).
15   All quotations in this and the following two paragraphs have been taken from Falsani, "Lynch: 'Bliss Is Our Nature,'"

what Lynch most loves – those delicate abstractions. Though films should not be solely made of abstractions, pictures that "hold" abstractions delight him. These pictures, he suggests, evade clear meanings and instead inspire rich feelings. These images are, Lynch claims, like "seeds," or, more interestingly, like the "Vedas, the laws of nature."

These are remarkable claims. They intimate, on the one hand, that the imagistic ideas that arise during meditation are manifestations of stable, unchanging laws. On the other hand, these statements suggest that the delicate abstractions of meditation are inflections of wispy, lubricious feelings. The picture of the seeker as a bulb overflowing with light captures this duality: the adept is a pattern of the whole, a revelation of pervasive consciousness, but also a condensation of the boundless, a distortion of the absolute.

Lynch's thoughts suggest that the seeker should take his relationship to spirit very seriously, for he is a unique manifestation of this numinous power. But Lynch's ideas also intimate the opposite. Because the seeker is ultimately an incomplete and inaccurate representation of the numinous, he should not take his connection to spirit very seriously at all. Finding himself in this middle ground between extremes, he must reach for the playful third term.

Other statements from Lynch nicely encapsulate this earnest playfulness. When asked if his films reflect the principles of Transcendental Meditation, Lynch responds in the negative, claiming that movies that exemplify a "message" are as uninteresting as telegrams. He then emphasizes that his films actually have nothing to do with his "religion." "Film," he observes, is not a vehicle to "sell" his religious "thing" but an expression of "ideas" that he has "fallen in love with." If Transcendental Meditation does appear at all in his films, it shows through in an inadvertent, "innocent" way. Obviously, on the one hand, Lynch's movies are not mere allegories of the dogmas of Maharishi Mahesh. However, on the other hand, his films are precisely sites of Transcendental Meditation – revelations of the full emptiness of being.[16]

There are numerous revelatory images in Lynch's films, structures that push viewers toward the bliss that might come with experiencing some kind of eternal consciousness, some sort of ubiquitous being. These images are overtly apocalyptic, sites where one can't help but meditate on the transcendental.

Lost Highway ends with Fred driving at night down a lonely highway. He has already allegedly killed his wife, transformed into another man, repeated some of the ills of his former identity, and turned once more into his old self. As he stares blankly into the cold darkness, we wonder if he has been condemned to hell on earth, to an endless journey over a wasted desert. But we also imagine that he might have broken out of the vicious cycle of repeated mistakes to a plane where time has no meaning, to eternity.

The conclusion of *Mulholland Dr.* is one of Lynch's most cryptic. The characters of the labyrinthine plot lines have all faded away, and we find ourselves in an old theater, the Club Silencio. A woman with blue hair and a white face appears in the balcony. She whispers, "Silencio." The film

<hr />

[16] Falsani, "Lynch: 'Bliss Is Our Nature.'"

ends. This image emphasizes the artificial quality of the movie, the fact that it is a construct occurring in a theater. But this startling picture also suggests that this silent theater is reality itself, the third realm generating and destroying both illusion and fact, mere mimicry and moving experience. The silence, then, becomes the ground of all sounds, the fecund abyss out of which all emerges and then fades, endlessly.

One of Kierkegaard's most famous books is called *The Sickness unto Death*. For Kierkegaard, this sickness is despair, a state in which one is out of alignment with God, incapable of faith, and thus without hope. Whether he knows it or not, Lynch with his sacred images revises the Danish philosopher. His pictures often throw us into a sickening hopelessness – an ill feeling that no final meaning or purpose is available, that life as we know it is meaningless. But these same visuals also show us that hopelessness might well be the proper condition for an experience of being's fullness.

Think of it: when we are without hope, we are also without expectation, and therefore devoid of a desire for things to be different. Empty of this desire, almost always selfish, we accept the world as it is, here, now, in the present. Doing so, we open ourselves to the ungraspable grandeur of existence, its horrors and its beauties, and thus, for a moment, enjoy an immediate experience of sublime wholeness.

A few years back, Lynch released one of his most obscure and disturbing works yet, *Inland Empire*. Whatever the film might mean – and it means so much and also so little – it is definitely an unforgettable encounter with the mystery of the inland, the imperial interiors that stay forever unmapped. In undertaking the task of sounding the abysmal insides of the heart, this picture is deadly to the rational mind, the faculty that wants to make sense, to say that "A" is "A" and this woman, Nikki Grace, is this woman, and no one else. But out of this death rises new life, the turbulent polarities of existence, the bracing fact that you are who you are, right now, but also everyone and everything else besides. This latter state might feel like insanity, mental illness, schizophrenia, but it might also be a feeling of wholeness, of healing, oneness with all creatures in the expanding cosmos.

FRANCOIS-XAVIER GLEYZON
LYNCH, BACON & THE FORMLESS

The work of Francis Bacon, according to Gilles Deleuze, stems from a logic of sensation whose unifying principle operates at the border, at the very limit of the abstract and the figurative by which subjects offer themselves to the gaze in a movement of disfiguration or progressive disfiguration without for as much affecting/distorting the theatricality or the staging in which they are represented (framework, structure and props). If the concept of the *informe* or "formless," as it was developed by Georges Bataille, plays a predominant part in the work of Francis Bacon, it is also remarkably present in the cinematographic work of David Lynch. As with Bacon, Lynch shows us faces that have lost their human form and lifts up in their place a head without a face and without a form so that the human head is unmade to reveal instead the head of an animal: *The Elephant Man*. The question of the animal and of becoming animal through the formless haunts the picture/the screen. "Perhaps art begins with the animal" and its pre-eminence could be said to consist in its primitiveness in which the sufferings, the convulsions and the vulnerabilities of body and flesh are ingrained.[1] Here, we shall need to create a scene of intensity and of correspondence through which experimentation and experiment both pictorial and cinematographic in Bacon and Lynch are implemented, set in motion, interact and tend to illuminate the fundamental question of the formless.

A BATAILLIAN VISION OF THE FORMLESS
But, to begin with, what is there to say about the formless and how do we approach it in the work of Francis Bacon and David Lynch? We will need first of all to effect an initial theoretical reconnaissance/framework as to the proper definition of formlessness. In the strange yet no less erudite review entitled *Documents* which Georges Bataille directed between 1929 and 1930, Bataille demonstrates in stupefying fashion his radical will to go beyond "les fondements propres de l'esthétique classique" ("the very foundations of classical aesthetics"). He does not rest then, to use an expression which is close to his heart, to "decompose" the image. In the production of theory as much as in the pragmatic manipulation of the concept, Bataille mounts and dismounts certain images *against* and *with* certain others in order to prove and to feel their efficacity even going as far as to abuse them, if not as Georges Didi-Hubermann terms it, in order to "mistreat them." In this practice and concept of montage, of the treatment-mistreatment of the image is contained all the intensity of

---

[1] Gilles Deleuze and Felix Guattari, *Qu'est-ce que la philosophie* (Paris: Editions de Minuit, 1991) 174.

Bataille's work. His creative concept does not consist simply of turning upside down, modifying, de*forming* the forms of images, but in elaborating something new in the sense that Bataille operates with *displacement*, with the surreptitious *deferral* of form towards formless. The formless does not arise in any way from the categorical refusal of form – quite the contrary. It is more about the setting into motion of forms, a quite special operation which, in contradiction to what is preached by philosophy "demanding in general that each thing has its own form" commits itself to the work of forms all the better to defile them:

> Ainsi informe n'est pas seulement un adjectif ayant tel sens mais un terme servant à *déclasser*, exigeant généralement que chaque chose ait sa forme. Ce qu'il désigne n'a ses droits dans aucun sens et se fait écraser partout comme une araignée ou un ver de terre. Il faudrait en effet, pour que les hommes académiques soient contents, que l'univers prenne forme. La philosophie entière n'a pas d'autre but: il s'agit de donner une redingote à ce qui est, une redingote mathématique. Par contre affirmer que l'univers ne ressemble à rien et n'est qu'informe revient à dire que l'univers est quelque chose comme une araignée ou un crachat.[2]

> (The formless is not only an adjective having a given meaning but a term that serves to *defile* (déclasser), requiring in general that each thing have its form. What it designates has no rights in any sense and gets itself squashed everywhere like a spider or an earthworm. It is necessary, in fact, in order for academics to be happy, for the universe to have a shape. All of philosophy has no other goal: it is a matter of giving a frock coat to what is, a mathematical frock coat. On the other hand, affirming that the universe resembles nothing and is merely formless amounts to saying that the universe is something like a spider or a gob of spit.)

If the formless arises from a certain type of defilement or from a defiling category, it arises at the same time from margins and the marginal or such as Marcel Schwob could state it himself in relation to the definition and the function of art: "L'art est à l'opposé des idées générales, ne décrit que l'individuel, ne désire que l'unique. Il ne classe pas, il *déclasse*."[3] ("Art is the opposite of general ideas, only describes the individual, only desires the unique. It does not file away, it *defiles*.") The formless, just like art, thus finds its definition, its proper meaning, its relevance and its efficacity in a *defiling* proposition and therefore in "the transgression" which, according to Bataille, will be translated into a form as subversive as it is prodigious "like a spider or a gob of spit." Georges Bataille will never deny the existence of form. The formless, he argues, is not to be found in a sense deriving from "a non-form" or "nothing at all" but in a certain painful and yet fertile effort that we could describe as giving birth, a death rattle-tearing and a cruel suffering and which nevertheless in its negativity will bring to the light of day a new artistic creation, in brief an overturning of the image by the formless, i.e. a new thought, a new *knowledge*. Perhaps Saint Augustine, *avant la lettre*, will formulate better than anybody the definition of the formless. An isolated moment accom-

[2] Georges Bataille, "Informe," *Documents* 7 (December 1929): 382.
[3] Qtd in F. Leperlier and Claude Cahun, *L'écart et la metamorphose* (Paris: J-M. Place 1992) 85.

panied by funereal doubts as mystical as they are heretical, this text seems to designate, echoing Bataille, the genesis of the formless such as Saint Augustine conceived of it as much as he feared it:

> My mind was in a whirl of hideous and horrible forms which utterly denied the order of nature; yet they were forms all the same; and I conceived the formless not as totally lacking form but as possessing such a form that, if it were seen, my senses would recoil from its strangeness and grotesqueness and my human weakness be utterly confounded. But in fact the concept I had was formless not by the absence of all forms, but only by comparison with forms more beautiful. Right reason urged that if I wished to conceive the formless, I should strip away every smallest vestige of every sort of form. But I could not do it. I should have found it easier to think that whatever is totally without form cannot exist at all, than to conceive something between form and non-being, lacking form yet not nothing, formless and almost nothing. So my mind ceased to question my spirit, which was full of images of bodily forms, which it changed and re-arranged as it willed. I fixed my mind upon the bodies themselves, and looked deeper into the mutability by which they cease to be what they were and begin to be what they were not. And it occurred to me that this transition from one form to another might be by way of something formless, and not by way of absolute non-being. But I wanted to know [...].[4]

In a confidential, *confessional* tone and the tone of an internal experience in Bataille's terms, strictly speaking, Saint Augustine shows us both the very crucible itself of his aesthetic questioning and his struggle, his hand-to-hand combat I would say in an infinite relationship with images in their overturning and their transgressive mutability. It seems that Saint Augustine though dismissive of the phantasmagorical effects of forms within the image ("those phantoms of splendour") did not cease to pursue the particular movements of that visual experience – of "that infinitude of images," he will go on to say, "which throws itself right into the eyes of the soul with an impetuosity against which it is quite difficult to defend oneself."[5] Bataille, for his part, will not defend himself against them – on the contrary he will give free rein to the work of forms in their mutations, welcoming at the same time their transgressions, their own *informités* (literally "formlessnesses"). "Jouissance of transgression": all the fundamental aesthetic turning upside down/overturning of Bataille will consist in this work of transgressing the limits inherent to the forms of images. And it is indeed in these terms that Michel Foucault in his *Préface à la Transgression* will set out the creative plans of Georges Bataille: "La transgression est un geste qui concerne la limite; c'est là, en cette minceur de la ligne, que se manifeste l'éclair de son passage, mais peut-être aussi sa trajectoire en sa totalité."[6] ("Transgression is a gesture concerned with the limit; there it is, in the thinness of that line, that the flash of its passage is manifested, but perhaps also its trajectory in its totality.") What does transgression consist of *visually* once the limit is crossed?

[4] Saint Augustine, *Confessions* (354-430). Book XII, Caelum caeli et materia informis, Chapter 6. Trans. Francis Joseph Sheed. Ed. Peter Brown and Michael P. Foley. (Indianapolis: Hackett) 263.
[5] Saint Augustine, *Epistula*, Book CXLVII 42.
[6] Michel Foucault, "Préface à la Transgression." *Critique* (Paris : Editions de Minuit Aug.-Sept. 1963) 195-96, 754.

What does transgression open out on and thus the formless as defined by Bataille? Re-reading back issues from the surrealist series of *Documents* and the artistic and photographic input of Man Ray, Brassaï, Boiffard shows radically and blatantly that the formless corresponds in a lot of cases, if not all cases, to the bringing into play of a quite specific type of space. In this way we encounter close-up angle shots, plunging perspectives or methods in which framing, *détourage* and cutting of the object/subject photographed/portrayed is rendered vague or else deliberately taken out of frame.[7] It is indeed in such mind-boggling, special and sometimes – so it seems – grotesque details (*Big Toe, Lobster Claw, Open Mouth*, etc.) that the technical practices and processes of representation adopted by the artists represented by Bataille in *Documents* are put on display as much as the perceptive processes aroused in the spectator. But, above all, detail will have as its aim to *dislocate* and *defile* and, in this sense turn upside down, overturn and transgress the general economy of the form of the image and thus our understanding strictly speaking. Do we not find here in this detail and in these practices, as Roland Barthes was able to put it in terms, which would suit Bataille perfectly, "le commencement timide de la jouissance"[8] ("the shy commencement of jouissance").

FOCUS ON THE MOUTH

There are numerous connections, affinities and analogies between David Lynch and Francis Bacon with regard to the formless image. But it is not enough to enunciate their intrinsic affinities in order to find fruitful correspondences. Besides are not these more fortuitous than fruitful? Cinematographic criticism of Lynch and iconographic criticism of Bacon always seems to focus on the influence and effects exerted by one towards/upon the other to the point of making of them an interpretation which is unilaterally referential, even binary. Work, however, the creative plans of an artist can never be summed up by pointing out or summing up its influences such as it is possible to read them in the interviews David Lynch gave to Chris Rodley. Also, when David Lynch enunciates perhaps too easily the famous analogy – too famous and too cited – between his work and that of Bacon, Lynch does not thereby illuminate or show us *anything* of the creative process he is involved in. He prefers to indicate allusively – and deliberately – that "stuff," that "everything" that inhabits the work of Bacon and with which he finds himself in harmony. But what is this "stuff" and this "everything"? The analogy we thought would be useful seems to us from this point on to be quite trivial and sterile. In order to palliate such disappointment, we must take an interest in particular points and what I mean by that is the points of attachment and anchoring at the heart of which may be found the artistic plans of Lynch and Bacon through a creative exploration of the formless. Perhaps we will find in the

---

[7] *Détourage* is an expression chosen deliberately since it refers to the art of representation (painting, photography or engraving), which involves delimiting the subject's precise contours on a canvas or film, making it stand out from the background or eliminating this altogether.

[8] Roland Barthes, *Sollers écrivain* (Paris : Seuil, 1979) 70. See also on the subject of Bataillian jouissance the potent work of Wilson, Scott *The Order of Joy*: *Beyond the Cultural Politics of Enjoyment* (New York: SUNY, 2008) and notably the chapter "The Structure of the Real" where the term "jouissance" is explained and declined, cf. p.3 et seq.

motif of the *mouth* the concrete manifestation of this encounter or even a perfect triangulation between Lynch, Bacon and Bataille.

In Michel Chion's seminal study devoted to David Lynch, Chion shows that the *open mouth* occupies a major and particular place in Lynch's work.[9] The vision of an open mouth offers in Lynch the sign of the pleasure of orgasm *par excellence*, of *jouissance* in short. Such is the case in the photographic collection of the catalogue *The Air is on Fire* in which there is truly a focus/emphasis on the mouth (cf. photographs on pages 392, 394, 407-9 and 417)[10]. But this orifice undergoes with Lynch mutations/transformations so that the gaping mouth with red and well rimmed lips no longer displays itself to the gaze or the understanding as a photographic/filmic detail, but it divests itself of flesh – it becomes in itself alone an autonomous and central unitary figure. To such an extent that the process of magnification well and truly cancels out the human face in order to blow the mouth up, to make it meaningful in terms of a *body-mouth* and in this way to create, of that there is no doubt, an organic topology as fantastic as it is fantasmatic of the female body. In fact, if we refer to *Dune* we see that the Supreme Being merely consists in an abject organic mass in which the orifice of the mouth is magnified so that when Lynch zooms in on the mouth a semantic mutation takes place and the latter becomes a genital orifice: a *vagina* or an *anus*. This head-mouth, organic, floating and deformed, also puts us in mind of that of John Merrick in *The Elephant Man* – but it is without doubt closer to the baby in *Eraserhead*. Here again, the baby's whole body seems to be a formless body, harboring a mouth with thin lips: neither anus nor vagina, the baby's body turns this time into *meatus*.[11] The mouth in Lynch is clearly organized around a process which moves and progresses so well in the general economy of the work that it acquires (as in Bataille and Bacon we shall see) the power of illocalization and independence. The mouth, we could say, eats up the face, contaminates it, overflows it – swallows it. In this way the humid mouth, as horrendous as it is indecent, of Bobby Peru in *Wild at Heart* seems to lacerate his face and only opens in a close-up to reveal that it harbors a toothed orifice reminiscent of a *vagina dentata*.[12] Still in *Wild at Heart*, and in an even more explicit fashion, the lips of Lula, on which David Lynch focuses, bleed when she has just been raped by her uncle Pooch. The mouth, the lips become the metonymic expression of a sexual organ, they swell and are pierced to become *hymen*. In the same way, some scenes later, the abortion scene that constitutes a painful memory for Lula manifests itself to the spectator through an *orifice*-magnifying glass – an O – offering us in this way a magnified vision of Lula's mouth. This centering on Lula's mouth coincides at this moment in time with the aspiration of her blood that empties itself out of her body

[9] Chion, Michel, *David Lynch*, 2nd ed. (London: British Film Institute, 2006) 176.
[10] David Lynch, *The Air is on Fire* (London: Thames and Hudson, 2007).
[11] In point of fact, organs move about and seem to be constantly changing in Lynch's work. A phrase of Burroughs that Deleuze also cites in relation to his *Francis Bacon – Logique de la Sensation*, seems entirely in keeping with our remarks: "... no organ is constant as regards either function or position... sex organs sprout anywhere... rectums appear, open to defecate... the entire organism changes color and consistency in split-second adjustments..." William Burroughs, *Naked Lunch – The Restored Text*. (London: Harper Perennial Modern Classics, 2005) 9.
[12] Erich Neuman, *The Great Mother*, 168 and n42

and designates at the same time here through the round hole of the empty and open mouth the place of the O, the origin and the ori*gyne*. But in Lynch's work, the motif of the mouth and the lips advances-circulates in a polycentric and polyorganic dynamic. In other words the motif of the mouth in Lynch is constantly being *defiled*. In fact, there is no point in classifying it by endowing it with a general meaning as Michel Chion was able to do in spite of himself with his famous Lynch-Kit, for the motif does not cease to migrate, to escape from any category to which it may be assigned. The mouth seems to act in a displacement, an insatiable and uncontrollable movement like the gaping and devouring mouth of the worms on the planet Arakis in *Dune* with centrifugal forces and ambivalent sexual characteristics which envelop the mouth in a mixed semiotics both vaginal and tubular, phallic.[13] But still the mouth seems to be unsatisfied.

The rimmed, bright red mouths (blood red we might say) of Lula and Marietta Fortune in *Wild at Heart* seem to be the motif uniting mother and daughter. If the lips of Lula bleed and somewhat stain her then innocent face, the lips of the mother, as far as she is concerned, will be endowed with a peculiarity, an invasive function which will literally take hold of her face and proceed to what one might call a *dévisagéification*. At a moment as remarkable as it is intense in the film, Marietta Fortune, having ordered the murder of Sailor by Santos, is beset by doubt. In a moment of panic and remorse, she goes first of all to contemplate her face in a mirror so that she can afterwards literally un-*visage* herself. She tries out to begin with a simulated suicide using the red of her lips – her red lipstick – and pretends to cut her veins. A few moments later, in a veritably trance-like moment, intervenes the veritable will to expand that David Lynch confers on the mouth. Marietta Fortune's mouth suddenly invades the whole of her face and covers all of it in red. In fact, Marietta Fortune's cry no longer comes out of her mouth but the whole of her face – her head, her face turns into a mouth. This mouth-face blown up excessively that hollows out and throws up in the toilets, redoubles in vigour and vitality by the fact that it suggests *Stimmung* – that nauseous disposition that precedes vomiting – and these point at the same time towards the very experience of existence per se as Emmanuel Lévinas shows in *De l'évasion*: "On est là et il n'y a plus rien à faire, ni rien à ajouter à ce fait que nous avons été livré entièrement, que tout est consommé: c'est l'expérience même de l'être pur [...]."[14] ("We are there and there's no longer anything we can do, nor anything to add to that fact that we have been liberated completely, that everything has been consumed: this is the essence of the experience of a pure being [...].")

Mouths vomit in the films of Lynch just as they do in his works of art as we can realize for ourselves in the short film *Six Men Getting Sick* or then again in his paintings and the sketches of *The Air is on Fire* (cf. untitled artworks, 117, 119 & 121). Mouths vomit or foam in a prolonged

---

[13] On the homology between male and female genitalia, I refer the reader to the article by Thomas Laqueur, "Orgasm, Generation, and the Politics of Reproductive Biology." *Representations* 14 (Spring 1986), *The Making of the Modern Body: Sexuality and Society in the Nineteenth Century*. Ed. Thomas Laquer and Catherine Gallagher. (Berkeley: University of California Press, 1987), and more especially p.12 et seq. as well as figures 1,2,3 & 4.

[14] Emmanuel Lévinas, *De l'évasion* (Paris: Fata Morgana, 1982) 116.

groan which does not stop invading the space of the representation. What Lynch presents to us here – echoing Lévinas – is perhaps this extreme situation, this situation where people are vomiting, where "there's no longer anything we can do" in terms of the experience of the pure being and at the same time in terms of the experience of escape that imposes itself. There is in the vomiting a refusal to stay there, an effort to get out. What the mouth shows the eye here is repression and rejection. The mouth takes precedence inasmuch as it knows how to concretely incorporate the visible in order to render it all the better afterwards (if not to spew it up), or even, as Georges Didi-Huberman so admirably puts it: "la bouche sait réaliser ce que l'oeil ne sait souvent que désirer."[15] ("The mouth knows how to realize what the eye often only knows how to desire.")

When the mouth throws up, it shows us in a gush not only a string of nausea but also an optic-tactile (therefore haptic) space coming from the inside of the body. The mouth then expresses the organic life of the subject and also shows all the complexity of a representation in which the latter opens like an eye and comes to vomit the depths of the body as Worringer was able to describe it: "This will does not then consist in reproducing the things of the external world or in restoring them in their outward appearance, but in projecting externally [...] organically vital forms, the harmony of their rhythm, in short their whole internal being."[16] How can we represent this interiority if not by the spurt or the gush, organic rejection and all this through the orifice of the mouth? The mouth is both screen and the word – mouth – once it is pronounced is already a break-in and an opening towards internal depths and the deep rejections of the body. It is perhaps in this last proposition that the artistic thought of Lynch and Bacon is best articulated.

We would need to gather together at this moment in time all the paintings of Bacon so that we can contemplate therein a multitude of orifices, of gaping mouths that open and vomit. For, as Deleuze has written, the mouth is that hole, that organ from which vomiting is a visual process through which the whole of the body escapes.[17] So the painting *Triptych May-June 1973* (1973) offers to the gaze a series of both spasmodic vomiting and excretion. The pushes, the rejections which escape from the body are effected by the round contours of the mouth or the anus which, in their turn, affix themselves to the round form of the toilet. There is a certain continuity in which the organ of the mouth or the anus is prolonged and finds itself received in its circularity by a material structure (toilet or washbasin) which in its turn couples with it and forms/moulds a hollow volume so as to collect in a vanishing point the organic rejection (vomit/excretion). This is a prodigious development, a prodigious organic continuity whose final operation seems to consist in contemplating a *relic* (reliquat, remnant), or perhaps according to the expression of Paul Eluard to describe the writings of Bataille and the formless, "un vomi mystique"[18]

---

[15] Georges Didi-Huberman, *L'image ouverte* (Paris: Gallimard, 2007) 334.

[16] Wilhem Worringer, *Abstraction and Empathy: A Contribution to the Psychology of Style*, trans. Michael Bullock (London: Routledge, 1963) 28.

[17] Gilles Deleuze, *Francis Bacon, Logique de la Sensation* (Paris : Seuil, 2002) 24, 32.

[18] Qtd in Michel Surya, *Georges Bataille: An Intellectual Biography*, trans. Krzysztof Fijalkowski and Michael Richardson (London: Verso, 2002) 192.

or "a mystic vomit." Mystic vomit or then again, *vomi sacré* – for it is true that Bataille does not miss out himself on invoking vomit in his article in Document n°8 (1930) entitled "La mutilation sacrificielle et l'oreille coupée de Vincent Van Gogh" ("Sacrificial mutilation and the cut-off ear of Vincent Van Gogh"). For Bataille it is a question of grasping the logic itself of the sacred in the act of self-giving, of submission and to open up and whoever intervenes at the end of an operation involving rejection in which the sacrificing subject "libère les éléments hétérogènes [...], se laisse aller à lui-même [et vient] vomir son propre être comme il a vomi un morceau de lui-même [...] c'est-à-dire comme à la nécessité de se jeter hors de soi comme un galle ou un aïssaouah."[19] [...] ("liberates the heterogeneous elements [...], lets itself go to itself [and comes] to vomit its own being like it has vomited a piece of itself [...] i.e. as if to the necessity of throwing itself outside itself like a gallstone or an aissaouah.")

There then, in the foods vomited, the sacred is to be contemplated! This uncontrollable eruption-rejection that comes to lie immobile in a repugnant aqueous mass under our eyes corresponds perfectly to the paradigm of the *formless* in the sequence of actions that releases it: *hole-excretion-rejection*. Besides it was at the end of a similar operation that Bataille defined the formless itself by insisting and affirming that the *formless* comes down to saying that the universe is something like [...] *a gob of spit*.[20] Spit and/or vomit, this couple go together in the sequence action-repression-rejection and seems to be in perfect reciprocity with an exemplification of the formless. It is also in response to an investigation of the formless as an abject mass that Michel Leiris elaborated the definition of the gob of spit:

> Le crachat est enfin, par son inconsistence, ses contours indéfinis, l'imprécision relative de sa couleur, son humidité, le symbole même de *l'informe*, de l'invérifiable, du non-hiérarchisé, pierre d'achoppement molle et gluante qui fait tomber, mieux qu'un quelconque caillou, toutes les démarches de celui qui s'imagine l'être humain comme étant quelque chose.[21]

> (Spit is finally, by its lack of consistency, its indefinite contours, the relative imprecision of its colour, its wetness, the very symbol itself of the *formless*, of the unverifiable, of the non-hierarchical, a soft and sticky stumbling block which undermines, better than any pebble, all the procedures of he who imagines a human being to amount to something.)

What interests us here is the fact that the text of Leiris on spit "Crachat – L'eau à la bouche" is included first and foremost, as Georges Didi-Huberman has indicated admirably, in a study/consideration of the mouth that Leiris has identified in the first place as being the opening *par excellence* in which the "Human figure" is identified. Francis Bacon will be perhaps the painter who observes this definition of the mouth up to its

---

[19] Georges Bataille, in "La mutilation sacrificielle et l'oreille coupée de Vincent Van Gogh," *Œuvres complètes* (Paris : Gallimard, 1970) 269. See also on the subject of sacred sacrifice Alexander Irwin, *Saints of the impossible: Bataille, Weil, and the politics of the sacred* (Minneapolis: University of Minnesota Press, 2002) 35.
[20] Georges Bataille, "Informe," 382.
[21] Michel Leiris, "Crachat – l'eau à la bouche," *Documents* 7 (1929) 381.

very limits in order to transgress it all the better afterwards. In fact, Bacon reaches an extreme level which will extend perhaps as far as what one could call, to borrow the expression used by Leiris, a veritable "defilement of human likeness." For it is also this defilement of the human face/likeness which is radically called into question in the triptych of *Sweeney Agonistes* (1967). The centre of the picture reveals a powerful aesthetic emphasis/focus on the mouth so that the latter transgresses all limits of the conceivable and seems to come to hollow out the head of the person portrayed the better to disfigure his face. As Deleuze points out, the open mouth then appears like the section of a severed artery.[22]

The blood flows through this mouth/artery by which the head and face are defiled and is cancelled out. Bacon idealizes the mouth – it is that essence or then again that antrum of the organic in which is realized and thereby *idealized* the human face in the defilement of its own form. Or in other words, the mouth – the open orifice par excellence – would be the vector of the formless. This is why all organic pushes from the body in Bacon escape via the mouth. To quote just a few examples – for we would have to bring together all the mouths in Bacon's work here in order to appreciate their full magnitude – the mouth in *Head II* and *Head VI* (1949), that of the wet nurse in *Study For The Nurse In The Film Battleship Potemkin* (1957), or even *Three Studies for Figures at the Base of a Crucifixion* (1944) and the famous sacred-sacrificed mouth of *Pope Innocent X* (1953) which opens to scream through a curtain of chromatic rain.[23] In this way the mouth – that wet mucous membrane of the oral cavity – redoubles in power in its cry while it seems at the same time to double its visible saliva. It is slaver that the painter will want to present as the organic rejection of the cry and it is also in these terms that Francis Bacon will explain and define his art in the catalogue of the Modern Art Museum of New York in 1955 making use of a quite special and quite organic analogy, that of snail slaver: "I would like my pictures to look as if a human being had passed between them, like a snail, leaving a trail of the human presence and memory trace of the past events as the snail leaves its *slime*."[24] This slaver, this *slime*, like spit, this type of white and shining froth, is perhaps the very condition of existence – the elementary trace of an aesthetic – of Francis Bacon's painting. The white foam (spit – slaver) that manifests itself at the corners of sick, senile, mad or epileptic people's mouths always comes from – in its figurative sense – castoffs, the vile and abject matter which presides over the definition of the formless. But in its literal sense we find that this same foam also manifests fermentation, a fertile medium, aesthetic creation *par excellence*, and notable that of the birth of Aphrodite:

> And Heaven came, bringing on night and longing for love, and he lay about
> Earth spreading himself full upon her. Then the son from his ambush

22 Gilles Deleuze, *Francis Bacon*, 30.
23 On the subject of the motif of curtains in the painting of Bacon, I refer the reader to the study by Luigi Ficacci, *Bacon* (London: Taschen, 2006) 37: "The strokes of the curtain whose identity had become complicated in the course of evolution [...] Here they appear as a sort of chromatic shower that cloaks and leaches the body's features."
24 Quoted in Michael Pepiatt, *Francis Bacon in the 1950s* (New Haven: Yale University Press, 2007) 166, *my italics*.

stretched forth his left hand and in his right took the great long sickle with jagged teeth, and swiftly lopped off his own father's members and cast them away to fall behind him. And not vainly did they fall from his hand; for all the bloody drops that gushed forth Earth received, and as the seasons moved round she bare the strong Erinyes and the great Giants with gleaming armour, holding long spears in their hands and the Nymphs whom they call Meliae all over the boundless earth. And so soon as he had cut off the members with flint and cast them from the land into the surging sea, they were swept away over the main a long time: and a white foam (*leukos aphros*) spread around them from the immortal flesh, and in it there grew a maiden.[25]

The genital potency of this scene in which Ouranos, mutilated by Chronos, sees his genitalia cut into pieces and thrown far off into the sea demonstrates well how this abject matter (slaver-spit-sperm), this frothy foam (*aphros*) with regenerative properties gives *form*, birth to Aphrodite. The ambivalence between dirt/abject matter and the beauty of Aphrodite with which the text plays, makes us think that it contains a certain eroticism or at least a phenomenology of the fantastic. Still with the same axiom of foam as spit and its sexual analogy, we should point out that Michel Leiris, still in the same article "Crachat – L'eau à la bouche," will himself express in his turn the defiling, demeaning, transgressive and (therefore) profoundly erotic character of spit. Also, after having established the mouth as a *sacred*, *divine* place, "ce lieu de la parole" ("that place of words"), of the intellect made sonorous and visible, Leiris will note in the same breath that its evacuative function, such as spit, makes the mouth "plus répugnante encore que son rôle de porte où l'on enfourne les aliments" ("even more repugnant than its role as a portal into which food is shoved"). He will only need a few more lines to underline that the sacred nature of the mouth finds itself daily soiled by the sacrilege of saliva or spit.

Le crachat touche de très près aux manifestations érotiques, parce qu'il introduit le même "à vau l'eau" que l'amour dans la classification des organes. Comme l'acte sexuel accompli au grand jour, il est le scandale même, puisqu'il ravale la bouche – qui est le signe visible de l'intelligence – au rang des organes les plus honteux, et par la suite l'homme tout entier à la hauteur de ces primitifs animaux qui, ne possédant qu'une seule ouverture pour tous les besoins et étant par conséquent exempts de cette séparation élémentaire de l'organe de nutrition et de celui de l'excrétion à quoi correspondait la différenciation du noble et de l'ignoble, sont encore plongés tout à fait dans une sorte de chaos diabolique où rien n'est démêlé. De ce fait le crachat représente un comble en tant que sacrilège. La divinité de la bouche, par lui, est journellement salie.[26]

(Spit comes very near to manifestations of eroticism because it introduces the same "go with the flow" as love in the classification of organs. Like the act of sex in broad daylight, it is scandal itself, since it relegates the mouth – which is the visible sign of the intelligence – to the rank of the most shameful organs and then the whole man to the level of those primitive animals which, only possessing a single opening for all their needs and be-

[25] Hesiod, *The Theogony*, trans. Evelyn White (Stiltwell, Digitalreads.com Publishing) 45-6.
[26] Michel Leiris, "Crachat – l'eau à la bouche," 381-82.

ing consequently exempt from that elementary separation of the organ of nutrition from that of excretion to which used to correspond the differentiation of the noble and the ignoble, are again plunged completely into a sort of diabolic chaos in which nothing is distinguished. Because of this, spit represents a high point as far as sacrilege goes. The divinity of the mouth is soiled by it on a daily basis.)

The abject evacuation of spit could be said to confer a certain eroticism or at least a certain fantasm in its transgressive formula: the sacred (mouth) – sacrilege (spit). But spit still plays on its ambiguity. Or, to be more precise, it envelops a semantic fluidity as pointed out by the article of Marcel Griaule who, in collaboration with Michel Leiris, retraced a short history of spit through its ethnological meanings:

On peut sans être déshonoré, recevoir en plein visage un coup de matraque ou de pistolet automatique; on peut dans les mêmes conditions être défiguré par un bol de vitriol. Mais on ne saurait accepter sans honte un crachat volontaire ou involontairement lancé [...] C'est que le crachat est plus que le produit d'une glande, et il faut bien qu'il soit de nature magique puisque, s'il dispense l'ignominie, il est aussi un grand faiseur de miracle: la salive du Christ ouvrait les yeux des aveugles, et "le baume de mon coeur" des mères guérit les bosses des petits enfants. Le crachat accompagne le souffle, qui ne peut sortir de la bouche sans s'en imprégner. Or, le souffle est l'âme, à tel point que certains peuples ont la notion de "l'âme de devant le visage," qui s'arrête là où le souffle ne sait plus sentir, que nous disons "rendre le dernier soupir," et que "pneumatique" signifie, au fond, "plein d'âme." [...] La salive est de l'âme déposée ; le crachat est de l'âme en mouvement [...] En Afrique occidentale, pour donner l'esprit à l'enfant, le grand-père, quelques jours après la naissance, crache dans la bouche de son petit-fils.[27]

(We can, without being dishonored, receive full in the face a blow from a cosh or an automatic pistol; we can, under the same circumstances, be disfigured by a bowl of vitriol. But we cannot accept without shame a gob of spit voluntarily or involuntarily launched at us [...] This is because spit is more than the product of a gland and it must have something magical in it since, though it dispenses ignominy, it is also a great performer of miracles: Christ's saliva opened the eyes of the blind, and "the balm of my heart" of mothers cures the humps of little children. Spit goes with breath, which cannot come out of the mouth without being impregnated by it. The breath is the soul, to such an extent that certain peoples have the notion of "the soul before the face" which stops where the breath can no longer feel anything, which we call "giving up the ghost" and "pneumatic" basically means "full of soul." [...] Saliva is part of the soul deposited; spit is part of the soul in motion [...] In West Africa, to breathe spirit into a child, the grandfather, a few days after its birth, spits into the mouth of his grandson.)

What are we to make of the paradoxical status of spit? Better than anyone perhaps, David Lynch, in his adaptation of Frank Herbert's novel *Dune*, has been faithful to the meanings of spit in its movements and its paradoxes so as the better to reconcile them. Thus, for the Fremen community living in the arid desert of the planet Arakis, spit is considered a

---

[27] Marcel Griaule in Michel Leiris, "Crachat - l'eau à la bouche," 381.

distinguished and honorable way of greeting people. Apart from the projection of humoral matter into faces understood as a social code of *contact*, of politeness, the Fremen recycle all bodily liquids for they are, including spit, highly *sacred* and a source of life. However, still in *Dune*, we find in Baron Harkonnen a very different meaning for spit. The purulent face of the Baron covered with pruritus and pustules is already extremely reminiscent to us of a formless vomit. In a remarkable moment in the film in which Lady Jessica and Paul find themselves made captive and at the mercy of Baron Harkonnen, the latter floats above the royal family and stops for a moment to contemplate the *aphro*disiac beauty of Jessica's face. In a moment of ecstasy and intense excitement, the Baron leans over and then opens his mouth to spit on Lady Jessica:

127. The Baron floats across the room with suspensor-borne lightness.

BARON
Goodbye, Jessica and goodbye to your sweet
son... I want to spit once on your
head... just some spittle on your face –
what a luxury.

He spits on her cheek. The Baron floats out of the
room into the passageway.[28]

The mouth that opens and spits in this sequence of David Lynch's film puts us without doubt in *contact* with the eroticism of spit and at the same time with its sacrilegious and transgressive function that the director marries so well with its sacred character. What Lynch touches here and shows us through the mouth and the dejection of spit consists in a combinatory and dialogue mode between sacrilege – the *secular* and the sacred – *religious*. It is through this movement of dialogue that a correspondence is established for all the instability of the meaning both sacred and secular of spit, one that comes to resound in the mouth. Through this dialectical investigation, this movement of dejection of spit (which is "the soul in motion" according to Griaule) perhaps we rejoin a taking into consideration of what Bataille used to call "the symptom" in all the strangeness and instability of its own meaning: "le symptôme, s'il est encore un signe, est le signe le plus équivoque qui soit, le plus déroutant [...] De surcroît, c'est un signe incarné, organique, mouvementé [...] Il possède cette étrange exubérance qui fait de lui une composition théorique de paradoxes enchâssés les uns dans les autres."[29] ("The symptom, if it is still a sign, is the most equivocal and the most disconcerting of signs [...] Moreover it is an incarnate, organic, mobile sign [...] It possesses that strange exuberance which makes of it a theoretical composition of paradoxes set one inside the other.") For Bataille the symptom is staged, manifests itself *visually* by the interference, the collision created by the duality/the paradox of the mouth and its humoral dejection. In his article on the *Mouth*, Bataille clearly explains the moment when the symptom

28   David Lynch, *Dune Script* from The Internet Movie Script Database (IMSDb).
29   Georges Didi-Huberman, *La ressemblance informe, ou le gai savoir visuel selon Georges Bataille* (Paris: Macula, 1995) 360.

manifests itself in all its glory or then again in a dazzling and tearing violence in which reconciliation becomes impossible – unless it is by the
dislocation of the Human Face:

> Et dans les grandes occasions de la vie humaine se concentre encore bes-
> tialement dans la bouche, la colère fait grincer les dents, la terreur et la
> souffrance atroce font de la bouche l'organe des cris déchirants. Il est facile
> d'observer à ce sujet que l'individu est bouleversé, relève la tête en tendant
> le cou frénétiquement, en sorte que sa bouche vient se placer, autant qu'il
> est possible, dans le prolongement de la colonne vertébrale, *c'est-à-dire*
> *dans la position qu'elle occupe dans la constitution animale.* Comme si des
> impulsions explosives devaient jaillir directement du corps par la bouche
> sous forme de vociférations.[30]

> (And in the great events of human life, still bestially concentrated inside the
> mouth, anger makes us grind our teeth, terror and atrocious suffering make
> of the mouth the organ of piercing cries. It is easy to observe on this count
> that the individual is overwhelmed, raises his head stretching out his neck
> frantically so that his mouth comes to position itself, as far as it can, as a
> prolongation of the spinal column, *i.e. in the position that it occupies in the*
> *make-up of an animal.* It is as if explosive impulses were to spurt directly
> from the body through the mouth in the form of vociferations.)

It is in the very place that the mouth occupies that for Bataille is organized the genesis of everything primitive or then again of a certain
animality: "la bouche est le commencement, ou si l'on veut, la proue des
animaux: dans les cas les plus caractéristiques, elle est la partie la plus
vivante, c'est-à-dire la plus terrifiante [...]" ("the mouth is the beginning,
or if you like, the prow of animals: in the most characteristic cases it is
the part which is most alive, i.e. the most terrifying [...]") We may note
here that the analysis of Bataille's mouth tends ineluctably towards a de-
composition, a tearing ("explosive impulses"), a defilement of the Human
Figure, in short towards an incipient *formlessness*. In fact, we should note
here too how Bataille's will does not cease to inform the painting of Francis Bacon, in other words, and Deleuze affirms it: this will is unwearying
not in making restitution or representation (in the order of figuration or
narration), but in presenting, harnessing-capturing the forces, the intensities, the dynamics of the Figure of the body itself which come into play
and come to liberate themselves/to escape through the outlet of impulses,
spasms and pushes.[31] In fact, the Figure of the body is deformed and escapes in a cry, but for Bataille as for Bacon, the deformations that pass
through the body are infinitely *animal*. So much so that the face loses its
form and undergoes what Jacques Aumont calls a process of *dévisagéifi-*
cation after which a head emerges, an *animal* head.[32] "Il arrive que la tête
d'homme soit remplacée par un animal" ("It happens that the man's head

[30] Georges Bataille, "Le Gros Orteil," *Documents* 6 (1929): 299-300, *my italics*. Let us note with
regard to/as an echo of the text of Bataille which positions the mouth in the prolongation of the
spinal column, Bacon's picture, *Three Figures and Portrait* (1975) where the spinal column is
also painted through a contorted Face. Also quoted and commented on by Gilles Deleuze, *Francis Bacon* 28-29.

[31] Gilles Deleuze, *Francis Bacon*, 25.

[32] Jacques Aumont, *Du visage au cinéma* (Paris: Éditions de l'Etoile/Cahiers du Cinéma-Essais,
1992) 185.

is replaced by an animal") writes Deleuze with regard to Bacon. Such words are highly apt to describe the hero of the film *The Elephant Man*, John Merrick, directed by David Lynch. Merrick, having been afflicted by an incurable illness, neurofibromatosis, had a huge head deformed by monstrous protuberances. Owing to the curling up of his upper lip, John Merrick's mouth revealed an enormous oral cavity, very similar to that of the elephant, hence his name of Elephant Man.[33] The maternal gestation of John Merrick is retraced at the beginning of the film by a sort of series of fantasmatic/goric images in which shots of the mother of John Merrick are juxtaposed with those of the animal-elephant. In fact, the image of the mother is married to that of the elephant. If for Chion the scene makes one think of a difficult, not to say disastrous birth, the juxtaposition of images that Lynch shows us between the drawn-out cry of John Merrick's mother stretched out on the ground of a country that looks exotic and the trumpeting coming-and-going of the animal's trunk make us envisage a sort of savage *coupling* between the mother and the elephant.[34] It is not about showing us a sterile and binary game of correspondences between man and animal but to show that the coupling that intervenes here is what Deleuze identifies precisely as a "zone d'*indiscernabilité* et d'*indécidabilité* entre l'homme et l'animal." ("a zone of *indiscernability* and *undecidability* between man and animal.") If John Merrick constitutes this zone of indiscernability, he also represents "ce fait commun" ("that common fact"), according to Deleuze, of the animal-human and it envelops at the same time that sovereignty of symptomal dialectics according to Bataille. What can we say? The case of John Merrick opens not as the antithesis of the human as the medical entourage of Doctor Treves might think, but it reveals itself as the unfathomable point of contact between *resemblance* and *lack of resemblance* in the human, i.e. on the one hand, the tragically *animal-bestial* (deformed, violent, torn) and, on the other, the tragically *human*. Man is coupled with his animality and the animal is coupled with its humanity. It is also in this sense that Deleuze could write in a similar axiom (with regard to the paintings of *Two Studies for a Portrait of George Dyer* 1968) that man does not turn into an animal without the animal in its turn taking on the spirit of a man. It is in this sense that Doctor Treves will reveal under bestial formlessness and deformity, the refinement of John Merrick, starting with his use of language and, subsequently, his pronounced taste for culture.

However, in this symptomal dialectic, or then again in this duality between lack of resemblance and resemblance coming together in a single body, the formless body of John Merrick still remains that mass of meat, bruised in its flesh. In fact, it is not by accident that when Doctor Treves, looking for John Merrick, plunges into the labyrinthine alleyways of Victorian London only to find repulsiveness and abjection, he should walk through abattoirs in which the carcasses of dead animals are hanging. This paradigm of the abattoir cannot help but bring to mind once more the photographs that Eli Lotar took in order to illustrate Bataille's article on

---

[33] I refer the reader here to the work by Michel Chion, *David Lynch* (London: British Film Institute, 2006) 46.

[34] Chion, *David Lynch*, 50.

"the abattoir." For Didi-Huberman the butcher's slaughterhouse, meats and carcasses illustrate in a fundamental way the *formless* for they express by themselves "les formes *lamentables* d'un vivant écrasé, mais donnant vie à ce qu'*informe* veut dire" ("the *woeful* forms of a living being crushed, but giving life to what is meant by *formless*").[35] The Elephant Man, John Merrick, also perhaps himself best embodies in his flesh, his repugnant meat, the formless *par excellence*. All the pains, the convulsions and vulnerabilities are here catalyzed/embodied in his flesh, in his meat. It is perhaps also in this sense that Lynch makes of Merrick a pitiable and suffering being just as much as a *sacred*, *religious* one. In the same way, we know, Bacon will be for Deleuze, the religious painter whose sole object of pity will be meat, that *formless* mass which, like John Merrick, suffers and cries and nevertheless remains human:

> Pitié pour la viande! Il n'y a pas de doute, la viande est l'objet le plus haut de la pitié de Bacon, son seul objet de pitié, sa pitié d'Anglo-Irlandais. [...] La viande n'est pas une chair morte, elle a gardé toutes les souffrances et pris sur soi toutes les couleurs de la chair vive. Tant de douleur convulsive et de vulnérabilité [...]. Bacon ne dit pas 'pitié pour les bêtes' mais plutôt tout homme qui souffre est de la viande. La viande est la zone commune de l'homme et de la bête, leur zone d'indiscernabilité, elle est ce 'fait,' cet état même où le peintre s'identifie aux objets de son horreur ou de sa compassion. Le peintre est boucher certes, mais il est dans cette boucherie comme dans une église, avec la viande pour Crucifié ('peinture' de 1946). C'est seulement dans les boucheries que Bacon est un peintre religieux.[36]

> (Have pity on the meat! Meat is undoubtedly the chief object of Bacon's pity, the sole object of his pity, the pity of an Anglo-Irishman. [...] Meat is not dead flesh – it retains all the sufferings and assumes all the colourings of living flesh. So much convulsive pain and vulnerability there is in it [...]. Bacon does not say: 'have pity on the beasts' but rather that every man who suffers is a piece of meat. Meat is the common territory of man and beast, their zone of indiscernability, it is a 'fact,' that very state in which the painter identifies with the objects of his horror and of his compassion. The painter is definitely a butcher but he stands in his butcher's shop as if he were in a church with the Crucified One represented by meat (cf. 1946 painting). It is only in butcher's shops that Bacon is a religious painter.)

Francis Bacon, painter of flesh and meat: religious painter! It is perhaps through a contemplation-investigation of Bataille's concept of the *formless*, of the abject, of the repulsive and of the defilement of the human figure (set free henceforth from all qualitative judgment) that not only all the art of Francis Bacon and David Lynch is unveiled, but that we also find a way in (difficult, even impossible to look at) to a certain negative mystic theology. This reflexion/meditation is apprehended at the very heart of an internal experience which the heterogeneous but combinatory modes of reflexion of Bacon, Bataille and Lynch succeed in running alongside and in freely interacting with so as to open out onto a *mystical theology* such as Pseudo-Dionysius could call up and in this way "to know unveiled this non-knowledge that knowledge hides in each being that we

---

35 Georges Didi-Huberman, *Resemblance Informe* (Paris: Macula, 1995) 163.
36 Gilles Deleuze, *Francis Bacon*, 29-30.

can have from this being so as thus to see that suressential Darkness that all the light contained in beings hides."[37]

[37] *Abbot Suger on the Abbey Church of St.-Denis and its Art Treasures*, ed. trans. and annotated by Erwin Panofsky, 2nd ed. (Princeton: Princeton University Press, c1979) 18-21.

GARY BETTINSON & FRANCOIS-XAVIER GLEYZON
DAVID LYNCH & THE CINEMA D'AUTEUR: A CONVERSATION
WITH MICHEL CHION

Michel Chion was born in 1947 in Creil, France. A musicologist and composer, he worked as assistant to Pierre Schaeffer in the early 1970s, experimenting in musique concrète at the Paris Conservatoire national supérieur de musique. His research into music theory and cinema climaxed in several authored studies of film sound, making a far-reaching impact on Anglophone film theory and criticism. Two seminal volumes – *Audio-Vision: Sound on Screen* and *The Voice in Cinema* – explored the acoustic capabilities of cinema, and launched a new lexicon for describing sound-image relations. Many of Chion's discoveries in this area have informed both his critical studies of particular filmmakers (including Charles Chaplin and Jacques Tati) and his book-length commentaries on individual films (such as Stanley Kubrick's *Eyes Wide Shut* and Terrence Malick's *The Thin Red Line*). His monograph on David Lynch appeared in 1992. As well as holding a teaching post at the Université de Paris III, Chion has ventured into film directing and composing, and served as film critic for *Cahiers du cinéma*.

Chion's study of Lynch reveals the *Cahiers* heritage, but it adopts a less fervent approach to authorship than did the auteur-centered criticism of the 1950s. Swerving from the *politiques des auteurs*, Chion affirms the notion of film as collective artistic creation – hence *The Elephant Man* (1980) can be discussed as "a great film made collectively."[1] Artistic importance is attached to Lynch's cadre of actors and especially to those personnel spearheading music and sound. Furthermore, Chion asserts the primacy of the artwork, *prima facie* downgrading the rank of the auteur. He contends that Lynch's films manifest their maker and not vice versa; thus the artwork, in effect, authors the author. Despite the echoes of Barthesian theory – the text precedes and can outstrip its creator(s) – Chion hardly espouses the death of the author. A theory of multiple authorship does not displace the role of the auteur, but distributes that role among various workers. Such views notwithstanding, Chion treats Lynch as the films' principal creator. To this extent he preserves the classic auteurism fostered in *Cahiers du cinéma*. Even certain minutiae of 1950s criticism are ripe for preservation, as when Chion argues below for the definitiveness of a director's maiden work, thereby echoing François Truffaut (and before him, Jean Renoir). (The authorial traits harbored in the debut film also underpin Chion's "Lynch-kit," the set of materials out of which Lynch's *oeuvre* is built.) If Chion's concept of authorship at times seems murky, it is best grasped as springing from a confluence of proxi-

---

[1] Michel Chion, *David Lynch* (London: British Film Institute, 1995) 57.

mate forces, an attempt to fuse disparate premises from Parisian film and literary criticism.

Auteurism and other aspects of Chion's *David Lynch* hover over the following interview, conducted in November 2009. Chion's book – among the first large-scale monographs to center on the filmmaker – remains a landmark in the Lynch literature, and has been reprinted several times and in numerous languages. The interview takes as its broad purview the development of both Lynch's cinema and Chion's central thesis since the book was first published in the early 1990s.

In your 1995 monograph on David Lynch, you argue that by the late 1980s Lynch is striving toward a "non-psychological cinema."[2] Could you elaborate on this claim, which perhaps runs counter to most commentators' assumptions about Lynch? Do you feel that Lynch in subsequent years continued to pursue the kind of cinema you describe?

I would like to make it clear that the first edition of my book dates back not to 1995, but to 1992 (before *Lost Highway*). I finished it just as *Twin Peaks: Fire Walk with Me* was being released in cinemas, a film which was very badly received by the majority of critics and shunned by the general public. I can recall very well that, for a certain time, Lynch stopped being fashionable in France – he was thought of rather as a skilful manipulator of public opinion. I am anxious to remind you of this for it was after this first version that I inaugurated what I called the Lynch Kit, a series of key words in French alphabetical order, but which I made correspond to English words: Link, Alphabet, Void. In editions brought out subsequently, I haven't changed a thing with this Lynch Kit, even though it is based on films prior to *Lost Highway*, and nobody has noticed. This can be taken to mean that these signifiers are still valid in the eyes of those who discovered Lynch through *Lost Highway* or *Mulholland Drive* or *Inland Empire*, and who buy the new editions of my book.

I think that for a certain category of artist, to which Lynch belongs, everything falls into place very quickly from the first finished work: the themes, the key signifiers, the universe, and so on. He makes me think in some ways of Olivier Messiaen, who I was slightly acquainted with. His universe was so surprising and original, and he behaved in life with so much calm and decorum that some people tried to see in him a manipulator and a cheat. I am convinced that he was sincere – he was a bit of a displaced person.

The theory was that Lynch was an emotional director, which seems obvious now, after *Mulholland Drive*, but was not at the time. Already, however, during that period some people were surprised at the discontinuity in his work between *Eraserhead* and *The Elephant Man* (a tear-jerker *par excellence*), which they interpreted as evidence of an absence of personality on his part.

By "non-psychological cinema" I mean that it is not a cinema in which the characters are defined by a behavioral logic corresponding to that which is most often found in real life. Their psychological coherence is not that of "likely" characters, moderately neurotic, and so forth; they can

[2] Chion, *David Lynch*, 123.

change their attitude completely and can come across as mad or what-ever. On the other hand there is a psychological coherence in this cinema itself, which functions on the basis of archaic fantasies. I think that Lynch effectively went on in this direction; there is a great stability in his uni-verse, and *Inland Empire* is by the same director as *The Grandmother*.

Lynch's characters, of course, are not marionettes or abstractions. They live, love, have both pleasures and agonies. It is in this respect that Lynch is not a cerebral filmmaker, playing with two-dimensional charac-ters or making fun of them. The latter have emotions.

Writing in the original foreword, you note the risk of characterizing the *oeuvre* of a still-working, young auteur whose subsequent works "may refute some of [my] propositions"[3]. From today's vantage point, are there significant arguments in the book that you would want to recast or reject?

I could try to say certain things better, but I believe that my book has its unity and that's why I haven't modified it radically. No, I can't see that I ought to change anything essentially. I also believe that I must let this book exist without me; I merely add a few pages when Lynch brings out a new film. In 1992 I had the idea of a shock therapy cinema for depressive mothers, as an epigraph borrowed from the psychoanalyst Françoise Dolto indicates. I had the idea of a vitalist cinema where everything is good. That's why the end of *Inland Empire*, which features the sumptuous "Sinnerman" sung by Nina Simone, delights me but does not surprise me.

A female friend told me that what I had done with my book was to bring back to the fold of common humanity that "degenerate Lynch," as she affectionately called him. It is as if I had meant to say that he seems odd, like a displaced person, but he's still human, he's still one of ours.

Lynch is traditionally linked most closely with the American independent cinema, but his films intersect with the mainstream industry in a host of ways. Can Lynch be categorized predominantly by an individual cinematic mode (e.g. popular, indie, art)?

No, I don't think you should put Lynch into a category – nobody can be defined just by a category and I could say the same thing about any direc-tor, about George Lucas, Robert Bresson or Gus Van Sant. In France it is fashionable now to define as "atypical" all these interesting directors. If everyone is "atypical," nothing stands out. Once we've defined Lynch more as "populart," more as "art," so what? We wouldn't be much fur-ther on and we wouldn't have said anything worth saying.

Where do you think Lynch currently stands in the pantheon of American directors, and on the world stage in general?

For me, he's a genius. When my book came out, this genius was not yet obvious to everybody and I am happy that young movie buffs discovered

---

[3] Chion, *David Lynch*, xii.

him with *Lost Highway* and above all with *Mulholland Drive*, for this last film is particularly loved in France. Now I don't try to rate Lynch in a list of "best directors." Personally, when I give out ratings (purely for pleasure), I rate the film and not the director. For example, *Blade Runner*, directed by Ridley Scott, is one of my favorite films, on a par with those of Lynch and Fellini, while Ridley Scott is certainly not as great a film-maker as Lynch or Fellini.

How would you characterize the evolution of Lynch's film career generally, and perhaps most particularly since your Lynch book was first published?

At the risk of appearing provocative, I would say that there is no evolution in Lynch's work. I firmly believe that for certain artists, their personality is defined quite early on. Afterward their works will vary externally according to circumstances.

Luck has a great part to play. What would have happened to Lynch if Mel Brooks (praise be to him for it) had not thought of him to direct *The Elephant Man*? He might perhaps only have made two or three experimental films.

The evolution of his career is of necessity largely determined by the success or lack of success of some of his films. Success and lack of success are, by and large, random things. He has succeeded as an artist in remaining himself in his films. Of course, I can see that he does a lot of exhibitions, performances, and so on, but it's his films especially that I deal with in my book and his films always succeed in being films by him – they come from that part of him that is immutable and which is already expressed in its totality in his first "shorts."

I deeply believe that a genuine artist carries in himself his work, his feeling of the world and then his works bear of necessity the trace of what happens to him, but he expresses himself in spite of everything. There is an artistic metabolism which, as long as nothing too untoward befalls him, makes the artist use the things that happen to him.

You have stated that Lynch tries to "renovate [cinema's] forms."[4] What, in your view, has been the most transformative aspect of Lynch's film-making on contemporary cinema?

Great artists, alas, often set bad examples, and there have been a lot of strange films after Lynch, just as there were a lot of carnival films after Fellini. When I said "renovate," I didn't mean: have an influence on films other than his own, that is, films by other directors. I was thinking especially of his own work. The influence of Lynch is bad, precisely because he is unique and too personal – you shouldn't try to imitate him.

Film scholars have theorized Lynch's work from many different angles. Do you consider that any particular theoretical paradigm can adequately explicate Lynch's cinema?

---

4 Chion, *David Lynch*, 159.

I don't think it's a matter of "explicating" Lynch's cinema, but of under-standing life and the world better through it. I think that my approach in the Lynch-Kit is the best and I am happy and flattered that Slavoj Žižek should have found in my formulations a stimulus for his own ideas.

Lynch tells us that we live in a mysterious world, and we think that he is trying to hide a truth from us, that he himself knows the truth behind the mystery. Not at all! His films tell us that we live in a mysterious world, and he is right.

There's a phrase of Jules Renard: "the less I understand life, the more I like it." This is exactly what I feel as I get older.

As an interviewee Lynch is notoriously guarded, cryptic and evasive. How much should critics accept, or read into, what he says about his films?

An artist says what he wants to, what he can. Critics – and I mean crit-ics, not the journalists who write "gossip columns" and asides – must keep themselves aloof from the discourse an artist generates about his work. It's the work itself that counts.

I find anyway that Lynch is not as "cryptic" as he is said to be. I inter-viewed him once for the special edition of a DVD in France of *Inland Empire*. He answered my questions very directly and very honestly. It is because he says simple things with simple words that people find him vague.

Your overview of Lynch's film and television productions presupposes an *oeuvre*, a body of collaboratively-produced work overseen by a single creative figure. You describe Lynch as an "author."[5] You also incorporate a good deal of biographical detail. Yet you express caution at embracing auteurism whole-heartedly. Could you elaborate, in relation to Lynch, your views on the auteur theory?

This question is crucial. I think we need to use "auteur theory" intelli-gently and not mechanically. First of all, it isn't legitimate to apply it to everybody; on the other hand, we need to combine it with "a politics of the work," an idea I express with regard to *Eraserhead* right from the start: to begin with there is a work. It's his works that make Lynch, not Lynch that makes his works.

I use in my book few biographical details, just what is needed for the reader to locate him, but I never use biography to explain the work: I'm not interested in his childhood, his relationships with women, his philoso-phical or religious beliefs, his personal attributes and so forth. I quote some of his reflexions because they are poetic and interesting. But there isn't a single line on his relationship with Isabella Rossellini. It's not a bi-ography. The epigraph in which I quote Françoise Dolto on unbearable children and their mothers is not about Lynch's childhood, Lynch's life, or his relationship with his mother. I talk about the Mother Figure who is present in his work from the first film onwards! It makes little difference to me if his real mother was a depressive or not, it's none of my business.

---

[5] Chion, *David Lynch*, 28.

I am very proud of having noticed from 1987, when I was writing a criticism of *Blue Velvet* which had just premiered, the importance and intensity of very short images that show us "women sitting on eternal couches" (the image of the hero's mother in front of a television, the sound of which seems muted). *Inland Empire* is the development of that image. I am much more interested in things like that than in the question of knowing if Lynch was traumatized during his childhood. If Lynch touches cinema-goers all over the world, it is because he addresses himself to what is universal in us.

FILMOGRAPHY

1408. Dir. Mikael Håfström. Perf. John Cusack, Samuel L. Jackson, and Mary McCormack. Dimension Films, 2007. Film.

Absurda. Dir. David Lynch. Cannes Film Festival, 2007. Film.

The Amityville Horror. Dir. Stuart Rosenberg. Perf. James Brolin, Margot Kidder, and Rod Steiger. American International Pictures, 1979. Film.

Blade Runner. Dir. Ridley Scott. Perf. Harrison Ford, Rutger Hauer, and Sean Young. Warner Bros, 1982. Film.

Blue Velvet. Dir. David Lynch. Perf. Kyle MacLachlan, Isabella Rossellini, Dennis Hopper, Laura Dern, and Dean Stockwell. De Laurentiis Entertainment Group, 1986. Film.

Donnie Darko. Dir. Richard Kelly. Perf. Jake Gyllenhaal, Jena Malone, and James Duval. Newmarket Films, 2001. Film.

Dumb & Dumber. Dir. Peter and Bobby Farrelly. Perf. Jim Carrey and Jeff Daniels. New Line Cinema, 1994. Film.

Dune. Dir. David Lynch. Perf. Francesca Annis and Kyle MacLachlan. Universal Pictures, 1984. Film.

El Topo. Dir. Alejandro Jodorowsky. Perf. Alejandro Jodorowsky, Brontis Jodorowsky and Mara Lorenzio. 1970. Film.

The Elephant Man. Dir. David Lynch. Perf. Anthony Hopkins, John Hurt, and Anne Bancroft. Paramount Pictures, 1980. Film.

Eraserhead. Dir. David Lynch. Perf. Jack Nance, Charlotte Stewart, and Jeanne Bates. Libra Films, 1977. Film.

Eyes Wide Shut. Dir. Stanley Kubrick. Perf. Tom Cruise, Nicole Kidman, and Sydney Pollack. Warner Bros., 1999. Film.

Frenzy. Dir. Alfred Hitchcock. Perf. Jon Finch, Alec McCowen, and Barry Foster. Universal Pictures, 1972. Film.

Ghost Dance. Dir. Ken McKullen. Perf. Leonie Mellinger, Pascale Ogier, Robbie Coltrane, Jacques Derrida, and Dominique Pinon. 1983. Film.

Gilda. Dir. Charles Vidor. Perf. Rita Hayworth, Glenn Ford, and George Macready. Colombia Pictures, 1946. Film.

The Grandmother. Dir. David Lynch. Perf. Richard White, Dorothy McGinnis, and Virginia Maitland. AFI, 1970. Film.

The Harder They Come. Dir. Perry Henzell. Perf. Jimmy Cliff. New World Pictures, 1972. Film.

Harold and Maude. Dir. Hal Ashby. Perf. Ruth Gordon, Bud Cort, and Vivian Pickles. Paramount Pictures, 1971. Film.

Harvey. Dir. Henry Koster. Perf. James Stewart, Josephine Hull, and Peggy Dow. Universal International Pictures, 1950. Film.

The Haunting. Dir. Robert Wise. Perf. Julie Harris, Richard Johnson, Claire Bloom, and Russ Tamblyn. MGM, 1963. Film.

Industrial Symphony No. 1. Dir. David Lynch. Perf. Laura Dern, Nicolas Cage, Julee Cruise, and Michael J. Anderson. Warner Home Video, 1990. Film.

Inland Empire. Dir. David Lynch. Perf. Laura Dern, Jeremy Irons, and Justin Theroux. Studio Canal, 2006. Film.

Lady in the Lake. Dir. Robert Montgomery. Perf. Robert Montgomery, Audrey Totter, and Lloyd Nolan. Metro-Goldwyn-Mayer, 1947. Film.

L'année dernière à Marienbad. Dir. Alain Resnais. Perf. Giorgio Albertazzi, Sacha Pitoëff, and Delphine Seyrig. 1961. Film.

Les Enfants du Paradis. Dir. Marcel Carné. Perf. Arletty, Jean-Louis Barrault, Pierre Brasseur, and Pierre Renoir. 1945. Film.

Lost Highway. Dir. David Lynch. Perf. Bill Pullman, Patricia Arquette, and Balthazar Getty. October Films, 1997. Film.

The Matrix. Dir. Andy and Larry Wachowski. Perf. Keanu Reeves, Laurence Fishburne, and Carrie-Anne Moss. Warner Brothers Pictures, 1999. Film.

Meet the Parents. Dir. Jay Roach. Perf. Robert De Niro and Ben Stiller. Universal Pictures, 2000. Film.

Mulholland Drive. Dir. David Lynch. Perf. Naomi Watts, Laura Elena Harring, and Justin Theroux. Universal Pictures, 2001. Film.

Night of the Living Dead. Dir. George Romero. Perf. Duane Jones, Judith O'Dea, and Karl Hardman. The Walter Reade Organization, 1968. Film.

Paris, Texas. Dir. Wim Wenders. Perf. Harry Dean Stanton, Nastassja Kinski, and Hunter Carson. Twentieth Century Fox, 1984. Film.

Philadelphia. Dir. Jonathan Demme. Perf. Tom Hanks, Denzel Washington, Jason Robards, Antonio Banderas, Joanne Woodward, and Mary Steenburgen. TriStar Pictures, 1993. Film.

Pink Flamingos. Dir. John Waters. Perf. Divine, David Lochary, and Mink Stole. New Line Cinema, 1972. Film.

Psycho. Dir. Alfred Hitchcock. Perf. Anthony Perkins, Janet Leigh, Vera Miles, John Gavin, Martin Balsam, and John McIntire. Paramount Pictures, 1960. Film.

Queen Kelly. Dir. Erich von Stroheim. Perf. Gloria Swanson, Walter Byron, Seena Owen, and Tully Marshall. United Artists, 1929. Film.

Rabbits. Dir. David Lynch. Perf. Scott Coffey, Rebekah Del Rio, Laura Harring, and Naomi Watts. 2002. Film.

Red Shoes. Dir. Michael Powell and Emeric Pressburger. Perf. Moira Shearer, Anton Walbrook, and Marius Goring. Eagle-Lion Films, 1948. Film.

Reefer Madness. Dir. Louis J. Gasnier. Perf. Dorothy Short, Kenneth Craig, and Lillian Miles. Motion Pictures Ventures, 1936. Film.

The Rocky Horror Picture Show. Dir. Jim Sharman. Perf. Tim Curry, Susan Sarandon, and Barry Bostwick. Twentieth Century Fox, 1975. Film.

Salome. Dir. William Dieterle. Perf. Rita Hayworth, Stewart Granger, and Charles Laughton. Colombia Pictures, 1953. Film.

Shadow of a Doubt. Dir. Alfred Hitchcock. Perf. Teresa Wright, Joseph Cotten, Macdonald Carey, Patricia Collinge, and Henry Travers. Universal Pictures, 1943. Film.

Shallow Hal. Dir. Bobby and Peter Farrelly. Perf. Jack Black, Gwyneth Paltrow, and Jason Alexander. Twentieth Century Fox, 2001. Film.

The Silence of the Lambs. Dir. Jonathan Demme. Perf. Jodie Foster, Anthony Hopkins, Scott Glenn, and Ted Levine. Orion Pictures, 1991. Film.

Six Men Getting Sick. Dir. David Lynch. Pennsylvania Academy of Fine Arts, 1966. Film.

Slacker. Dir. Richard Linklater. Perf. Richard Linklater, Kim Krizan, and Marc James. Orion Pictures, 1991. Film.

The Straight Story Dir. David Lynch. Perf. Richard Farnsworth, Sissy Spacek, and Harry Dean Stanton. Walt Disney Pictures, 1999. Film.

Sunset Boulevard. Dir. Billy Wilder. Perf. William Holden, Gloria Swanson, Erich von Stroheim, and Nancy Olson. Paramount Pictures, 1950. Film.

The Texas Chain Saw Massacre. Dir. Tobe Hooper. Perf. Marilyn Burns, Gunnar Hansen, Edwin Neal, and Allen Danziger. Bryanston Distributing, 1974. Film

There's Something About Mary. Dir. Bobby and Peter Farrelly. Perf. Cameron Diaz, Matt Dillon, and Ben Stiller. Twentieth Century Fox, 1998. Film.

Twin Peaks. By David Lynch and Mark Frost. ABC. 8 Apr. 1990 – 10 June 1991. Television.

Twin Peaks: Fire Walk with Me. Dir. David Lynch. Perf. Sheryl Lee, Moira Kelly, David Bowie, and Chris Isaak. New Line Cinema, 1992. Film.

Variety. Dir. Bette Gordon. Perf. Sandy McLeod, Will Patton, Luis Guzman, Richard Davidson, and Nan Goldin. Feature Narrative, 1984. Film.

Videodrome. Dir. David Cronenberg. Perf. James Woods, Debbie Harry, and Sonja Smits. Universal Studios, 1983. Film.

Wild at Heart. Dir. David Lynch. Perf. Nicholas Cage and Laura Dern. The Samuel Goldwyn Company, 1990. Film.

The Wizard of Oz. Dir. Victor Fleming. Perf. Judy Garland, Frank Morgan, and Ray Bolger. MGM, 1939. Film.

CONTRIBUTORS

LOUIS ARMAND is Director of the Centre for Critical & Cultural Theory in the Philosophy Faculty of Charles University, Prague. His recent books include *Literate Technologies: Language, Cognition, Technicity* (2005), *Event States: Discourse, Time, Mediality* (2007), *Solicitations: Essays on Criticism & Culture* (2nd ed., 2008); and *Incendiary Devices: Discourses of the Other* (2006). He is also the editor of *Contemporary Poetics* published by Northwestern University Press in 2007.

REBECCA ANNE BARR is Lecturer in English Literature at the National University of Ireland, Galway. Her work has appeared in *The Eighteenth-Century: Theory and Interpretation* and *Bone Dreams: Anglo-Saxon Culture in the Modern Imagination*.

GARY BETTINSON teaches Film Studies at Lancaster University, U.K. His work has appeared in *Film Studies: An International Review*, *New Review of Film and Television Studies*, *Asian Cinema*, and the anthology *Puzzle Films: Complex Storytelling in Contemporary Cinema* (edited by Warren Buckland, 2009). He is co-author (with Richard Rushton) of *What is Film Theory? An Introduction to Contemporary Debates* (McGraw-Hill, 2010).

JASON T. CLEMENCE teaches film theory and criticism at Tufts University. His article "Empty All Along: *Eraserhead*, Apocalypse, and Dismantled Masculine Privilege" recently appeared in the collection *Media and the Apocalypse* (Peter Lang Publishing Group).

DOMINIQUE DE COURCELLES is Director of Research at the *Centre National de la Recherche Scientifique*, France. She is also Director of Studies at the *Collège International de Philosophie*, Paris. She has authored many books and articles on art, semiotics, literature and philosophy.

FRANCOIS-XAVIER GLEYZON is Assistant Professor of English at the American University of Beirut. His research centers on Renaissance Literature, Visual and Cultural Theory. He is the author of *Shakespeare's Spiral* (UPA), and "Shakespeare and the Archaeology of Shadows" (MUP).

JOSHUA DAVID GONSALVES is Assistant Professor of English teaching nineteenth-century British literature and film at the American University of Beirut. His focus is Romanticism across the disciplines of geopolitics, cinema & animal studies, literary culture and cultural theory. He is at work on two books – *Keats Goes Global: Close Reading and the Geopolitics of Cultural Production*; and *Screening War: The Construction of "Geopoli-*

tics" in Pre-Cinematic Mass Culture: 1789-1914 – and has recently published work on Wordsworth, Swinburne and Byronic/Venetian geopolitics.

GREG HAINGE is Reader in French at the University of Queensland. He is President of the Australian Society of French Studies and serves on the editorial boards of *Culture, Theory and Critique, Contemporary French Civilization, Études Céliniennes, Studies in French Cinema* and the editorial advisory board of *Altitude*. He is the author of a monograph on Louis-Ferdinand Céline and is currently writing another on the ontology of noise.

TODD MCGOWAN teaches film and critical theory in the English Department at the University of Vermont. He is author of *Out of Time: Desire in Atemporal Cinema* (Minnesota), *The Real Gaze: Film Theory After Lacan* (SUNY), and *The Impossible David Lynch* (Columbia).

MICHEL CHION has written many books on the cinema, including a series of groundbreaking works on film sound. His study of the film and television work of David Lynch (*David Lynch*, BFI, 1995) has become, since its first English publication in 1995, the definitive book on one of America's finest contemporary directors.

ALANNA THAIN is an Assistant Professor in the Department of English, McGill University, where she teaches film and cultural studies. She is currently completing a monograph entitled *'Suspended (Re)Animations: Affect, Immediation and the Film Body,'* on Lynch, Hitchcock, Lou Ye, and Kore-Eda.

ERIC G. WILSON is the Thomas H. Pritchard Professor of English at Wake Forest University. He is the author of *The Strange World of David Lynch: Transcendental Irony from Eraserhead to Mulholland Dr.* (Continuum, 2007), *Secret Cinema: Gnostic Vision in Film* (Continuum, 2006) and *Against Happiness: In Praise of Melancholy* (Farrar, Straus, and Giroux).

SCOTT WILSON is Professor of Media and Cultural Studies at Kingston University. His books include *The Order of Joy: Beyond the Cultural Politics of Enjoyment* (SUNY, 2008), *Great Satan's Rage: American negativty and rap/metal in the age of supercapitalism* (Manchester, 2008) and, with Fred Botting, *The Tarantinian Ethics* (Sage, 2001).